THE CENTRE OF HILARITY

MICHAEL MASON

THE CENTRE OF
HILARITY

A play upon ideas about laughter and the absurd

SHEED AND WARD
LONDON AND NEW YORK

FIRST PUBLISHED 1959
BY SHEED AND WARD LTD.
33 MAIDEN LANE
LONDON W.C.2
AND
SHEED AND WARD INC.
840 BROADWAY
NEW YORK 3

PRINTED IN GREAT BRITAIN
BY PURNELL AND SONS LTD.
PAULTON (SOMERSET) AND LONDON

To

MY MOTHER AND FATHER

We are saved by hope

ST. PAUL

Bash on regardless

UNKNOWN SOLDIER
OF WORLD WAR II

CONTENTS

CONTENTS

I : "YOU CAN ALWAYS READ BROWNING"

Not long after the Second World War, I found myself one evening in the company of a number of other Cambridge undergraduates, who had gathered to read contemporary poetry. At that time, I was sufficiently more of a Yahoo than I am at present to have a straightforward crude prejudice against the poetry of my own day in general, on the simple grounds that I couldn't understand what it meant. And I wasn't made any more favourably disposed when I found that for our opening selection we seemed to hit, for the most part, on poems whose message was apparently one of total despair. Anyhow, after a while, during the discussion which followed the reading of one particularly dismal piece, I gave vent to my feelings sufficiently to say, "This stuff gives me the pip." Not what you'd call a reaction of decadent sensitivity, but honest enough as far as it went.

It was—to borrow an expression which the late Roy Campbell used of a slightly similar situation—as if I had belched in church. There was a moment's silence, and then someone said, in tones of indescribable contempt, "Well, of course, if you want to be *cheered up* you can always go and read Browning."

There's a passage in P. G. Wodehouse where he makes Bertie Wooster describe how you tread on a girl's dress at a dance and it tears and she says sweetly, "Oh, don't be upset, it doesn't matter at all, really", and then you catch her eye and feel as if you'd trodden on a rake and the handle had jumped up and hit you in the face. That was me; I went down for the count. Indeed, I was so taken aback that I didn't even try to work out,

1

then or later, which was the greater disgrace—wanting to be cheered up, or reading Browning.

As time went on, Cambridge made sufficient impression on my backwoodsmanship to dispel this hillbilly hostility of mine. For a time, it even converted me to, and instructed me in, the grim and rigorous orthodoxy of my deflator. But I don't think I was ever really convincedly committed to the acceptance of grimness as man's authentic condition. If I had been absolutely honest with myself I should have admitted, I'm sure, even at the time when my ideals of adult realism were at their starkest, that I had a basic sneaking sympathy with an attitude once expressed by my mother. Being asked why she hadn't gone to see some particularly harrowing film masterpiece of the year, she replied simply that there were more than enough things in the world that made her miserable free of charge, and if she was going to spend one and ninepence it was jolly well going to be on something that made her happy. I grant that if in those days I ever had the choice between Bob Hope and a Film Society showing of some UFA epic about homicidal maniacs, I always went dutifully to have a couple of hours of homicidal mania. But that was only because I didn't really have the courage of my convictions. Deep down I always retained a stubborn instinct of resistance to "being made miserable"; a thirst for joy, of the kind most simply expressed in the childhood demand for the happy ending. And this was something which I couldn't do anything about. However sincerely I tried to inculcate in myself the degree of grimness generally felt to be appropriate to the mid-twentieth-century intellectual, there always persisted an ineradicable childish taste for enjoyment. And in my heart of hearts I knew that in some quite fundamental way I was not what I was trying to be.

2

It's not easy to find a satisfactory description of the outlook in terms of which this childhood's longing —not forgetting Browning—had been so vigorously condemned; in terms of which I, too, subsequently, tried to weed out those particular "childish things" which I thought myself bound to put away in order to achieve maturity. If I fall back on the word "humanist", it isn't for lack of sympathy with the protests of many "humanists" at being so called, and at being labelled as adherents of any -ism whatsoever. As usually employed, the word is all too strongly associated with a quarrel between sacred and profane which does the non-believer a good deal less than justice, and deprives the believer of an essential part of his inheritance. Yet the temper of mind which my undergraduate companion was speaking up for—one with strong roots in the scientific and non-conforming tradition of Cambridge—is still, undoubtedly, very similar to that of the classical humanists, from the sixteenth-century grammarians to the nineteenth-century mechanistic scientists. Man still stands at the centre of the picture, even though with little of the crude self-confidence which he had even a few years ago. Indeed, the picture is as stark as it is just because he does so stand, and with a mind just so changed. The gods are dead; man isn't feeling so good himself. But at least, he says, he can face both facts without crying for Mother. All this may no longer be a formulated creed, as in the days of the great Victorian atheists and agnostics; but you don't avoid holding the assumptions by which you live just because you decline to give them explicit dogmatic status. So, the necessary qualifications being understood, I shall call this viewpoint a humanist one—a secular humanist one.

This humanist condemnation, then, of the childhood

3

insistence on the happy ending, was something which, in due course, much commended itself to me, as I have said. And it's not hard to see why. There's obviously so much in it that is sound. If the instinct to resist being made miserable implies nothing more than a desire to insulate yourself against suffering, then of course it is sense to say that we shouldn't want to be cheered up. In the grimness of this kind of stoicism there's a lot of plain honesty and an admirable refusal of selfish escapism. Yet for all this, in the long run it seemed clear to me that it was quite impossible to live on self-respect alone in this way. And when I came to re-examine, in the light of that conclusion, thought and writing which I had first come to know from a stoically humanistic standpoint, my original crude and simple reaction at the poetry reading seemed to demand, well, not readoption as it stood, certainly, but some sort of reconsideration.

Since modern secular humanism, in the sense in which I am using the term here, was created, partly at least, by a world in revolt against the Christian tradition, it's not surprising if a questioning of humanistic assumptions should find itself echoing those of Christianity. You can account very simply for the bitter climate of despair in which so many men live today by saying that it is the logical consequence of the abandonment of the Christian vision. And there's all too much truth in that. But truth is very complex as well as very simple, and there is something significantly un-human about a simple-as-ABC knock-down supernaturalism like that. It makes light, with a word or two, of the whole labyrinthine complication of the human situation. To start with, it is plain fact that this puzzle about joy hasn't presented itself, and doesn't present itself, in straightforward terms of a contrast between happy

4

Christians and miserable non-Christians. The ages of
faith produced plenty of men whose message of Christian
exhortation is just about encouraging enough to drive
you to drink. And for our own day you have to ask
yourself, in all seriousness: "If I owed my first acquaintance with the Christian world-picture to Mr. T.
S. Eliot [or Mr. Graham Greene, or M. Mauriac], would
the phrase which leapt to my lips, when I wanted to
describe it, be 'Good tidings of great joy'?"

For a great many of us, the honest answer could only
be "No". And this is a fact of some importance. Irreligion is less intellectually respectable today than it
has been for many years past. Because of the appalling
catastrophes which have erupted out of the secure and
optimistic world of the nineteenth century, the wholly
self-sufficient and self-confident aspect of the modern
humanist tradition has been viewed with decreasing
favour by many who are far from wanting to break
away from the tradition as a whole. So a good many
people are having second thoughts of some kind about
religion; and despite the growth of interest in the
spirituality of the Far East, and the syncretism which
is understandably popular because so undemanding,
this still probably means for most people second thoughts
about Christianity. But the question is: Assuming, for
the moment, that some kind of return to Christianity *is*
the right thing, what does it imply? Mr. Eliot, and Mr.
Greene, and M. Mauriac, for example, all profess acceptance of a Christian world-picture; and you may well be
all the more inclined to think them right because it
isn't their evident business as artists to do so—as you
would assume it *was* the business of an Anglican parson
or a Catholic monk. Poetry of the crisis in the classical
humanist tradition can well, as I blurted out so abruptly
at the reading, depress one to a disabling degree. But

5

once Cambridge had enabled me to respond to poetry more intelligently—which it did chiefly by helping me to digest Mr. Eliot—I found I was compelled to admit that I found the long-lost and much-desired joy of childhood almost as hard to discover in some Christian writing of the day as I did in some non-Christian.

The problem about being cheered up can thus appear, at least, to persist. What is, in fact, supposed to happen to the childhood taste for enjoyment in the vision of a man like Mr. Eliot, for example? Is the stoical humanist vision of tragic maturity a sort of prefiguring, at the natural level, of a similar drastic Christian revision of our attitudes which should make up the putting away of childish things described by St. Paul? Ought the common-or-garden joys of childhood, with all their innocent egotism, to be recognizable at all in Christian joy? What do you explain in terms of which? As Humpty Dumpty remarked to Alice, it's a question of which is to be master, that's all. And that's more than enough, too; for the problem is one of absolutely fundamental attitudes to life, and the complex of forces it represents is a structure built up out of immense psychological and spiritual energies. Those energies can be released destructively or creatively, like the energy in the uranium atom; and whichever way you pick, the results can be spectacular.

This, then, as I see it, was the problem which underlay my crude yet honest puzzlement at that Cambridge poetry reading in 1947, and the slightly more sophisticated yet equally genuine further puzzlement which arose as I found some kind of an answer to the first one. What, in a word, should the true Christian be trying to do with his natural self, in this matter of joy in particular, and in all else by implication? Christians know that they are supposed not to be miserable like

those who have no hope, and whose final assertion of
their human dignity thus has to be in terms of a refusal
even to want any. But what *kind* of a joy is this Christian
joy, as compared with that which we had (if we were
reasonably fortunate) as children, and which we lost
so painfully as the world's evil and our own broke
down the enchanted walls of childhood's short-lived
garden of paradise? What is the relation between the
good things which God hath prepared for them that love
him, and a young couple's sitting in the two-and-three-
pennies eating soft-centred chocolates and watching
Doris Day in a VistaVision musical? Are we faced with
an either-or between selfish and futilely escapist fixation
in, or regression to, the experienceless egotism of childhood, and a higher Christian joy which can't, of its very
nature, make any concession to the selfish hungers of
natural man?

In this book I am going to try to play with this problem within certain limits only.[1] I am not concerned
with the issues it raises in pure theology, but with how
it works itself out in the sphere of culture. Within
that field I shall concentrate on literature, and, within
the field of literature, ultimately on the work of two
twentieth-century Christian writers in particular.

The terms of the question—the relation between
natural joy like that of childhood and the supernatural
joy of Christianity—make its literary aspect of special
interest to an Englishman like myself. For in the English, for good or bad, the child tends to live on in the
man especially strongly. Surprisingly enough, considering the venerable picture of the Englishman as a
glum creature, the childhood capacity for enjoyment,
together with a tendency to react by laughter to the

---

[1] As I shall try to show later on, playing with something does not in
any way imply a merely frivolous attitude towards it.

absurd, gives the comic element a strikingly large share in our literature's great achievements. And the question is, once more, what is to be explained in terms of which? When you contrast on the one hand, the element of comic warmth in England's literary tradition—in Chaucer, in Shakespeare, in Dickens, to name no more— and the Eliotian bleakness on the other hand, the problem of the relation between Christian joy and that of the common natural man seems repeated in a more sharply particularized form. Is English comicality specifically non-Christian? non-Catholic?

We can only judge of pure theology, for the most part, by the actual fruits it bears in the world of our culture and agri-culture—the world of daily thinking and doing in which we express our ideals and earn our daily bread. And this question of the relation between English comicality and Catholic seriousness in the work of a poet like Mr. Eliot is of special interest to anybody who tries to relate his English inheritance to the Catholic tradition; as I did, not so very long after the embarrassing experience with which this story opened. It becomes easier to understand the rather abstract question, what is a Christian supposed to be trying to do with his natural self, when it is reformulated in the more concrete terms of, what may a Catholic be expected to make of an English literary tradition so largely built up in connection with the rejection of Catholicism? Yet far from restricting the relevance of the discussion, this particularized instance focuses the wider issues more sharply; the implications of this question reach out not only to the whole relation between nature and the supernatural, but also to sharply particularized problems of England's cultural health or disease which the non-Christian humanist, too, considers vitally important.

Chief among these, perhaps, is the split between the world of the "eggheads" and that of the common man. These two separated worlds are both, in their own ways, aware that their lack of common ground is a bad thing. The Church is aware of it too. On purely theological grounds alone, she is, in her series of doctrinal decisions as to what words are to mean, a determined champion of the cause of common ground. But she is its champion, too, in the field of culture. Cultural health is not her primary concern, but it cannot help being a concern of hers, and an important one too. For although a man isn't saved *by* his culture, he *is* saved *in* his culture, being not a spirit unfortunately imprisoned in matter but a wedding of the two, destined to remain so when taken up into the very life of the Trinity Itself. He works out his salvation in and through the making of houses and clothes, the cooking of meals and the singing of songs, the playing of games and the sharing of work. The Church teaches that it is man's primary duty to love God. But she doesn't teach that he is to do it by sitting down on the ground by himself and uniting his will to God until starvation transports him to the next world.[1] He loves God by living his life for him—whether that means building jet airliners, chanting the monastic Office, digging holes in the road or writing symphonies; by doing everything, from sowing seed to reaching the highest peaks of philosophical speculation, which goes to round out the total life of man. And one of the basic qualities of that life is that it cannot be lived except in common—with the help and co-operation of other men. That applies to all the things over and above bread alone by which man lives, just as much as to

[1] In case anyone thinks I am being whimsy, something of this kind was actually taught and practised by the thirteenth-century Albigensians, in the *endura*, the fast to death.

9

the elementary problems of feeding, self-protection and education which are the basic concern of the family and the social community. It applies to the world of culture as well as to that of agri-culture. Where the thinkers and poets and painters and musicians of a society are isolated one from another and all from the rest of the community by lack of common ground, intellectual, emotional and spiritual, their individual work suffers and is impoverished.

Not only that; the work of the world of daily bread-getting suffers too. It is obvious enough that if no crops are sown the artists and thinkers cannot survive to do their work; but it is equally true, though not equally obvious, that where there is no vision the people perish—the whole people, not just the intelligentsia. A diminution of creative instinct in the intellectual elite of a nation can involve, sooner or later, a decline in the creative vitality of its people as a whole; there is a direct connection between the productivity of a country's industry, the standards of its craftsmanship, and the nature of the spiritual insight embodied in the visions of its artists. The way in which a statesman approaches the negotiation of a treaty, or a factory manager the handling of his men, or a farmer the managing of his land, or an artisan the handling of his tools—all these things are profoundly conditioned by the kind of vision infused into the national consciousness by men whom statesman, manager, farmer or artisan may never have heard of. And it is because all these aspects of man's culture and agri-culture have their bearing on the way in which he lives his course towards his final destiny that the Church agrees with the humanist that what goes on in the world of the eggheads matters directly to what goes on in that of the common man. A man can save his soul in a sickly culture, just as he can save

it in a squalid home or a diseased body; but the Church
has never argued from this that it is a matter of indifference to her whether or not men create great art, or build
decent houses, or make war on disease. The Catholic is
certainly separated from all other men by that lack of
common ground indicated by the extent to which they
decline to assent to the Church's definitions of the meanings of key words in human discourse. But the reality
and importance of this must never make anyone lose
sight of the common ground of common humanity which
Catholics share with all men, and in terms of which
genuine communion between them is always possible—
indeed, essential. The special problems of the Catholic
are one with problems common to all men because of
their common humanity. And since this is so, it is only
to be expected that particular problems like an English
Catholic's attitude to certain elements in English literature should be inseparable not merely from the questions of national morale and cultural wellbeing which
concern his non-Catholic fellow-countrymen, but also
from those which face men of other countries.

To some extent at least the difficulties of a dis-integrated culture—a world of technologists, men-in-the-
street, artists, philosophers, statesmen, theologians and
so on all out of step with one another—are the problem of
all Europe. And the distinguishing feature of European
civilization, and its developed self-renewal in the New
World, is its pattern of general likeness between things
individually diverse. Just as the general problem of the
relation of natural to supernatural presents itself to us in
such concrete instances as the place of common childhood joy in great Christian poetry, so the universality of
Europe exists as a supra-national complex of sharply
distinct nationalities; historically speaking, Christendom. The national units composing the civilization

11

of the whole West flourish only in the seedbed of that civilization's greater whole. And so the problems and achievements of the Frenchman, the German, the American and so on create the indispensable background against which the Englishman must look at his own problems if they are to be intelligible. And it is because the great whole is built up of parts both similar and diverse (unlike the amorphous or monolithic societies of the East)[1] that the particular problems of the Englishman are relevant to those facing other westerners. Here again, to indicate the limits within which the discussion takes place is to extend the range of the audience to which it can be intelligible.

There's no need, then, of further justification for focusing such a question as, What may a Catholic be expected to make of the English literary tradition, even more sharply in a question like, What may a Catholic be expected to make of the achievement of that tradition's most distinguished contemporary architect—Mr. T. S. Eliot? Is the aristocratic austerity of his work the symbol of a revolutionary transformation which must go on in the English mind before it can be integrated once more with the Catholic-rooted world of Europe's culture—the highly serious and uncompromisingly adult world which produced, for example, the St. John of the Cross and the Baudelaire who figure so powerfully

---

[1] There is a striking parallel between the great central themes of European philosophy and the nature of the civilization within which they have been discussed. Medieval Christendom's central philosophical achievement was to resolve, via the controversy about universals, the conflict between things' likeness to, and difference from, one another. Its central political achievement was to reconcile, in the society of Christendom, the individuality of Europe's nations and the universality of her faith. But modern Europe's main philosophical preoccupation has been the exploration of the distinction between abstract thought and the concrete thing. And her main cultural preoccupation—even if against her own will—has been the exploitation of the distinction between the unity of the European spirit and the mutual antagonism of the European nations.

in the background to Mr. Eliot's work? Or is the English childishness, with its often-unsuspected capacity for common enjoying laughter, something whose under-development in Continental Catholic culture (and ex-Catholic culture) is one of the hurts inflicted by the Reformation? The thing forms a sort of mental jigsaw-puzzle, and the question is again, what is to be fitted to which? And that basic ambivalence in the problem —its optical-puzzle, facing-both-ways aspect—makes Mr. Eliot a particularly good focal point. For a key aspect of his achievement is its enigmatic quality, and the enigmatically significant position he occupies in the complex pattern of the relation between the English and the Catholic elements in the tradition of his country's culture.

In obvious contrast to his achievement stands that of the second well-known Christian writer whom I shall ultimately discuss—G. K. Chesterton. The extent of the difference between these men, and the extent to which the intellectual climate of England has changed in the past quarter-of-a-century, is sufficiently illus-trated by the fact that today many would consider it almost ludicrous to compare them. And whether or not you agree that Chesterton is unworthy of serious consideration in the same breath with Mr. Eliot, or whatever the qualifications with which you accept some part of that attitude, you can hardly deny that the contrast between them is extreme. Where Mr. Eliot is austere, Chesterton is genial; where Mr. Eliot is desperately earnest, Chesterton is scandalously playful; where Mr. Eliot conveys a painfully achieved approval of existence, Chesterton communicates a childlike exultation in it; where Mr. Eliot cultivates a pretty Christian wit, Chesterton bubbles over with laughter. Viewed in the light of humanism's increasingly stringent critique of the culture and society it has created, the first appears as essentially distinguished, the second as essentially vulgar. And it is really in virtue of that culminating distinction between "mass civilization and minority culture" that we have to account for the fact that Chesterton is hardly taken seriously at all by the intellectuals—the "clerks"—of the Second World War period, or their successors of the atomic age. To the majority of them, probably, there is no surer sign of his failure to achieve membership of the cultural elite than his fundamental happiness and pleasure in the being both of himself and everything else. Indeed, for many of the most sensitive and intelligent men of today happiness of any basic kind is either escapism or immaturity, and despair the very stuff of adulthood. It's hardly surprising that for such Chesterton invites a critical placing so easy as to involve little critical effort at all.

How far this view is a fair one is a point to be discussed later. But whatever Chesterton was or wasn't, it does seem that he was, in some respects, more in the central stream of English literature than Mr. Eliot is (which could, of course, be a smack in the eye for English literature). In his highly developed comic instinct, the uninhibitedly "popular" basis of his art, and the vigorous amateurishness with which he overspills the classical canons of form—in all these things he is in direct line with Chaucer, Shakespeare and Dickens. And thus once more (and for the last time, you may well be hoping), we see refocused our old question of what is to be explained in terms of which? Is the Roman Catholic Chesterton—at the cultural level, at least— more English than Catholic: and is the Anglo-Catholic Mr. Eliot more Catholic than English? And is a choice between the two a choice between "popular" bowels and "clerkly" head? Suppose we have on the one hand a Chesterton whose appeal to a vulgar English taste for enjoyment is made possible by smoothing off the tragically hard edges of Catholicism. And suppose we have on the other an Eliot whose power of compromise is robbed of comfort by the chill of a truly Catholic either-or. Is the choice between them a choice between a culture's fine flower and its gross soil? Is the "popular" nature of Chesterton's art achieved only in debasement, and the distinction of Mr. Eliot's possible only in virtue of its unintelligibility to the common man?

These two do indeed draw to a final focus the wide implications of the question about the proper place of joy with which I began. And this complementing of the particular by the universal indicates in itself the pattern which my discussion will tend to follow in its natural course. For although this dialectic certainly assumes a Catholic world-picture, its main appeal will be not to revelation, but to reason. Reason is common sense; and it's the natural complementarity between the common—the universal—and the extraordinary—the particular—which the Church endorses when she maintains that all the common sense of all mankind balances upon the mysterious axis of Rome; and that commonplace, flesh-and-earth Rome is the concrete centre to which the universal pattern of man's mysterious common sense refers. The appeal to mystery and that to common sense are always, inevitably, one.

I'm not, then, doing anything which either the Anglo-Saxon or Catholic mind should feel unfamiliar with when I begin my investigation into the problem of joy, and its implications, by recalling that all such discussions as these are discussions about the way in which we use words. That does not, of course, imply that they are nothing *but* discussions about how we use

15

words. But it is obvious that the answers you can give to a question depend on the way in which it is put, and that the conclusions which an argument will yield depend in part at least on the terms which it begins in.

When, in the past few pages, I have been talking about this oddity, joy, and about laughter, and the comic, and Englishness, and Catholicism, and all the rest of it, I have been talking about them all in terms of "ought"—what *ought* a Christian artist to think of the works of Mr. Eliot and Chesterton, and so on. And if you follow that "ought's" implications back to the beginning, you will find that this discussion has as its reference point a concept of human maturity. When the idea of being cheered up (particularly by Browning) was viewed with such contempt, it was against an implied idea of what a mature man *ought* to be; and that idea certainly included an element of spiritual fulfilment. All the argument about whether a man "ought" to want to be cheered up implied an idea of the fulness of man's being, of his becoming all that he had the power to be. And that idea is the reference point on which we can take our bearings when we begin to manœuvre the various pieces of this mental jigsaw-puzzle.

In this book, whether we are talking about secular-humanist ideas of human maturity, or Christian ideas in general, or Catholic ideas in particular, we are discussing them at the cultural level—pre-eminently, as they express themselves in the creations of literature. We are looking at spiritual maturity as it is incarnate in literary greatness. So the obvious thing to do is to begin by considering for a moment the nature of today's general ideas of greatness in literature.

The thing that stands out at once as soon as you do this is the extent to which such greatness is thought of in terms of the tragic vision. And it is obvious where you must look if you are to grasp the immediate historical roots of this particular concept of human maturity and fulfilment.

At the Renaissance there is suddenly turned inside out, with comparative and dramatic suddenness, that deep-rooted distrust of the "singular", and implied trust in the common, man, which—despite all the antidemocratic features of the Middle Ages—was the rock on which the mental world of the first Christendom, with all its social, political and cultural organization, was founded. You may be duly sceptical of the simplification which labels the Middle Ages "The Age of Faith" and the world of the sixteenth-to-eighteenth centuries "The Age of Reason"; a closer look shows all too hair-raising a capacity for unfaith in the one and all too sinister an irrationality heaving and boiling away under the beautifully symmetrical constructions of the other. Yet for all that, it is true that in the sixteenth century European man does round on his old world in a crisis of dominative self-assertion and critical analysis which is sufficiently different from the most sceptical thought-ventures of the Middle Ages to make label-sticking justifiable. The comparatively sudden advent of the titanist type of great artist is only one aspect of the whole dazzling apparition of the Renaissance New Man, whose very essence is the extra-ordinary. In the age that preceded this new world you had the concept of great kings, great bishops, great warriors, great scholars, great monks and so on—greatness worked out in terms of what is common, universal. Created beings were evaluated by their fittingness in the place they occupied in a great hierarchical pattern whose node was the Creator. Medieval men are great in virtue of the way in which they contribute to the common design composed by humanity as a universal whole; St. Louis is typical

17

of them, and the Emperor Frederick II, the Wonder of the World, the exception that proves the rule. But with the sixteenth century there disappears this idea of greatness as being rooted in what is common to men, and instead of great abbots, great kings and the like we begin to get Great Men pure and simple; titanic figures distinguished increasingly, not by the degree to which they fill their part in a pattern of common humanity, but by the degree to which they are different from the "common herd" of their fellows. They are not great with reference to some extrinsic standard; they are themselves the standards of greatness, and their pre-eminence is expressed in terms of pure human intensity, pure charge of being. It is the *virtù* of Machiavelli's ideal prince. And Machiavelli, of course, teaching as he does that every great ruler should make up his own moral code as he goes, in the interest of his own success, is one of the clearest of all the foci in which you can see in little the whole brilliant vision of the New Man: singular, a law unto himself, making his own world, moral and mental and material, in an astounding titanic gesture towards the uniqueness and omnipotence formerly attributed only to divinity.

In this revolution in the concept of man the two elements of the un-common and the new are inseparably connected. There's an individualistic breakaway from the common man and his common world, towards the uniqueness of divinity and the singularity of the titanic man who aims towards it; and this is also a breakaway from the familiar towards the unprecedented. Instead of a vision of vitality as a "dearest freshness deep down things"—a wonder close to us in the very heart of what we know well—we get an identification of the wonderful with the unprecedented. The age born of the Renaissance is not, like its predecessor, one whose desire is to

18

arrive at the point from which it started and know that place for the first time. It is one whose passionate desire is to get somewhere else. More abundant life is looked for not in the depths of the ordinary but in the further reaches of the extraordinary—"outside". And this sudden powerful desire for what is "outside" shows itself in the archetypal pattern of the "New World" which underlies so many of the forms the dynamic energy of the Renaissance takes. Extra-ordinary may mean the flesh-and-blood (or should we say spices-and-gold?) geographical world of the sailors and conquistadors. It may mean that overpowering experience of the Protestant Christian, dizzy with excitement and fear at finding himself, implicitly if not consciously, his own Pope, ultimately an autonomous one-man Church in a constellation of autonomous one-man Churches outside the one-and-only common or universal Church of previous Christian tradition. It may mean the exploring empiricism of the natural sciences, with Galileo claiming to discover by observation and experiment things which, on the supposed authority of Aristotle, shouldn't even have been there to be discovered. It may be Machiavelli stepping right out of the old framework of morality to make each great man the author of his own private Ten Commandments, with political success as the final end to which they are designed to bring him. All these New Worlds have in common a movement very different from the rythm of the dance of the Middle Ages. To the repose which *that* movement implied succeeds a dynamic restlessness; life as progress from the outmoded to the unheard-of. The pattern of the way of the new man is not a circling voyage of rediscovery which is a homecoming, but a rising arc of departure from communion in what is common towards godlike isolation in what is not.

I have described this New World of new worlds by contrasting it with the preceding world of the Middle Ages. And indeed, one of the main aspects of the Renaissance and the age to which it gave birth is revolt against them. To be sure, that is not the whole of the Renaissance story, by any means; there is continuity as well as rupture. But whatever else there may be to be said when you talk about the essence of the Renaissance crisis, still in the event it did manifest itself very largely as a revolt against the medieval order. It was a revolt of philosophy against loyalty to theology; of natural science against the overlordship of metaphysics; of nations against Christendom; of individual judgement against religious authority; of trader and merchant against feudal lord; of king against the customary restraints of feudal order; of politics against even a theoretical subjection to the Christian code of morality. A breakout from the accepted cosmic order of the medieval world in a titanic enterprise of establishing a new order by the dominative assertion of man's own powers—that is the ultimate pattern of the spiritual and mental and psychological revolution of the Renaissance. And it is a pattern of revolt against what the Middle Ages would have called man's "creaturely" status—the concept of essential dependence implied in the notion of being created. The change of standpoint is, ultimately, from one which sees man as part of a greater pattern to one which sees him as pattern's creator.

The quickest of glances at the literary scene in England during the first upsurge of this titanist revolution shows the link between titanism and the tragic vision of human maturity. For there you have, springing up almost overnight, the amazing flowering of Elizabethan and Jacobean tragic drama, from Sackville and Norton to Beaumont and Fletcher. The literary creation of

Elizabethan tragic drama is a "new world" in the fullest
Renaissance sense of the term, fit to stand on an equal
footing with the astronomy of Galileo and Copernicus,
the superman-morality of Machiavelli, the voyages to
the Indies, the despotic monarchs, the cannon and the
printing presses and all the rest.

One very interesting point about this particular
literary voyage of discovery is the way in which it
stands on its head, so to speak, a pattern fundamental
to the life and thought of the Middle Ages. Medieval
man's aim was, as I have said, re-entry into a freshness
of being that might have been lost but was always known
to exist. Insofar as he was interested in New Worlds it
was only in the sense indicated in the Scriptural text
"Behold, I make all things new"; the new was the
original in the strict sense, something to do with the
state of affairs in the beginning. The Renaissance world,
revolting from this idea of discovery as homecoming,
and setting out to achieve *total* discovery, totally new
worlds, did so in this particular case by returning in part
to an old one. The medieval world-picture had been
formed on a concept of redemption, so daring that the
like of it had never been entertained before; it was a
picture of a divine comedy in which the worst of evil
was mysteriously turned to account by a greater and
triumphant good. In such a world, tragedy in the true
sense is not possible, and does not, indeed, exist; insofar
as "tragedy" exists at all in the Middle Ages it is a
straightforward edifying recital of the Falls of Princes
and the turning of the Wheel of Fortune, an object-
lesson against the sin of pride. To rediscover and re-
create a new world of tragedy English Renaissance drama
has to return to an older world; that of antiquity. And
in that world the tears at the heart of things are not
viewed as destined to be wiped from our eyes in a

comforting which, for all its cosmic scale, is in its own way just as homely as the hug and sweet a mother gives her baby when it has fallen over. The new age's rediscovery of the old world is a rediscovery of unresolved conflict, and a consequent basic criticism of existence. The medieval *Weltanschauung*[1] was one of fundamental acceptance. But the new age, revolting against the familiar repose of such a cosmic order, re-encounters, raw and naked, the shock of that intolerable clash between good and evil as it appeared outside the unique resolution offered by the Jewish-Christian tradition. It re-entered a mind that saw the conflict between the goodness of being and the evil of suffering as unresolved; a mind forced, through that vision, and by its own very honesty, into a criticism of existence pushed, when need arose, to the spine-chilling finality of Sophocles' "Not to be born is best" or Aristotle's "Death is the greatest of terrors, because it is the end."

Yet for all this similarity between antiquity and the Renaissance there is a profound difference too; a difference because of the continuity which the new tragic vision has, for all its revolutionary nature, with the vision of divine comedy underlying the order of the Middle Ages. The old Christian morality and mystery drama, with its roots in the liturgy and its centre in the Mass, is almost as important an ingredient in the dazzling achievements of the Elizabethan stage as the neo-paganism of the Renaissance intellectuals. One and a half millenia of Christian optimism do not go for nothing; no matter how heavily the Elizabethans draw upon the stoicism of Seneca, their heroes cannot help but inhabit a world much less inhuman than that of the Greeks, who provided Seneca with his. Semitic thought, and the

---

[1] I apologize for the term, but it is one of the infrequent cases where there just isn't an English word which will do as well.

Christian thought which flowers out of it, is nothing if
not intensely personal; and even a world-picture which
is no more than ex-Christian is something very different
from one in which *themis*—the impersonal principle of
cosmic "fittingness"—crushes its violators with a re-
morselessness suggesting some kind of infernal auto-
mation and the very gods themselves are recognizably
personifications of the non-human. Even if Christianity
has left no stronger or more positive a trace upon new
European man than a tendency to atheistic blasphemy,
he still inherits a mental picture of the world which
does not provide a really incongruous framework for
the human. The very intensity of his revolts against
existence presupposes, among other things, viewing the
horrors which life can produce against ideas of divinity's
benevolence in which personal and human terms play
an essential part.

Which means, of course, that the presence of Christian
elements in the tragic critique of existence cuts both
ways. The Christian world, whether in the glow of its
heaven or the glare of its hell, is a warmer place than
the world of the ancients was; it lacks that curious
chill at the heart which casts an invisible shadow over
the brightest sunlight of pagan Greece. But greater
expectations of God imply a sharper anguish when these
appear to be unfulfilled. The world of antiquity expected less of divinity to start with. It lacked the comfort of the concept of a God who is infinite love, and
whose mercy is above all his works; but lacked, too, the
correspondingly sharper pain of the suffering which
arises when you experience evil as seeming to make
nonsense of just that idea of divinity. To that extent
its serious tragic play works to achieve a release from
tension which takes place at a lower level than that
aimed at by the Elizabethans. Yet if the world of Hamlet

is free of the glacial and lunar bleakness which pervades that of Orestes and Oedipus, still the modern tragic stage is permeated with a kind of nostalgia which the Greeks did not suffer. For somewhere behind its partial satisfaction and basic inadequacy lies the lost playground of the medieval ritual, with its echoing chant of *Agnus Dei, qui tollis peccata mundi*; and the Greeks, at least, could feel no hankering after a kind of liberation which had no place in the "folk-memory" of their civilization.

When, therefore, John Donne summed up the vertigo of the New Ages in

The new philosophy calls all in doubt

the challenged order of the "all" is something very much less impersonal and fatalistic than the order which was subjected to the criticism of Euripides; and the anguish arising from its being called in question is correspondingly keener. Thus, the dark underside to the brilliant mental world of Elizabethan drama, the interaction of which with a typically Renaissance self-confidence and exaltation provides the dynamic light and shade of these plays. The dramatic critique of existence develops a sharp enough edge when it bites into the substance of a world which has tears at the heart of its loveliness; but it develops an even sharper one when it is working on the concept of a world redeemed. The resurrection of tragedy was possible only on the condition of a *Götterdämmerung* of the medieval world, and indeed it is precisely a disintegration of the medieval cosmos which provides the "atomic fission" that powers the dazzling and intoxicating firework display of the Renaissance. The dissolution of order and the release of energy go together.

You can say, then, that the intervening Christian
experience has spoiled modern tragedy's chance of repeating the full naked starkness of its ancient prototype;
the Christianizing process through which the mind of
Europe has been passed has left its vision of the natural
world obstinately impregnated with the atmosphere of
Christian hope. The Renaissance's very substitution of
belief in progress for the ancient world's cyclical fatalism
is a typical example of this. But the very fact of this
neo-pagan substitution of the movement of hope for
the full stop of stoical endurance means that the new
tragedy has in it possibilities of a kind of finality which
was out of the reach of the Greeks even at their bleakest.
"He who has never hoped can never despair", says
Bernard Shaw's Caesar; but he who puts the world-
picture of Christian hope itself to the supreme test of an
ultimate tragic critique opens up possibilities of a kind
of nihilism which makes the mind dizzy. To see how
this works out in practice we shall have to consider for
a moment the work of M. Sartre; for it is only with him,
I think, that in the world of drama proper[1] the new
tragic critique is pushed to its ultimate conclusion in
the disintegration of tragedy itself and the creation of an
evil "comedy" of the absurd.

I have put the word "comedy" in inverted commas
here; and indeed you might say that M. Sartre's world
has been, exactly, a world in which everything is in
inverted commas. For it is a world in which meaning is
jarred clean out of being, and an attempt is made to
assent to the cross-eyed unfocusing of vision implied,
as being the only kind of stereoscopy which accurately
pictures reality. Encountering M. Sartre's earlier thought

---

[1] It had, of course, been anticipated in philosophy by Nietzsche's proclamation of the "death of God", and his aim at a life "beyond good and
evil"—to say nothing of the actual insanity into which he followed,
with a strangely heroic consistency, the lead of his own thinking.

is rather like being suddenly presented with an alchemist's alembic or a medieval astrolabe or a stone slab with an inscription in Aztec; you can hardly take no notice of it but there doesn't seem to be anything sensible you can do with it. Perhaps he provides the finest focal point there has ever been for the ordinary Englishman's fascinatedly ambivalent attitude towards the French; his feeling of inferiority in the face of so much intelligence being so remorselessly intelligent, and his compensating secret conviction that for practical purposes it often works out as more or less the equivalent of being cracked. I don't think that anybody but a true French café intellectual could have worked out into a formal "ism" the idea of man as an impossible attempt at being a non-existent God.

It is only in the existentialist drama of M. Sartre that the more horrific potentialities of post-Christian tragedy are worked out to their final dead end, and the critical, dominative

> . . . appetite, an universal wolf
> . . . Must make perforce an universal prey,
> And last eat up himself.

In his existentialist drama the modern tragic criticism of existence in the actual form of tragic drama is worked out not so much to its logical conclusion as to that final blind alley of absurdity which is the finish of all logic. It is a contra-natural performance which can be carried out only with the material provided by the Christian super-natural underwriting of the purely natural world. The idea of the intrinsic goodness of being was inherited by even the most violently rebellious post-Catholic dramatists from the medieval world on which they rounded; and it formed the indispensable ground against which alone the evil of tragedy could be seen as such.

26

But at the logical focal point of M. Sartre's dramatic thought, that resisted bite of evil into good vanishes, and we are left with a mental sensation equivalent to the physical one of stepping onto the stair that isn't there. The anvil on which the hammer of tragic critique has struck such brilliant showers of sparks disappears, wholly disintegrated at last by the hammering of a wholly bitter wonder; tragedy has eaten up itself. Man's dominative, accusing and self-excusing analysis of his world that is "not quite itself" here emerges as a nakedly murderous onslaught under which being itself chokes into absurdity—in the subjective world of the mind, at least. There is no longer any meaning in the "Why, why, why?" of the tragedian, for the very ground of being that made that cry meaningful is now seen as totally absurd. Modern tragic drama labours its artistic-religious redemptive "work" to an insanely logical close in a kind of evil play. In the medieval world there was redemptive "play" in the true sense—something which both doesn't matter—"without me you can do nothing"—and which nevertheless demands the best that we are capable of—"strive to enter by the narrow gate". Then there is a complete turning-inside-out of this into the self-sufficient "work" of tragic self-redemption, which, for all its desperate necessity and anxious effort, "doesn't matter" in the ironic sense; the greatest of tragic heroes and tragic dramas can only offer the shadow of an answer to the question which the earlier age had summed up in "Who shall deliver me from the body of this death?" And then this second stage of sacred play profaned into a humanistic and secular tragic "work" undergoes yet another turning-inside-out. Carried to its logical end, its dominative critique eats into the very sanities that form its own vitals, and those who practise it take a nightmarish and vertiginous plunge into a "new world" of evil play where tragedy destroys its own point. There is no tragedy in *Huis Clos*; the tragic point has been lost in the wider context of an ultimate bad joke. The shabby and old-fashioned hotel waiting-room which constitutes the hell of the characters in the play symbolizes that ironic apotheosis of Renaissance titanist man, with all his deadly serious-ness and diminishing capacity for play, which Mr. Eliot referred to when he made one of the speakers in *The Waste Land* say

> I think we are in rats' alley
> Where the dead men lost their bones.

The worst of the pointless point of *Huis Clos*' grim joke is that conscious appreciation of it which the author invites his audience to share with him. The critique of existence voiced by the tragic hero turns upon himself, and the new world of man's self-assertion ends not in a bang but a whimper—or shall we say, a lunatic chuckle. For the ultimate point of the tragic hero turns out to be that he has no point whatsoever; there is not in his private world of absurdity even enough of sanity for rebellion to get a purchase on. That very honesty which drove the New Man of the sixteenth century to make his tragic critique of existence has driven him on to make a further and devastating critique of the critique itself; his titanic leap upward towards the unattainable divine reveals itself as a plunge into the unplumbably clownish. For the whole point of the relationship of the inhabitants of Sartre's second-class waiting-room in hell is that it is an attempt at an impossible denial of all relationship and all community. The patternless constellation of private worlds which is that Sartrian universe holds all men violently together in the mutual repulsion of an interminable and unresolvable conflict. "Hell is other people." To each would-be human god of his own private universe the other would-be human gods, with *their* private universes, are in themselves and by their mere existence so many immovable obstacles to the irresistible force of the drive to self-assertion—the "useless passion". Merely by existing, they turn his godlike reign over his own private universe into a bad joke. It is a shabby hotel waiting-room eternally shared with other similar human caricature-gods. None of them will turn their community from torment to comfort and communion by free acknowledgment of their creaturely lack of self-sufficiency. Yet none can abolish it by making good against the others his unrelinquished claim to godlike total freedom and dominion. This is the tragic fate—man's inevitable yet impotent revolt against his condition—finally stripped of that element of grandeur which makes it tragic. All that is left is a total clownishness laughing laughterlessly at itself with a sound like "the crackling of thorns under a pot".

In this decisive bankruptcy of neo-pagan tragic sacrifice is the heart of the breakdown of man's dominative attempt to master the destructive tensions in experience and redeem himself from the sufferings inseparable from his condition. For the ultimate meaning of that attempt can only be what is in fact the essence of titanism—the attempt to achieve divinity. And the only possible "realization" of that aim reveals itself as entirely ironic. Man embraces as an absolute, divine freedom his ability to reign as "god" over a nightmare private world of the absurd.

II : THE MAGIC MIRROR OF
SELFCONSCIOUSNESS

To start off, then, by aiming at the heavenly throne (even if partly unconsciously) is, if you are consistent with that initial impulse, to end up in Rats' Alley. That is not a piece of sermonizing digestible only by those who accept Christian assumptions; it is a truth demonstrated for us by a highly logical non-Christian work-out of the implications of rejecting them. Incidentally, we may note in passing that the dominative humanist critique's ultimate fine "flowers of evil" have a certain ambiguity about them. At first sight atheist existentialism can be so determinéd-to-be-a-villain that its very nihilism has about it something a trifle ludicrous. You might be tempted to write it off as rather an unpleasant variety of the old game of blinding 'em with science. But the Continent, and France especially perhaps, has a habit of taking itself very seriously. It is a sobering reminder of existentialism's negative potentialities to recall that not so long ago a young man was charged with inciting a woman to drown her small child for the sole purpose of providing them both with an exercise in existentialist moral freedom. In all this I-wants-to-make-yer-flesh-creep talk there is, unfortunately, far too much seriousness of purpose for us to dismiss it as the mental acrobatics of the conventionally unconventional. A really diabolical element of perversity is there, and quite real; and contact with it, even of an indirect kind, is a correspondingly unpleasant experience; not least because here, as always, evil is not in the very least the exciting thing which the romantically-minded sometimes think it. Yet when you've given this element its full weight, it still doesn't wholly exclude an element of unintended comedy. For there is always something childish in the spectacle of a grown man declaring solemnly that he is going to be just as bad as bad can be, if not worse; something which made the Middle Ages, who took the devil seriously enough, make him also, in their mystery plays, a figure of fun. And this should remind us that, quite apart from the fact that it is an impertinence to sit in judgement on the souls of our fellows, we shouldn't be too quick to discuss this devil-less diabolizing simply in the terms of the Frenchman who wrote a book entitled: *Sartre: Is He Possessed?* There is plenty of twisted courage and honesty tangled up with the perversity; and we do not know their full power for making M. Sartre retreat, ultimately, out of Rats' Alley. Indeed, in some ways it would seem almost impossible for anyone to remain there permanently; though the late André Gide, I suppose, found a solution of sorts to even that problem by popping in and out like (appropriately enough) the lover in the traditional French farce. And up to the time of writing Mr. Samuel Beckett seems to be displaying an unprecedented capacity for staying where "one can neither stand nor lie nor sit".

But the fact remains that in his time M. Sartre has worked out the modern tragic critique *ad absurdum* with a vengeance. And the important point for our immediate purpose is that it has been an overripe fruit of the dominative tradition itself who has described the type of man which it creates as an inevitable but futile attempt at divinity—a "useless passion". It is a titanist to end all titanists who describes titanist self-assertion as absurd.

A crisis of just that kind of self-assertion was what I looked back to, earlier on, when I was considering the roots of the modern tragic conception of human maturity and literary greatness. On this point, then, the final verdict on the Renaissance of modern secular humanism at its most consistent agrees, however reluctantly, with that which the Middle Ages would have pronounced. They would have seen the crisis as a denial of humanity's creaturely condition—to say nothing of humanity's fallen condition—and viewed it as, fundamentally, a violation of mere sanity. In that final evaluation they would have been in agreement with many moderns who are as far as can be reasonably imagined from accepting medieval Christendom's Catholic axioms. To that extent the Renaissance experiment has confirmed, however unwillingly or unwittingly, the assumptions implicit in the medieval world-picture against which it revolted.

Here, the important point is that we have reached solid grounds for questioning the assumptions under-lying the tragic concept of human maturity; and that we have done it by following the work-out of that concept's implications, not by appealing to that very Christian world-picture which it criticizes. It is by reflection on the nature of man as revealed to his own reason, and on the kind of limitations which give form to his greatness, that we are led to discover the destructive chain-reaction which is potential in the tragic vision. Whether or not you accept the Christian view that tragedy began in an attempt to embrace the absurd as real (of which view, more later), you can see for yourself the existentialist demonstration that it ends that way. To reject the tragic concept of human spiritual maturity because it implies an ultimately absurd attitude to the absurd is to reject it on grounds of common sense; that particular department of common sense which is called metaphysics. And I myself came to think more respectfully of my original instinctive resistance to being made miserable largely because of being forced into a groping rediscovery of some of those common man's

inarticulate, obstinate sanities; what Chesterton referred
to as "the dumb certainties of experience" and Mr.
Eliot, perhaps, had partly in mind when he described
the eyes of the Sweeneys of this world as being "assured
of certain certainties".

A sympathetic refusal to accept the tragic standard
of spiritual greatness doesn't, then, have to be simply
a frightened recoil from the strains of a secular humanist
world, back into the reassurance of a world of faith.
Because it is the result of an appeal to common sense—
to reason—it is something supremely humanistic. Reason, common sense, sanity, are precisely what give the
animal, man, his humanity, making him a "he" and not
an "it". It is in search, not denial, of the essence of
humanism that we are compelled to shift the tragic
vision from being a standard of criticism to being a
subject for it. If this were not so we shouldn't, I think,
have much to say to those who argue that any questioning of the tragic standard is in itself a failure to bear the
burden of maturity.

It is with reference to the natural, then, that we come
down at last to the bedrock of solid grounds compelling
us to query the tragic concept of human maturity. But
it is true, of course, that "natural theology", though in
itself a perfectly fitting term, can be a misleading one;
for all metaphysics—that is, the study of being as such—
should end in the study of the ultimate ground of being
—the supernatural God. Natural theology deals with
the supernatural. Which reminds us again that there is
no such thing as the natural pure and simple, so to
speak, suspended in the void by an unshakable grasp of
its own bootlaces. Seeing the true nature of the natural
involves seeing it in the greater setting of the supernatural. And it's highly significant that in order to
work out into its ultimate terms his final development

of the modern titanist, with his tragic criticism of existence, M. Sartre is compelled to make use of the traditional Christian concept of hell; that is, the condition of a creature who finally and totally insists on trying to be a god. This makes it not unreasonable to view in terms of the medieval assumptions our humanistic reaffirmation of common sense in criticizing the tragic vision, and some of the main attitudes which underlay the creation of the modern mental world. Here common sense and mystery speak with one voice. Faced with the ironic revelation of the only "divinity" achievable by man—godlike dominion over a private world of absurdity—you can in fact find in that worst self-imprisoning perversity of pride what the Middle Ages would have called a *felix culpa*, a happy guilt. In the face of the Huis-Clos world of the ultimate bad joke, with all its deadly seriousness, you can in fact legitimately give rein to what is the natural, if slightly shamefaced, reaction of most Englishmen to such things; you can begin to laugh. The titanically serious assertion of total, godlike freedom for man ends, ironically, by shutting him up in the narrowest prison imaginable—a nightmare paralysis which is the ultimate and chaotic caricature of all order. But the clownishly playful enjoyment of his marvellous ridiculousness can build out of topsy-turvydom the implications of an order particularly solid and serene.

"Great wits are sure to madness near allied", wrote that master of particularly sane poetry, Dryden. In an age faced with mental situations inconceivable to him, we may make the further application of his words, that sane greatness of wit, which is the greatest type of all, derives its essence from that loving play with the *in*sane—the absurd—which constitutes a true sense of humour. There is nothing complex about this play

34

reaction; it is so commonplace as to be elemental. As proverbial speech wisely says of those misfortunes which suddenly reveal our vulnerability and helplessness, "You've either got to laugh or cry." But you won't laugh if you demand first that laughter should justify itself at a philosophy congress. If you can't see anything funny at all—that is, anything at all like your own foolishness—in the world of the Parisian intelligentsia, then that's that; if you cannot feel free to laugh at the Goon Show until you have done a thesis on *Goonismus in der Weltanschauung der Gegenwart,* then there's nothing for it but prayer. Any argument designed to *prove* to a man that there is something laughable in the absurd is heading for Rats' Alley just as surely as any argument designed to prove to him that he exists.

What it comes to, then, is this. The modern re-establishment of the ancient tragic critique of existence meant a "transvaluation of values", to use the phrase coined by Nietzsche at the end of the last century; the common sense which the Middle Ages had, in principle, endorsed as man's standard of judgement was subjected to the challenge of uncommon genius, throughout thought and art. The pushing of that tragic critique of being and thought to its logical conclusion leads you into the dustbin world of M. Sartre's second-rate hotel-room in hell; the only way out is a fundamental reversal—another "transvaluation of values" that undoes the work of the first one. Reason divorced from faith—that is, common sense divorced from its roots in mystery—leads from the medieval world of divine comedy via the world of human tragedy to the world of inhuman absurdity. And when you awake from that nightmare in the saving knowledge that true laughter is justified in the face of the absurd, it is as obvious as ridiculousness itself that the "transvaluation of values" to which you're then

35

committed is one which will reinterpret tragedy in the wider context of comedy.

We have got thus far, then, in justification of the childish impulse to be cheered up, to enjoyment, reading Browning and all the rest of it. But we are talking about all this in terms of England's culture and English literature; what does this kind of revaluation mean in such terms?

Clearly, Elizabethan drama is the crisis point at which the matter of the old medieval world is transformed in an "atomic fission" of dazzling energy. The old values are by no means wiped out in a twinkling, in fact from some aspects they are never totally wiped out at all; but none the less they do form the fuel on which the long blaze of the dominative revolution feeds, and the greater the brilliance of the explosion, the greater the progressive consumption and disintegration of the old sanities. In the whole brilliant panorama of this critique of the old world of supernatural redemption, conflict-resolution and hope, the most dazzling part of the fireworks is provided, of course, by Shakespeare—the most dazzling tragic fireworks, perhaps, which have ever been provided. If you want to see how the picture changes when you shift from the viewpoint of tragic humanism, there is no better place to see it than in him.

It is true, of course, that the Shakespearean scholarship of the last twenty years or so has paid a great deal more serious attention to the less famous among Shakespeare's works—the "dark comedies", for example, and the last plays—than was customary before. Yet the fact that this particular focusing of attention should have seemed necessary is in itself an indication of how far the approach to Shakespeare has been governed by the assumptions implicit in the tragic-humanist concept of maturity. And we are still predominantly inclined to think of the shape of the Shakespearean achievement in terms of the great tragedies—*Hamlet, Othello, Macbeth, King Lear, Antony and Cleopatra*—with the "histories" as their basis, and the comedies as their setting, the "dark comedies" and the "last plays" providing two rather baffling satellite constellations which, for all their beauties, fit somewhat awkwardly at best into the system centring round the "big five". The "dark comedies", on this view, are most conveniently regarded as artistic enigmas in which their creator found a therapeutic release for a then unbearable intensity of experience which only found integration in plays like *Lear* and *Antony and Cleopatra*. And the "last plays"— *Pericles, Cymbeline, The Winter's Tale* and *The Tempest* —are thought of as intrinsically of less weight than the works of the tragic centre of the pattern. Indeed, so decided is that basic evaluation that some, in the name of very honesty, have felt compelled to develop it further. It has been argued that here as so often in Shakespeare's career, the pattern of events fell in pat with the development of his genius; or, if you prefer, his genius showed itself, precisely, in a brilliant exploitation of the pattern of events. Only in this case the "development" of his genius was the retrograde one of the kind which we see wherever a high civilization passes on into decadence. Box-office taste was dropping steadily towards musical-comedy standards—masque and elaborate spectacle. And this fell in neatly with the inevitable and mysterious fatigue of spirit which made Shakespeare fall away from the titanic heights of his central tragic achievement; as also with his final refinement of technical virtuosity which tuned the blank-verse instrument to a pitch where it seems in fact to have had no further possibilities apart from the internal collapse which it in fact suffered at the hands of the later Jacobean dramatists.

37

That is one picture of the pattern of Shakespeare's final development, and by no means an unintelligent one. It is, I think, one with much to commend it to men like the neo-classical Continental purists of the seventeenth and eighteenth centuries, and to the Romantic champions of the "divine English madman" in the nineteenth. The Latin mind, deeply stamped as it is with the tragic critique of antiquity, would perhaps see just such an incapacity for enduring the glacial altitude of naked tragic truth as typical of that woolly English deficiency in high seriousness which makes us a species of interesting yet ultimately childish barbarians.

Such is the kind of estimate of Shakespeare's work which we inherit from the mental world which Shakespeare helped to create. Turning that world inside out again, in the cause of sanity, means turning the estimate inside out too. And so profoundly are we conditioned by acceptance of the modern critique of existence that our initial sensation in doing this is almost sure to be one of violating the natural order of things. It comes almost as a surprise to realize that challenging this tragedy-centred concept of the pattern in Shakespeare is in fact restoring a pattern indicated to us by the sequence of the plays themselves, in the order of their composition.

It won't do, of course, to be too simple-minded in this reappraisal. It is clear enough, certainly, that there has been a good deal of overemphasis on that vein of nostalgic agnosticism in Shakespeare's last plays which is summed up in the famous speech about the cloud-capped towers. Yet the element is there and cannot be merely explained away; and it is based upon a kind of experience impossible to Dante, or even the Chaucer of *Troilus and Criseyde*, for all his sophistication. Certainly it's true, I think, that we are not justified in assuming that Shakespeare didn't indulge in "working out a philosophy of life", or that the matter is irrelevant to literary appreciation of his work. Yet for all that he is not, of course, a "philosophical poet" like Dante or Milton or Goethe, and his work gives, of its own nature, every indication that it is not to be approached as a cumulative attempt to formulate a "message". Shakespeare doesn't, in the Romantic tradition typified by artists like Beethoven, utter a "last word" from the mountain top and pass into silence. On the contrary, *Henry VIII* is well in the central Shakespearean tradition of combining box-office success with the free play of true creativeness; it is no super-apocalyptic book of revelations, but a leisurely return to the well-tested history genre of his early days. And the political tastes of the period are just as shrewdly catered for as before —though it is interesting to note how the meeting of the requirements of the Tudor version of history is here combined with the "religious" motifs of the "last plays" taken as a whole; particularly, I think, with their preoccupation with the theme of mercy.

Whatever is involved, then, in revising the traditional interpretation of the Shakespearean pattern, we certainly shan't be justified in identifying the ordering of experience worked out in these last plays purely and simply with that medieval ordering of experience which lies under the early histories. Whatever value you finally accord to the mental world of *The Tempest*, it contains new and cryptic elements strange to the Catholic mental order out of which Elizabethan drama was exploded; and of these elements there will be more to say later. Yet provided you accept this fact, and resist the temptation to pick upon any isolated speech or line as giving us Shakespeare's poetic last will and testament, you are, I think, quite justified in exploring the idea that these last comedies are what their chronological position

naturally suggests—a further advance on the great tragedies and a consequent deepening of the vision achieved
in them. In a word, it's a question of trying to take
something of a fresh look at Shakespeare's final maturity by at once respecting the pattern of his own development in time and the demands of our own commonsense revaluation of his tragic mental world with reference to the wider context of a greater comedy.

Of course, you find yourself at once swimming against
a strong stream of mental habit. There is an unashamed
and uninhibited element of the fairy-tale in the world of
The Winter's Tale, *The Tempest* and the rest. And we,
with five centuries of titanism in our blood, can't help
feeling that any claim to set up the world of the nursery
in judgement on the thoroughly grown-up world, where
men kill for power and strangle their mistresses, is plain
perverse paradox-mongering. You can't, we feel instinctively, possibly accord to this set-up of enchanted
islands and witches and sprites and long-lost-children-
suddenly-turning-up the kind of serious attention rightly
demanded by Hamlet's existentialist musings over the
possible uses of a bare bodkin or Antony's "I am dying,
Egypt, dying", or Iago's workings upon the mind of
Othello. And in a sense this feeling is quite right. The
same kind of seriousness of response is not demanded.
But the mistake is to conclude from this that no kind of
seriousness is demanded; whereas in fact a new kind is
—a seriousness not distinct from, but essentially dependent on, a thoroughgoing playfulness. The last
plays stand to the great tragedies in some ways as
Elizabethan polyphony stands to Wagnerian opera; and
we, conditioned as we are, tend, as always, to judge the
scope of the achievement in terms of the amount of dust
and uproar raised. In actual fact, the work of even so
archetypal a titanist as Beethoven reminds us, by the

form of its development, that this is not necessarily true. What we are accustomed to regard as a super-adult heavyweight quality constituting the essence of great artistic vision may be something quite different —a sort of magnificent expiatory disease incurred by art for trying to take over the role of religion, and create out of its own resources the mental order which it formerly accepted, explored, exploited and made manifest. You might almost say that Wagner, for example, was setting himself up as a new culture-hero, like those dim and legendary beings said to have brought the art of writing, the use of fire, the secrets of the plough and the like to primitive civilizations. He seems to aim at artistic creation on a really godlike scale; not only the music but the dramas which it is to body forth; not only the dramas, but their actual libretti; not only one great opera but *The Ring of the Nibelungs*—a whole new musical universe; not only that, but the whole theatrical apparatus and technique which is to bring that universe to life; almost, you might say, not only that but a whole new public, who are to be initiated, through this great aesthetic liturgy, into a new dimension of existence and response—perhaps ultimately a world as far beyond the good and evil of the old as that of Nietzsche in his lunatic asylum, or that of the Master Race to come when, as Heine prophesied, the old gods of the north reawoke and the strange and terrible attempt was made to create a New World of blood and iron. Where the sixteenth-century polyphonists, for example, could employ the most powerful dynamism of their music in serious play before the face of a wisdom which it did not have to create, Wagner had to direct his beyond the confines of his art itself in an impossibly serious attempt to make art create a new wisdom altogether; to write the book of genesis in a new holy

41

scripture of human artistic inspiration. Hence the profound disturbance to the human soul which inevitably accompanies the enormous stimulation of such music; hence the tremendous vital activity that is hidden in the contemplative repose of music like that of Palestrina or Josquin des Prés. Renaissance polyphony still displays that essentially playful internal balance of energy that marks a culture acceptant of, and dependent on, spiritual foundations thought to be independent of cultural creativeness. Titanic musical achievement such as that of Wagner displays a shattering exteriorization of energy, so that the hearer is thrown back upon his own naked individuality by a challenge, rather than drawn out of it in transforming contemplation. And that is very much the mark of a culture whose essence has changed from play to work—whose energy is turned outward in a desperately serious and overwhelmingly dominative labour; the superhuman effort of establishing its own spiritual foundation through its own creative vision.

That is the kind of conditioning experience which you have to recognize and allow for when you try to accustom yourself to the idea that Shakespeare meant us to take seriously the playfulness of that nursery world of fairy tale and happy ending which is, chronologically at the very least, the further New World lying beyond the traditional Renaissance New World of his tragedies. However, if you look deeper into the limpid clarity of these later plays, you can soon begin to see elements which make this revaluation of the nursery world seem a little less odd. To say that Shakespeare seriously accepted fairy-tale playfulness, with its happy endings and wondering simplicity of vision, as the fit vehicle for conveying his deepest insight into the truth of things, is not to imply any denial of the reality of the tragic *agon*, and the forces which create that conflict. The predominant pattern of reconciliation does not eliminate the full intensity of the stresses and strains of the great tragedies; it takes them up in a wider context. And this repossession of mental order is, as we shall see, a repossession of that world of medieval divine comedy which provides the point of departure for the early histories; a repossession of that controlled play between the sweet and the bitter wonders which formed the pattern of the hierarchical medieval order of the mind. The sweet wonder that it is so good to be, and the bitter wonder that it can be so terrible. It is indeed a New World in the medieval rather than the Renaissance sense of the term; a world of "Behold, I make all things new", in which all tears are wiped away, rather than a world of the hitherto unconceived, the beyond-the-ultimate-limits, with all the element of isolation which that implies. Yet for all that it is not a simple return to the pre-Renaissance mental world, nor to the world of individual experience that lies before bad dreams like Hamlet's or waking nightmares like Iago's lucid perversity. The deadly seriousness of Leontes's jealousy, the grim reality of Caliban's depravity, and the rest of it, provide just that wholly real element of *agon*, of tragic conflict, the control of which constitutes the very being of comedy. And if you examine a little more closely how this is done, it begins to become clear that it is not mere whimsy perversity to maintain that the final old wives' tales do in fact go even deeper than the titanic analyses of the great tragedies.

Caliban provides us with a very useful focus for all that is going on in this world of the last plays. For he is a symbol, in the true sense of the word, of that incredible and intolerable intruder, evil, which first sets up the conflict between the sweet and the bitter wonders, and must be taken into account, in any order that claims to resurrect the paradise of our first innocence. In a modern production, and to a modern audience, Caliban is something of a puzzle. Usually, I think, he tends automatically to become a sort of Walt Disney grotesque—a trifle strong in flavour perhaps, but still distinctly on the pantomine-demon-king level. Hence a corresponding puzzle appears in Prospero; the threats he levels at Caliban and the general watchful severity of his rule over him seem to strike a jarring note in the kind of idyllic harmony which we take the play to be generally offering us. If, on the other hand, Caliban be presented in the full realism of his grimmer moments— as, for instance, that of his attempt to rape Miranda, or that when he propounds his plan for "paunching" the sleeping Prospero with a stake—then he is simply an unfortunate attempt to make funny something which is not so in the least. The world of the last plays becomes an escapist retreat from the grim honesty of the great tragedies, and the fairy-tale harmony becomes strictly phoney. Indeed, we may yet see some tremendous angry-young-man production of *The Tempest*, which will reveal Caliban as its Sartrian hero.

Both these views of Caliban have in them an important part of the truth. Certainly he cannot be regarded as an obstinate skeleton which Shakespeare's reluctant honesty has compelled him to preserve in the closet drama of his new nursery world; to that extent the Walt-Disneyites are right. But equally certainly he cannot be looked upon as a Punch-and-Judy grotesque and no more; and to that extent my imaginary Sartrian producer would be right, too. In fact, I don't think we can see Caliban rightly except through the stereoscopy of both visions held in the mind simultaneously. With him, as with the devils and Herods of the old mystery plays, both the horrific and the comic elements have to be accepted pure and at full strength. There is a realism here which won't let us tone down Caliban's gruesome aspects in any way, and yet also refusal of a certain kind of "seriousness", which won't let us allow that gruesomeness to hypnotize us. Prospero's attitude clearly opens a stereoscopic vision in which Caliban's comic and horrific aspects are not mutually exclusive. When he says that Caliban is a creature who can take no imprint of good he means exactly what he says; and as we have seen, the watchful rigour of his control makes clear that Prospero is far indeed from underestimating the danger Caliban represents. Indeed, the mere recall of Caliban's evil antics is sufficient to drive him from the triumphant celebration of his "masque of spirits" to walk a turn or two

> To still my beating mind.

Yet none the less the worst Caliban can do is also taken so "unseriously" that his punishment for plotting, in deadly earnest, the "paunching" of Prospero, is no more than being put on extra fatigues cleaning out Prospero's cell. This is all a thoroughly Renaissance re-creation of a thoroughly medieval attitude. Julian of Norwich, writing of her vision of the "overcoming of the fiend", said:

> Also I saw our Lord scorn his malice and naught his unmight; and he willeth that we do so. For this sight I laughed mightily, and that made them to laugh that were about me, and their laughing was a liking to me. I thought that I would that all mine even-Christians had seen as I saw, and then would they all laugh with me.[1]

[1] *Revelations of Divine Love*, ed. Hudlestone, London, 1952, p. 26.

It is an attitude we meet again, obviously, in the carvers of the medieval gargoyles; with them an uninhibited playfulness doesn't exclude, but rather presupposes, an intense seriousness. And it is an attitude which we, despite the singularly grotesque and bizarre forms which great evil has taken in our own day, do not find it at all easy to accustom ourselves to. It is one in which the stresses and strains of the tragic *agon* are resolved and contained by being both taken seriously and not taken seriously, in a sober recognition which is also a sane evaluation.

The word "sane" is a reminder that this vision of divine comedy is also a vision of common sense—that common sense in the name of which I began this criticism of the tragic critique. And in turn that consideration pinpoints the axis about which this balance of contraries in Caliban is resolved—his relation to the absurd.

Caliban is a poetic image, a poetic incarnation, of the point at which the funny and the horrific meet. Thus much, of course, might be said of innumerable creations of the modern anti-Christian existentialist tradition, from the sound like gurgling water-pipes with which the Murderer of God begins his great oration in *Thus Spake Zarathustra* to the second-rate-hotel waiting-room which Sartre substitutes for the ponderous splendours of Milton's infernal palace of Pandemonium. The absurd is, precisely, the point at which the funny and the horrific meet; everyone, perhaps, would agree upon that. The vital thing, the elemental thing, is whether a man is capable of giving way, freely and joyfully, to his natural instinct of laughter at the absurd, or whether he determines to wipe that primal smile off his face in the titanic and indiscriminate seriousness which is one concept of human maturity. And on this point there is no doubt as to the attitude suggested to us by the vision embodied in Caliban's creation. In him that absurd thing which is evil stands with the horrific plain as a pikestaff behind it and its face plainly turned towards the light of comedy; Iago lies behind Caliban but Caliban is very definitely not an Iago. And the laughter whose matter he points to in the absurd is not, of course, the dominative, critical laughter-at which disowns the absurd in satire's bitter exorcism of the bitter wonder. It is an acceptant laughter-with which recognizes and accepts in Caliban something of our own selves and acknowledges it freely and un-resentfully as a vital element in that limitation which gives the human creature his very shape. And it is in this connection that the dominant theme of grace, mercy and repentance in *The Tempest*, and in all the last plays, acquires its vital connection with laughter. In a world racked throughout with the conflict reflected in the clash of the sweet and bitter wonders—what Christian theology calls a fallen world—these essential creaturely limitations don't show themselves merely in, for example, the fact that man, proud man, can slip on a banana skin. You see them too in grimmer terms; he can also play such fantastic tricks before high heaven as make the angels weep indeed—tricks like those of Macbeth and Iago; like Adam's, when he convinced himself that he knew better than his Creator the things that were to his peace. Unsqueamish yet basically joyful acknowledge-ment of the Caliban in us, with his double face of horror and ridiculousness, is a reaffirmation of the kind of attitude the Middle Ages had when they sang in the *Exultet* of Adam's happy guilt, that brought us so great a Redeemer. And like that attitude, it inevitably implies acceptant recognition of the relation between the creature and its Creator. For you can only stand re-alistic recognition of the Calibanly possibilities of our nature on the strength of an implied awareness of what

47

mercy infinite love must extend to beings so pathetically dependent and vulnerable. That is the element which makes the lyrical idyllicism of these last plays so steel-strong, for all its lightness, and gives their sweetness its cleansing astringency. This optimism is of the most soberly realistic kind, and its joy in being has been tempered in the fiercest heat that the bitter wonder can provide. And it is because of this that the Shakespearean progress is indeed a voyage to the place from which the poet started, and the discovery that lies at the end of it a knowing of the place of beginning, for the first time.

This becomes clearer yet when you pause to consider the lines in which the element of absurdity in Caliban is summed up:

> 'Ban, 'Ban, Ca-Caliban
> Has a new master: get a new man.

> Freedom, high-day! High-day, freedom! Freedom,
> high-day, freedom!

You can think back there to the irony which hovers over an earlier proclamation of a similar "existentialist" absolute liberty; Richard the Third's

> Conscience is but a word that cowards use,
> Devis'd at first to keep the strong in awe:
> Our strong arms be our conscience, swords our law.

Although it is perfectly true that the Renaissance did produce, on a large scale, the cultivation of this type of superman mentality, it is also true that the earlier sanities were so strong that the new extravagances could, as a whole, only find meaningful expression in

48

terms of them; a typical Renaissance slogan is not "Man is a useless passion" but, for example, the motto of the *condottiero* Werber von Urslingen: "The enemy of God, of pity and of mercy."[1] Chesterton was wholly right in attacking Bernard Shaw's facile reading of Nietzschean overtones into Shakespeare's Richard; the whole dramatic potentiality of such Elizabethan "Machiavels" lies exactly in the fact that they provide an exciting counterpoint to the older themes of moral order, and the social and political order which that implies. That is what makes their tragedy meaningful; that is the kind of evaluation which it involves. Richard the Third's significance can only be grasped in relation to the background of plays such as *Henry VI* and *Richard II*, which explore the nature of that very law and order which Richard III seeks to replace by the law and order of the strong arm and the sword. And the brilliance of his figure is made possible only by that setting of the medieval order, cosmic, social and political, within which it is firmly placed. Richard is seen as the final conclusion of a process which begins in the disorder of Bolingbroke's deposition of Richard II and develops through the Wars of the Roses; his "freedom" to create his own ten commandments is as much an illusion—even though a dazzling one—as Bolingbroke's "freedom" to break the framework of Christian loyalty and political order. And Caliban's "freedom" to break the limits of the order in which *he* exists is equally illusory and destructive. That order of the last plays is a hierarchical one arising out of a basic submission and acceptance, and patterned in the image of that mercy which acceptance of the creaturely condition opens up to man. Shakespeare's power of dominative critique achieves a reconciliation with his

[1] Jacob Burckhardt, *The Civilization of the Renaissance in Italy*, London, 1944, p. 278.

power of submissive acceptance not unlike the kiss between justice and peace which the Bible describes as the context of the Nativity. And when, in the figure of Prospero, he achieves a hitherto unprecedented integration of himself, as artist, into the world of his own procreation, it is, ultimately, in a place of humility, as we see in that final speech which is obviously a uniquely personal communication between Shakespeare and his audience:[1]

> Now my charms are all o'er thrown,
> And what strength I have's my own,—
> Which is most faint . . .
>   . . . now I want
> Spirits to enforce, art to enchant;
> And my ending is despair,
> Unless I be relieved by prayer,
> Which pierces so, that it assaults
> Mercy itself, and frees all faults
> As you from crimes would pardoned be,
> Let your indulgence set me free.

It is not necessary to point the difference between *this* concept of freedom, on the part of Caliban's master, and Caliban's own "existentialist" ideas on the subject. If Caliban is a Renaissance mind's re-creation of the medieval gargoyle, Prospero's dignity—typically Renaissance creation though he is, too—is formed in the image of the dignity of those medieval tomb effigies with hands folded in prayer; the dignity of realistic acceptance of human limitation—and its implied assertion of human greatness.

To say, however, that Caliban is a re-creation of the medieval gargoyle, is not to imply that the greatest

[1] Though *not*, as I have said, a "last word" summing up a Shakespearean "message".

achievement of Shakespeare's mature genius was no more than a putting together again of a medieval Humpty Dumpty. Here, re-creation really means re-creation and not just repair work, however brilliant. The dazzling beauty of this final apocalyptic "new heaven and new earth" mustn't blind us to the fact that it is the old medieval heaven and earth made afresh; but this fact too mustn't blind us to the fact of the remaking, with all that it implies; new and distinctive elements have arisen in the representation of the old vision.

To get an idea of the nature of this new element all you need to do is to use Caliban as a mirror in which to look back to figures like that of Iago. When F. H. Bradley discussed and rejected "motiveless malignity" as an interpretation of Iago he voiced what must have been a perfectly honest and quite understandable puzzle-ment in his generation before a figure of this type. It was, of course, accentuated in Bradley's case by his naïve insistence on "psychologizing"—on discussing Shakespearean characters as if they were historical per-sonages, and had an independent life of their own outside the play. In what I have to say about Iago here I shall try to steer midway between this Bradleian oversimpli-fication, and that of Professor Stoll, who opposes to the "psychologized" Iago of Bradley an interpretation based on the Elizabethan convention of the "slanderer believed".[1]

To us today, with a long panorama of surrealistic atrocities unrolled, on a colossal scale, for our con-sideration, "motiveless malignity" may still remain as big a puzzle as it did for Bradley, but at least its existence is not incredible, as it could quite reasonably be to the

---

[1] For a (to my mind) conclusive criticism of both Bradley's and Professor Stoll's viewpoints, see F. R. Leavis, "Diabolic Intellect and the Noble Hero", in *The Common Pursuit*, London, 1952.

average man of Edwardian England; we have seen the well-nigh-unbelievable happen in the most horribly spectacular fashion. Yet to many a modern reader or spectator *Othello* may well still seem—in retrospect, at least—to provide no really adequate motive for the devouring passion, the obsessive intensity, with which Iago sets about the destruction of the Moor and Desdemona. His passing hint

> And it is thought abroad that 'twixt my sheets
> 'Has done my office

—is never seriously developed, and gives every evidence of having been presented by the author as the character's passing rationalization of an impulse coming from a far greater depth than that at which sexual jealousy operates;[1] something we come nearer to touching on when Iago says of Michael Cassio

> He hath a daily beauty in his life
> That makes me ugly.

That Iago "comes off", for practical purposes, is undeniable; the question that underlies Bradley's laboriously "reasonable" analysis is, Ought he to come off? Or is he a really dazzling tour-de-force on Shakespeare's part, a sort of brilliantly-designed robot monster skilfully contrived for theatrical tactical purposes? He is certainly the most negative major figure in all Shakespeare. Macbeth has not a little in common with him in this direction, admittedly. But Macbeth's dehumanization is something which we see in gradual progress from the beginning of his tragedy to the end, and as the development of his own weaknesses and vulnerability; Iago begins where Macbeth leaves off and is,

[1] Iago's own words shortly afterwards strongly support this, I think.

from start to finish, completely integrated in evil. Yet
if there is one thing that is certain it is that Iago is a
character, in the fullest and richest sense of that word,
and not the symbol of an abstraction or a stock figure,
a super-Dracula. He always remains a human being,
even if a supremely enigmatic one. Dramatic convention
in the Elizabethan theatre does not provide a sufficient
answer here; the most rigid dramatic convention is
rooted, however remotely, in some concept of human
nature, and must reinforce that concept if it is to be
really effective.

Iago's enigma is real enough; yet curiously enough it
is precisely the enigma which provides the key to the
whole puzzle. In this "motiveless malignity" we have
something which is by now familiar, and which we have
just seen in Caliban so presented as to predispose us to a
reaction of laughter: the absurd, the nonsensical. The
whole point about Iago is that he is a perfectly serious
embodiment of that which does not make sense. And
here we must remember that although Iago cannot
validly be discussed from the critical standpoint as if
he had a life independent of the play, he can, as a con-
ventional type, be referred to a picture of man existing
outside the immediate context of the work of art *Othello*
itself. From this standpoint we can say that his an-
archism, his utter destructiveness, his nihilism, are a
summing up of the very essence of the Renaissance New
Man's attempts to be a god unto himself, dictating his
own ten commandments. They are in a direct line with
Richard III's

Our strong arms be our conscience, swords our law

—which is itself a rousingly rhetorical summing-up of
the principles of Machiavelli's *The Prince*, which in

turn, in the very preciseness and moderation of its tone reads horribly like a memorandum for the use of the civil service in hell. But Iago, of course, goes far beyond Richard and is the creation of a deeper insight. Richard's superman-amorality is aimed, with an almost childlike directness which is part of the secret of our sympathy with him, at the golden sugar-plum of the English crown; the moral anarchy is a means to an end. In the case of Iago the moral anarchy is an end in itself. He does not make sense, as Bradley seems to have suspected. He is not meant to make sense. He is not supposed to be trying to make sense; he is supposed to be trying to make nonsense; he is supposed to be committed to realizing in action the slogan "Nonsense, be thou my sense". And this he is implicitly conceived as doing in an attempt to achieve the kind of godlike freedom which makes mere political power seem as inadequate as it makes seem the accepted aura of the divine which medieval kingship claimed as its most prized glory. He is depicted, implicitly, as trying to achieve total self-assertion; as, being a man, driven by the very limitations against which he is rebelling, to achieve it in the only way possible to man—by destruction; destruction of all that moral order which men normally accept as something deriving from outside and above themselves. It is only through utter negativity that such a character can be conceived as achieving that kind of absoluteness, thirst for which is the impulse that underlies the whole character-pattern at a depth to which the spectator does not have to penetrate. That is the impulse which Iago is made to rationalize so strangely and yet so naturally in his perfunctory reference to the stock motive of sexual jealousy; it is nowhere explicitly formulated in the words of the play because it is implicitly formulated throughout the whole of it, in the whole great, terrible, dazzling movement of the Renaissance soul which it summarizes. The sheer perversity of evil for evil's sake is something which is the final logical outcome of a measureless thirst for unqualified self-assertion in man.

Granted, you can (as I have pointed out in connection with Richard III) be a thorough-going "Machiavelli" without necessarily following the implications of your aping of God to this very Huis-Clos-ish Rats' Alley of total negative self-assertion. Indeed, Machiavelli himself was far from being concerned about any ultimate "existentialist" implications of his prescriptions for successful power politics; he would indeed have described himself (with what unconscious irony!) as a "practical man", whose business was not with exotic philosophizing but the successful practice of cultivated *Realpolitik*. And in that Richard is his faithful follower. Yet the ultimate implications of the "new morality" were there, for all that, and could not be ultimately escaped; and there's all too much evidence, unfortunately, that Italy, in particular, produced not a few real Iagos. Dante had consigned traitors to the lowest pit of hell; and indeed the whole structure of medieval society had been built up out of the theologically derived concept of loyalty of the lower towards the higher. Treachery was the wrecking of the order of faith and obedience; as was also the final and total self-assertion of creature against Creator which underlay the social crime and gave it its image. And it was precisely in terms of this basically theological idea of evil, as the wrecking of a personal relationship, that the Machiavellians of the Renaissance conceived their artistry in amorality, with treachery, really breathtaking treachery, as its *chef d'oeuvre*.

The key word in the definition of the Renaissance superman was, significantly, *virtù*, which our more anthropologically-minded age might best render as *mana*.

The artistically-conceived frightfulness of some of the Renaissance despots and *condottierri* really does have about it, in its more extreme manifestations, a definite flavour of sin for sin's sake—the traditional concept of the assertion of the creature's "freedom" against the Creator re-expressed in terms of the new idolization of man, of his man-ness, his *mana*, his *virtù*. The mingled fascination and repulsion with which the Elizabethan theatre regards the "Machiavel" has much deeper roots in reality than could have any mere pleasurably-frightening literary exercise in making one's flesh creep; "Italianate Englishman—devil incarnate" was something more than a catch-phrase.

Yet, throughout, the Renaissance bricks are, inevitably, made out of medieval straw—as you see particularly in Shakespeare. The canonized absurdity of *Huis Clos* is something hardly possible as yet; and indeed it is the medieval formulae in the Renaissance revolt which provide it with half its thrill and fascinating power. The medieval world picture had provided plenty of room for the relative villain, on whatever scale: the man who, giving way to lust, anger, fear or what have you, chooses the lesser good of his own immediate satisfaction when that is conceived as involving the rejection of his ultimate satisfaction—participation in the divine life of his Maker. But it also provided a concept now almost totally blurred out of the minds of many. It was that of the absolute villain; the being who, with full knowledge and in absolute freedom, made such a choice of self definitive and total.

In other words, the Middle Ages believed in the devil and damnation. And it was this element in the medieval subsoil of the Renaissance mind which gave to the "motiveless malignity" of an Iago a sober significance which it is hard for a modern audience to grasp. For today, to describe Iago as "diabolical" is in most cases simply a way of saying picturesquely that he is ethically perverse; or perhaps, at one stage nearer reality, of investing him with some of the trappings of the "dark" aspect of Romanticism; or perhaps, a little nearer the truth yet, of describing him in terms of the symbolism of a reaction against the optimism of the nineteenth century. But to the men of the Middle Ages, and the Elizabethans who inherited, as well as rejected, so much that had been theirs, the word "diabolical" carried a perfectly straightforward and literal connotation of sheer horror. The traditional world-picture of medieval Christendom had a perfectly reasonable place for the attempt to take the absurd deadly seriously.

The mere fact of finding in the scheme of things a reasonable place for that wholly unreasonable act underlined those qualities in it which made a healthy response to it partly one of laughter, the spark struck by sanity off the absurd. The medieval background made it possible for Renaissance "existentialists" to go up with a bang like Tamburlaine the Great and not out with a choke like the characters in *Huis Clos*; it lent to absolute self-assertion the temporary meaningfulness of phrases like "The enemy of God, of pity and of mercy", or of Machiavelli's power politics, and shielded its practitioners from the lucid lunacies of a Nietzsche or a M. Sartre. But this background also preserved, in the deep subsoil of the mind, a powerful residual consciousness of the claim to absolute "freedom" as absurd. To the Middle Ages the self-assertion of the devil, and Adam after him, was absurd above all things; for, it was held, both beings had seen and grasped the nature of their creaturehood and their Creator with a clarity possible to no man now, and were thus free, in a way now unknown to us, to refrain ever from denying what they knew by what they

did. The unclouded intellect and unweakened will of the
unfallen Lucifer and the unfallen Adam made their
attempts to be God inconceivably absurd; pieces of
unrealism without parallel before or since. That was
what made the devil and Herod clowns as well as villains
in the mystery plays. And a persistent "folk-memory",
even in Renaissance man, of that essential absurdity of
evil, is what accounts for the ultimate evolution of Iago
into Caliban. In Shakespeare at least titanist self-
assertion receives, in a final "nursery world" of highly
significant fairy tale, that judgement of the people en-
shrined in the warning of innumerable nannies, nurses and
governesses to innumerable small rebels against order:
"Now you're getting past yourself."

Self-assertion as the destruction of order—material
order (which is life), mental order (which is sanity),
spiritual order (which is grace): that is the concept which
you have to concentrate on if you are to understand the
deepening of insight which Shakespeare's final world of
comedy gains over his midway world of tragedy. Othello,
at the beginning of that supposed overturning of the
order of wedded loyalty which constitutes his tragedy,
says to himself, "Chaos is come again"; and that chaos
is one in kind with the chaos symbolized in the storm
and madness of *King Lear*. The tragedies do indeed
sum up, with unrivalled mastery, something that is
typically of the Renaissance; the releasing of the energy
stored within the medieval order in a brilliant firework
display of disintegration, critically precipitated atomic
fission. It is, precisely, an essentially destructive transition from order towards chaos which turns the matter
of the old mental world into fuel for that "expanding
universe" of dazzling explosion which is the new one.
In Shakespeare, it is true, this "atomic explosion" is
made to harness itself in mid-career to provide the

58

energy which is to reconstitute the "new world" of the last plays; a crucial point in the operation being, significantly, the vision of human love, in all its grandeur and foolishness, worked out in *Antony and Cleopatra*. But the feat is a unique one, unique as is the world of the last plays itself; and Shakespeare only achieves it, as we shall see, by means of a quite extraordinary capacity to be Mr. Facing-Both-Ways.

It is in terms of a thoroughly medieval and Christian world-stuff, an ordered and hierarchical cosmos, that the thoroughly Renaissance and in one sense thoroughly pagan tragedies are constructed. And this is only possible because the creative mind involved is in some sense, and for a time, dispossessed of its Christianity. In virtue of that, it becomes possible for Shakespeare to treat the matter of the medieval cosmos as atomic fuel. And plays like *Troilus and Cressida* and *Timon of Athens* confirm that this dispossession of Christian conviction was something much more serious—and much more fruitful—than any piece of artistically utilitarian let's-pretend, such as W. B. Yeats, I feel, so often half-consciously indulged in. The destructive aspect of putting the old Christian order through its alchemical "mortification" seems at times to come near occupying the mental horizon so completely as to shut out all possibility of the "vivification" to which the trial by fire is traditionally designed to be the prelude. The tragedies may be considered as a sort of literary alchemists' crucible, in which—at the artistic level, at least—the inherited medieval cosmic order is put to the "death" of ultimate critical challenge and dominative analysis. That process of disintegration is mirrored in the actual language of the plays of the central period— increasingly intricate and convoluted, till the verse itself seems to be on the very edge of flying asunder

under the pressure of the intensity of the experience it articulates. In *Troilus* and *Timon*, for example, the crucible does in fact very nearly crack under the stress of the process it channels. The crescendo of disintegratory criticism comes near to running away in a chain reaction which would ultimately destroy the very possibility of coherent artistic expression and leave nothing but an evil, still small voice laughing a meaningless crackle of laughter somewhere on the far side of sanity and intelligibility. "That way madness lies"—it is the path to Rats' Alley and *Huis Clos*. But in point of fact extraordinary depth of artistic insight manages to control this great atomic explosion from within the fireball itself, turning the cataclysmic release of energy inside out, into a nebula from which a new universe is born.

It is in one of the moments when things seem nearest to getting quite out of hand—*Troilus and Cressida*—that the element of medieval order appears, like the phoenix in its shroud of fire, in one of its most brilliant formulations:

> . . . how could communities,
> Degrees in schools, and brotherhoods in cities,
> Peaceful commerce from dividable shores,
> The primogenity and due of birth,
> Prerogative of age, crowns, sceptres, laurels,
> But by degree, stand in authentic place?
> Take but degree away, untune that string,
> And, hark, what discord follows! each thing meets
> In mere oppugnancy; the bounded waters
> Should lift their bosoms higher than the shores,
> And make a sop of all this solid globe:
> Strength should be lord of imbecility,
> And the rude son should strike his father dead:
> Force should be right; or rather, right and wrong—

Between whose endless jar justice resides—
Should lose their names, and so should justice too.
Then everything includes itself in power,
Power into will, will into appetite;
And appetite, an universal wolf,
So doubly seconded with will and power,
Must make perforce an universal prey,
And last eat up himself.

It is a vision of the hierarchy of creaturely dependence; of the organic order which follows from recognition and acceptance of this, and the ultimate chaos implicit in its denial.

If you look at it in the light of the order of the last plays, and Prospero's freedom of humility, grace and repentance, you can see too how this latter world is an end which is a beginning—the resurrection of the world from which Shakespeare's artistic vision begins. What you see beyond *Troilus* in terms of the most intimate personal issues of spiritual balance you see earlier in terms of the problems of political and social order which are explored in the histories. If studies such as Iago or Macbeth are developments of themes outlined in *Richard III*, the world of *The Winter's Tale* and *The Tempest* is the repossession of that world whose disintegration is studied and worked out in *Henry VI* and *Richard II*, and forms a constant undertone of preoccupation in the positive syntheses of *Henry IV* and *Henry V*.

You greatly oversimplify, of course, the nature of this Shakespearean vision of the medieval world, with its order of "degree" and implications of divine comedy, if you overlook the fact that the very attack which the Tudor monarchy had made on the foundation of medieval "degree"—the Catholic faith—made it necessary for

the concept of political "degree" to be underlined all
the more heavily. Shake the foundations of that system
of religious authority which invests royal power with its
aura of the sacred, and you send a tremor through the
edifice of royal power itself: "No bishop; no king."
The tremor set up by Henry VIII was to trigger off the
forces which brought Charles I to trial and execution.
And there was perhaps some obscure premonition of
this in the heightened emphasis on the absoluteness of
royal power; the attempt to build the "new monarch"
into a being altogether outside the limits of that playground of customary law within which medieval kings
were for the most part restrained, however rough the
sport which they set on foot within these limits and
however strong their tendency to break the rules when
losing. The medieval concept of "degree" was appro-
priated with the utmost readiness by the Tudors, as a
most powerful weapon in their psychological armoury,
and very much stamped upon the popular mind from
above in order to enlist the whole persistent power of the
medieval hierarchic conception of society in the service
of a type of absolutism fundamentally different from the
medieval brand:

> For to the king God hath his office lent
> Of dread, of justice, power and command;
> Hath bid him rule, and will'd you to obey.
> And to add ampler majesty to this,
> He hath not only lent the king his figure,
> His throne and sword, but given him his own name,
> Calls him a god on earth.

Of course, this powerful response to the theme of
political and social "degree" is by no means something
merely inculcated, selfconsciously and even cynically,

from above. The whole complex pattern of impulses—personal, economic, ideological and the rest—which impelled the Tudors down the path of the new Renaissance despotism, is itself in part an expression of the national mind's deep revulsion from the appalling internal warfare which had led up to Henry Tudor's victory at Bosworth. The horror of rebellion and internal discord, and all the anarchy that accompanies them, is something sufficiently vivid in the folk-memory of Elizabeth's time to make her childlessness and the problems of succession which it created, a haunting spectre to the new national selfconsciousness.

These two aspects of Elizabethan "degree-mindedness", the dominative assertion from above and the acceptant intuition from below, symbolize in their interaction that state of affairs which provides the theme of "degree" with the special punch which it lacks where the present-day reader of Shakespeare is concerned. Behind the Elizabethan sense of "degree" in society and politics lies the thought-world of the Middle Ages, in which are balanced (at least in theory) the forces of dominativeness and acceptance which fly apart in the brilliant explosion of the Renaissance. And it is of course because the sense of "degree" dates much further back in the English mind than does the work of the Tudor propaganda machine that the work of that machine could be so effective. It turned to account a psychological force far more elemental than any it could have created on the spot. Behind and beneath the order of an England newly come to self-awareness lies, historically, the order of the medieval hierarchical society—an order transcending the limits of sociology and politics.

Shakespeare's early "histories" thus exploit immediate Elizabethan social and political issues exactly at the depth of the popular mind—and also safely within the limits of the views sanctioned by the regime of the day. But they do also express an insight of the Renaissance mind into the nature of the old world out of which the new one was being born, and of the process of the birth. And despite the undoubted and understandable sense of thrill and fascination at the prodigies this new mental world embodied itself in—from the ferocious brilliance of Richard to the vast autumnal glow of the setting-sun-like Anthony—the ground bass of the whole of this opening movement of the Shakespearean symphony is the vital value of order and degree, and the sense of horror and sacrilege attendant upon its overturning. From time to time this motif is focused in a single incident or symbolic situation. For example, in the scene of the Battle of Towton in *Henry VI* there enter to the saintly king in a sort of ritual ballet, first a son who has unwittingly killed his father, and then a father who has likewise killed his son; a crude yet forceful image of the violation of natural and cosmic order which is felt to underlie the violation of loyalty, and social and political order, in civil war and rebellion.

O pity, God, this miserable age!—
What stratagems, how fell, how butcherly,
Erroneous, mutinous and unnatural,
This deadly quarrel daily doth beget!

And the same sense of "unnaturalness"—of the breaking of those links of hierarchical unity which give the very matter of the social cosmos its organic pattern—lies again beneath the foreboding sense of sacrilegious horror which attends upon the revolt against and murder of the irresponsible and exasperating Richard II, and becomes passionately articulate in the speech of the Bishop of Carlisle:

> . . . O, forfend it, God,
> That in a Christian climate, souls refined
> Should show so heinous, black, obscene a deed!
> I speak to subjects and a subject speaks,
> Stirr'd up by God, thus boldly for his king
> My lord of Hereford here, whom you call king
> Is a foul traitor to proud Hereford's king
> And if you crown him, let me prophesy—
> The blood of English shall manure the ground,
> And future ages groan for this foul act;
> Peace shall go sleep with Turks and infidels;
> And in this seat of peace tumultuous wars
> Shall kin with kin and kind with kind confound . . .

And it is the same sense of clinging guilt and unnatural violation of a sacred order which echoes through Henry IV's yearnings to take the cross and liberate Jerusalem, and, of course, in the meditations of Henry V before Agincourt.

The development of this theme of the hierarchical order of being and the consequences of its rejection is also a shift of emphasis from the social and political sphere to that of the individual soul (though that soul is often, by virtue of its heroic position in the scheme of things, a kind of incarnation of social and political order as well—as in the case of Macbeth, for example). And it is in this transition, which coincides with the phase of the tragedies properly so called, that the truly Renaissance aspect of Shakespeare's achievement works itself out, and the suspension of assent to the traditional Christian world-picture makes possible the exploration of a new paganism. The "histories" are certainly not comedies, but neither are they tragedies; they are the new dominative critique's exploration of the old world of divine comedy as seen in the process of being violated.

65

The tragic critique has the scope of its play defined by a fundamental acceptance of the order violated. But in the tragedies the play of this critique of existence breaks bounds into a deadly earnest, and is carried on to the very substance of the old sanities; it is a typical example of the Renaissance's challenge to the claims of the old order and all its assumptions pushed *à outrance*. "The new philosophy calls all in doubt"; although we cannot (as has sometimes been done) use lines like

> As flies to wanton boys are we to the gods
> They kill us for their sport

as summaries of Shakespeare's "philosophy of life" yet the mere fact that they could be written at all shows us that this brilliant "calling in doubt" of the very foundations of the old order of divine comedy is no play. The pushing of dominative analysis and question to the very roots of man's sanity accounts for the place which madness and near-madness—completely uninteresting to medieval authors—takes in *Hamlet*, *Macbeth*, *Lear* and *Othello*. This poetic Good Friday of the old order is a genuine one, an absolutely honest working-out of the Renaissance impulse to self-assertion in dominative critique of existence. And that is why the resurrection of the world of divine comedy which emerges from it is a genuine re-creation and repossession of the beginning in the end. It is perfectly true that the great translation of "degree" from the social and political terms of the histories to those of the individual soul—the new fairy-tale settings —is a far-reaching admission of the profound change which the Renaissance crisis has made in the life of European man. The old social and political incarnation of Christian order has been lost. But that losing has been also a losing of its inadequacies and abuses. And the process of interiorization which moulds the form of the traditional Christian in the new de-Christianizing, disintegrating world, offers the chance of achieving one day a new Christendom which has explored its own implications in ways undreamed of by the first one. As we shall see, the disaster has redemptive potentialities. The essential principle of the old order is regained none the less because it must be embodied in a new way and create, out of the difficulties of communication which now beset it, a new symbolism in which to express itself.

A dynamic balance of "game" and "earnest" in reposeful play indicates the persistent identity of what first went into the titanic crucible of the great tragedies and what comes out of it. You can see this clearly in little if you set side by side the relation between Falstaff and Prince Hal in *Henry IV* and that between Caliban and Prospero in *The Tempest*. The rejection of Falstaff by Prince Hal, once the serious business of his life begins, and the ruthless judgement it implies, seem nothing more than an inexplicable piece of cold-blooded callousness to those for whom Sir John is first and last a "character" in the Dickensian sense. And certainly it is clear that we are not meant to feel an unqualified admiration for this sudden and ruthless assumption of kingly behaviour as traditionally understood. Come to that, we are not meant to feel a wholly unqualified admiration for the indubitable hero later depicted so skilfully for a justifiable popular taste in *Henry V*. Yet the relation of Prince Hal to his gross fellow-debauchee is not simply part of the sudden Elizabethan budding of all modern characterization's psychological complexity. It also involves the simple black-and-white pattern of the medieval morality play. The humanly endearing qualities of the glutton, drunkard, fornicator and coward don't, even in the first flush of the humanist

67

revolution, obscure a blunt estimate of sin for just
what it is. Even the grossest Elizabethan groundling
would, I think, have been shocked at any suggestion that
Falstaff's characteristics were in themselves either
picturesque or admirable, or that a truly kingly king
was not right to banish them from his company as ruthlessly as might be. The abstract justice of the situation
in all its tragedy and the concrete mercy of it in all its
comedy—these two things are given to us undiluted and
at full strength, and they are not meant to be viewed
as incompatible. A similar complementarity of justice
and mercy in Prospero is, significantly, more subtly and
humanely worked out. In the earlier instance the mercy
on the sinner which rounds out judgement on the sin
is only conveyed implicitly by the terms of the characterization, and their relation to the dramatic action.
In the later one the balance is explicitly set out in the
very structure of the plot itself. But one and the same
balance of strictness and forbearance runs right through
from the early histories to the last comedies.

The analysis of justice disintegrates a man, revealing
his righteousness as filthy rags and his pride as puny
and futile, remorselessly exposing the way in which his
being is forever falling to pieces through sin and weakness. The synthesis of mercy is forever putting together
again this disintegrating Humpty Dumpty; looking at
the redemptive possibilities of the destructive elements in
man, it uses them to reveal the deep ground of goodness
on which they get the purchase of their existence, and
finds, in the very inadequacies on which justice fixes,
the shape of that healing synthesis which is mercy's
vision. It is the balance in creative play of these opposing powers of analysis and synthesis, of domination
and acceptance, which is the fundamental distinguishing
mark of the world of order and "degree" from which

Shakespeare sets out. And the same thing is the hall-mark of its rediscovery at the end of his tragic voyage into the Renaissance New World of the unknown. You might say that his artistic development is one from epic through drama to epic again; for it is of the essence of epic to explore and exploit an accepted mental order (which is why the purest form of epic is comic), and of the essence of drama to criticize existence in the attempt to establish or discover a mental order (which is why the purest form of drama is tragedy). In the epic world the dynamism of the artist's creativeness is, in the last analysis, playful. His critique is controlled within the bounds of his acceptance. In the dramatic world its energies are released boundlessly in a shattering, brilliant and desperately urgent piece of *work*—the attempt to establish the kind of cosmic security formerly accepted. And it is not without significance that Shakespeare's work both opens and closes with the vision of a basically objective historical world; and that the core of the work separating *Henry VI* from *Henry VIII* is a seething alchemical nebula in which remote, mythical and legendary matter is furiously wrought upon in order to create, out of the power of an individual artist's vision, a new and hitherto unimaginable mental world.

At the heart of the fireball this is hardly conceivable; and it is only at the heart of the fireball that the forces of the explosion lay themselves open to recontrol. To say that Shakespeare's final utterances provide us with nothing so vatic and titanic as Goethe's

> Das immer Weibliche
> Zieht uns hinan

does not mean that they aren't the expression of a pro-foundly mature wisdom which has been tried in the very

heart of the furnace. The essential playfulness of the
last comedies is possible only in virtue of a complementary intense seriousness. And in this lies the focus
of the light Shakespeare sheds as a key study in the
revaluation of the tragic concept of maturity. It was
with reference to the very core of the human—commonsense rationality—that I argued the necessity of revising
the standards imposed on our literary judgement by
the modern humanist revolution. It is with reference
to the titanic seriousness of the great tragedies itself
that you view the playfulness of the last fairy-tales as a
further advance into reality, and not a graceful retreat
from it. There is a vision of an intrinsically ordered
world which provides both setting and matter for the
drama of the early histories. And there is a similar
vision which, in the last plays, provides an amazingly
light and yet amazingly strong vessel for containing
the full force of evil. The two are, in essence, one; and
the great passion of intellect and imagination which
separates them shares in the deeply Christian quality
of both through the Christian concept of spiritual "loss"
as preceding all spiritual "finding". The final Shakespearean Renaissance vision is a resurrection of that
primal acceptant wonder which is the uncriticizing
vision of the child, arising from the "death" suffered in
that dominative and critical secondary vision which
succeeds it.

The stable element in the contents of the Shakespearean crucible—the controlling inertia of sanity which
prevents his vision leading him right round the bend
like Nietzsche or M. Sartre—is, then, the medieval
straw out of which the Shakespearean type of Renaissance
bricks are made. To turn inside out the titanist interpretation of the Shakespearean pattern, and revalue, in
the work of this its greatest poet, the order of values

set up by the Renaissance, is to deepen your awareness
of that fact, automatically. You see that in this particular manifestation of the sixteenth-century spiritual
revolution the break with tradition doesn't by any
means destroy all organic continuity with the past, and
that this persists to a far greater degree than is accounted
for simply by the fact that no artist can be wholly an
innovator. In particular, Shakespeare inherits from his
medieval subsoil a particular kind of attitude to the
absurd which separates his mind decisively from that of
a man like Nietzsche, and prevents the admittedly
spectacular bang of his tragic explosion from developing
into a chain reaction which runs right out of hand. For
him, the very brilliance of the flash of the tragically
exploding medieval cosmos is a blinding illumination on
how to turn the explosion inside out and re-balance its
rending energies as the architectonic stresses holding
together the matter of a world both old and new, a
world reborn beyond its own grave. The Shakespearean
pattern is, in fact, what its plain chronological shape
makes it look like—the medieval pattern of "In my
end is my beginning". In him we see the integrating
vision of medieval divine comedy reborn, phoenix
fashion, in and through that very crisis of critical dis-
section and bitter wonder which provides the dark
underside of the Elizabethan glitter and is the decisive
experience separating the mental world of Chaucer and
Langland from that of Dickens. The forces that split
apart at the Renaissance in a dazzling disintegration of
either-or—either superman or sub-man, either natural
or supernatural, either faith or reason—are made, by a
unique kind of spiritual judo, to explode themselves
together again in a synthesis of both-and—both justice
and mercy, both tragic critique and comic acceptance.

Since this typically medieval play of opposites is an

71

element in Shakespeare's work which has been so seriously underestimated by his spiritual descendants, there is, of course, a temptation to overemphasize it. And that would be as much of a misinterpretation as the traditional titanist one. The most *outstanding* thing about his work is obviously its element of *dis*continuity with the world of medieval thought—the way in which his mind detaches itself from the medieval world-picture in the process of achieving a new, breathtaking and deeply disturbing viewpoint on it. The medieval element in his achievement, on the other hand, is the *deepest* thing in it. And to get a rounded picture of the whole you have, again, to manage that sort of stereoscopy which comes from holding both elements—the traditionalism and the revolutionism—together in your mind at full strength. You have to imitate the feat by which Shakespeare holds together in a fruitful *coniunctio oppositorum* both the horrific and the comic aspects of Caliban. It is not in his medieval or his Renaissance aspect exclusively that Shakespeare—and in him, the whole main body of English literary genius—reveals his full relevance to the present theme. It is in the conjunction of both at full intensity. The final "brave new world" (a symbol of English poetry's speciality—a peculiar freshness of innocence in experience) is really a resurrection, in essence, of the medieval cosmos. But that is because, for Shakespeare, that cosmos really died. The truth of talk about his repossession of the medieval world depends just as much on the "repossession" as on the "medieval". A comparatively sudden overwhelming upsurge of the dominative, assertive, critical "masculine" right-hand side of the mind has called forth a countering surge of power from the acceptant, submissive, synthesizing "feminine" left hand side of the mind. But this war is resolved at its very height; at the very vortex

72

of the Renaissance turbulence we have here a still point where the conflicting forces are reconciled in a comic, humane creatureliness which is a real turning-inside-out of true Renaissance "titanism". And indeed, titanism proper does not really become effectively incarnate in English literature till Milton. In Shakespeare the real and dazzling war between the Middle Ages and the Renaissance finally shifts from the restlessness of titanism's "divine discontent" to the dynamic serenity of play. And an exploration of the relation between war and play is the next stage in this present attempt to relearn the dance of joy.

III : GAME AND EARNEST

Y ou would, I think, have gone some way towards defining "play" satisfactorily if you were to say that it's conflict creatively controlled by a containing order. When you play rugger, or American football, you don't in fact say simply: "Our strong arms be our conscience, swords our law", although to the uninstructed spectator it often looks like it. You don't play the titan, creating each man his own universe and decalogue; you accept a given order, and agree that however violently you release your energies within its limits, you won't make a nonsense of the whole business by releasing them in destroying it. Adam was told by God that he could do what he liked in the Garden of Eden as long as he didn't eat of the fruit of the Tree of Knowledge; Cinderella was told that she could enjoy herself as much as she liked at the ball provided she was back by twelve; and even the largest All Black forward or Navy quarterback is told that his zeal to plant the ball over the line must not lead him to hide in an adjoining shrubbery until it's dark and then crawl to his goal via the back of the grandstand. He is ritually and ceremonially bounded in space and time by the white lines and cease-play whistles which mark off the limits, and consequently the very form, of the little universe which he must accept loyally and unquestioningly if he is to exist and make sense as a player of football. And thus even the beeriest and most barbarous oaf who ever helped to throw the college aesthete in the pond after the big match pays, on his Saturday afternoons, a profound if scarcely-conscious civilized homage to the metaphysical principle of order. Indeed (to shift our example for a moment) it is very silly to underestimate the depth of civilizedness implied

74

by that not undignified phrase, "It's not cricket", which we have been so frightfully superior about for so long. Not only to accept loyally the written law of a particularly reposeful "little universe" of play, but also to accept the unwritten law which keeps the spirit of the written one alive, and this so wholeheartedly that there is no need to try to write out what has been left unwritten, and so universally that a whole society of men can know what you are doing without explanation— this is in essence a highly civilized achievement. And they have been very foolish men who have allowed an affectionate amusement at its funny side to turn sour into a shoddy smart-aleck sense of superiority to the need for it. "The Party isn't the Boy Scouts" says one of the grimly-adult-realistic characters in M. Sartre's *Les Mains Sales*: to which the much-despised Empire-builders and pukka sahibs of a past age might reply by pointing out that if there had been a few more men who hadn't felt themselves too grown-up truly to "fear God and honour the king", the law of the jungle might not have returned to the modern world on quite the scale that it has.

But this is a digression. My immediate concern is with the creative conflict of play, and the world of accepted law and limitation within which it finds its creative freedom. My proposed definition of play as conflict creatively controlled by a containing order applied primarily, of course, to that variety of play which the specialists in this subject call "agonistic"— the play of contest and competition and striving. At first glance that seems to leave uncovered the whole wide field of play into which this agonistic element does not enter—a child absorbedly bouncing a ball against a wall, or running and jumping through the long grass, or crayoning bright blue the pigs and donkeys in the

75

colouring-book, or a baby rotating gravely and joyfully on unsteady feet to the accompaniment of burbling noises of indeterminate pitch.

Well, I don't in fact think that a definition in terms of controlled conflict does by any means exhaust the content of the term "play", or even the most important part of it. But a certain element of creative conflict does enter into a great many kinds of playing which are not games in the strict sense. It is simply that the conflict is with matter instead of persons—with the strings of a violin, or the colours on a palette, or the centre of gravity of a bicycle, or the pressures of wind and water on sail and rudder. And the play of comedy itself is, like tragedy, a conflict between the sweet and bitter wonders —between the triumph of man's walking on his two legs and the disaster of his sitting on his bottom in a puddle, between the miracle of his being able to talk at all and the monstrosity of his sinister ability to talk non-sense.

The epic world of comedy and the dramatic world of tragedy are structured by the same pair of forces, only in different relations to one another. The play of the sweet and bitter wonders in comedy is based upon the predominance of the sweet, and its implied attitude of fundamental acceptance. The soul, say the mystics, is feminine to God; and in that "feminine" submission and self-surrender to God, they add, you find your true self and the whole world as its possession. The war of the sweet and bitter wonders in tragedy is based upon the predominance of the bitter wonder, and its implied attitude of fundamental criticism. The soul, say the titanists, is the masculine progenitor of its own divinity. And if we may trust the logical conclusion to which M. Sartre works out the implications of this dominative self-assertion, the "true self" which is to be found at the end of the endless voyage into singular isolation is of such a kind that the finder will wish to God he could lose it.

The medieval world, whose essential element of hierarchical "degree" I have just been considering, was at bottom a world of play between the sweet and bitter wonders; a world of divine comedy, as the title of its supreme epic expression significantly put it. And its dynamic repose of the sweet and bitter wonders was, as I have said, a creative play between the dominative and submissive elements in man.

When you have said so much, you have to go on immediately to qualify what you have said. For it's very important not to let an awareness of medieval society's basic balance and order lead you into that pathetic and unfortunate medievalism which is little more than a regressive hankering after a peaceful world of quaint fancy dress and universal arts-and-crafts—which never, in fact, existed. Any picture, however sophisticated, of an idyllic medieval paradise, suddenly shattered by the demonic and prideful outbreak of the Old European Adam at the Renaissance, is grossly misleading. It does little justice to the furious barbarity, squalor, grimness and endemic internal revolt of the Middle Ages: to the intellectual rebelliousness which produced a stream of near-pagan philosophizing; the religious rebelliousness that sustained the idealized amorality of Provence and kept a near-animal peasantry stubbornly addicted to the pagan cults of their ancestors; the political rebelliousness that set Emperor and Pope at one another's throats and ravaged Europe in unending local war; the social rebelliousness that produced the Jacqueries and the Peasants' Revolt. Medieval Europe, with its gangster knights and blasphemously sceptical intellectual proletariat of poor scholars, was something vastly different from the pious world of colourful fancy

77

dress which the Romantics based on the manuscript illuminations. All the disintegratory forces of irreligion and social disruption which you can identify in the world born in the sixteenth century can be followed back into the very heart of medieval society.

But despite the massacres and the scepticisms and the anarchy, the manuscript illuminations *are* there none the less, with the *Divine Comedy* and the *Canterbury Tales* and the architecture and the music. And I think it is indisputable that the medieval vision, as formulated in medieval art, is characterized by a certain vivid positive vitality and a deeply energetic reposefulness. It is perfectly true that the Middle Ages contained a strong element of ferocious and gruesome pessimism; in fact, they revelled in it, very much as a certain kind of small boy revels in a real H-Certificate retreat sermon on hell, in the old tradition. And in the late Middle Ages there certainly develops, under the threefold impact of the Hundred Years' War, the Black Death and the Great Schism, an obsession with the macabre which goes a good deal deeper than the Chamber-of-Horrors gusto of the earlier centuries. Yet Villon, I think, with (for example) his final glittering line on the Assumption to balance a whole ballade of rotten-lush exploration of the feminine body's ripening and decay, clarifies for us the kind of principle on which the Middle Ages kept their basic balance, even on the most shivery of tightropes. The negative elements, however fierce, were always contained—even if only just—within the wider positive vision—the vision of submission and acceptance. Indeed, for Villon even the inevitable gruesome decay of that feminine loveliness after which he lusted had deeper undertones of unavoidable penance and redemption, as did the grim wages of sin which he reckoned up in his "Ballade of the Hanged Men". The harshness of medieval realism is secondary to an overwhelming savour of the intrinsic freshness and goodness of being: something that leaps at you from the glass of Chartres, or the carols of fifteenth-century England, or the Book of Hours of the Duc de Berry, or the opening lines of the *Canterbury Tales*. And it is highly significant that men living in so violent, uncomfortable and insecure a world should largely record their vision of it in terms of a vivid peace which is like the wonder of a child. The conflicts of the Middle Ages were real and terrible; their order was just that little bit more real yet. Despite their almost pathological turbulence medieval men, as far as their mental world was concerned, liked their energy in the form of good solid atoms, rather than explosions, however sunlike in intensity. And this was perhaps because of a deep instinctual awareness that as far as man is concerned fulfilment is a matter of being rather than doing. The fundamentally contemplative medieval view of life found it a truism that you fulfilled your destiny by becoming more fully what you had in some sense been all the time; just as the later activist view found it a truism that you fulfilled yourself by jumping out of your creaturely skin in the direction of some altogether nobler condition. Where the dynamism of the post-Renaissance world explodes outwards in an ambivalent "divine discontent", that of the Middle Ages is balanced in an internal play which does the work of holding in being a whole cosmic order.

The contrast and change between the two states is something which is, perhaps, most easily visible in music and architecture. Medieval polyphony, rocking end-lessly back and forth on the final note of the mode, creates out of strongly individualistic "voices" a melodic cosmos charged with architectonic energy. But dramatic tensions are in general conspicuously absent from it;

they slowly but increasingly characterize sixteenth-century music (Vittoria is a good example of the transition) and gain in power through the Baroque era to reach their height in the orchestral music of the great Romantic composers. Similarly the rushing mechanical fugues of Gothic tracery draw the observer out of himself in a worship-charged ecstasy; the dramatic sculptures and Atlas-like load-defying pillars of the Renaissance palace or the Baroque church stimulate his self-consciousness by throwing him back on his heels with: "Your admiration or your life!"

If, then, the arts of the Middle Ages incarnate an epic vision of existence as divine comedy, and consequently aglow with the luminous freshness of primal colour, this is not because its cities were "small and white and clean" (as William Morris startlingly imagined), or because everyone said his prayers regularly, or because fighting was conducted in a strictly sporting spirit. The world-picture is rather that of an existence in which despite filth and disease, stench and treachery, gross immorality and brutality, it is generally sensed to be good to be, and the evils attendant on being are generally sensed as being genuinely secondary, for all their appalling reality. The tension of life's conflict isn't removed; yet it is experienced as in principle resolved, as a pattern of forces manifesting the structure of an ultimate order in which "al maner of thyng" is well. And as far as the Middle Ages are concerned the point of resolution at which these mightily conflicting forces find their angle of repose is the person of the Redeemer. He is God and Man, the Man of Sorrows and the Hero bringing light and joy, the Unconquered Sun. And the paradox incarnate in this amazing figure is mirrored throughout the world remade in his paradoxical image. Whatever that world's ferocities, and whatever the strange harshness and violence of the men who endured them and contributed to them, the backdrop of the medieval spectacle remains the good tidings of great joy:

A babe is born of high nature
The Prince of Peace that ever shal be
Of heaven and earth he hath the cure
His lordship is eternity
What wondrous tidings ye may hear
That man now made is Goddës peer
That sin had made but fiendës prey.

But it is hardly possible, when one merely reads these words, instead of hearing them sung in their three-part setting, with its luminous open fifths and swallowlike melodic lines, to grasp to the full the *freshness* which the Middle Ages derived for their world and their art from the golden background of redemption. It is against the paradoxical happiness of the *felix culpa*—even when, as in the late fourteenth century of Avignon, the *culpae* are very culpable indeed—that the savagely vigorous pessimisms and barbarities of the Middle Ages must be viewed.

Where the modern world born at the Renaissance conceives vitality in the linear and temporal terms of progress from what is outworn to the unprecedented, the Middle Ages always conceive it in terms spatial and perennial. For them, there is a definite historic "point of intersection of the timeless with time"—the Redemption—which, perpetuated in the Mass, is the centre of existence; and vitality lies in the pattern in which all human activity organizes itself about that centre. The "lack of historic sense" which makes medieval men see Virgil primarily as a Christian prophet, and Homer as a "great clerk", is certainly in part the under-development of man's historical self-awareness; but it is also

something more positive. It is an inarticulate sense of
the freshness of eternity underlying the transiency of
that coming-to-be and passing-away which is the carrier
wave of history. And that is the freshness which glows
at us out of the primary colours of the manuscript
illuminations, and flowers in dynamic repose in the lithe
convolutions of medieval polyphony, or the patterns of
stress and thrust in medieval roof-tracery—to say
nothing of the "babooneries" which so confidently
counterpoint the solemn lines of the great churches.

That comic resolution of the sweet and the bitter
wonders is one of play between the submissive and
dominative aspects of man's response to his experience.
In terms of philosophy, this amounts to a play between
intuition and analysis—between man's power to know
trees and elephants and archbishops and so on, and his
power to dissect that knowledge; between his power to
submit to experience in acceptance and his power to
dominate it by mastery; between his power to appreciate and his power to criticize. By virtue of a basic
creaturely acceptance of the fundamentals of thought as
gifts to be received—as opposed to a titanistic lust after
them as spoils to be won—the Middle Ages intuitively
defined their mental world by certain lines of absurdity
within the limits of which a most bewildering and violent
play of critical analysis was possible. Since they had in
their bones an inarticulate determination not to sacrifice
common sense to singular brilliance, they could afford
to play games with scepticism. True, as time went on
the games began to get too rough, as the nannies say;
they got nearer and nearer to being in earnest. From
Peter Abelard to William of Ockham there was always
a line of dazzling left-wingers to conduct a philosophical
critique of theology which could, on occasion, assume a
startling intensity. In fact, it nearly always seemed to

be doing so to traditionalists such as those who brought
about the condemnation of that audacious innovator
Thomas Aquinas—a fact which should be more often
remembered by those who tend to use him as a club for
keeping non-Catholic thought at bay with. William of
Ockham is not an isolated Morning Star of Logical Posi-
tivism, and predominance of the analytical aspect of
philosophic thought is not something which rushed upon
us almost out of a clear sky in the sixteenth century. Yet
despite the nominalist movement—in a way, because of
it—it is not hard to see that the medieval mind, whatever its passion for the logical subtleties of disputation
(a most interesting kind of formal play), never allowed
the dazzle of critical analysis to hypnotize it away from
the intuitions of common sense. The medieval philosopher may have got worked up to the knives-and-
cudgels point by the passions aroused in trying to eluci-
date just how it was that he was able to apply the term
"animal" to lions and rabbits alike; or what exactly
were the characteristics of that mode of existing which
enabled him so to apply it. But he never doubted
seriously (as opposed to playfully) whether he did apply
the term, or whether he did exist. Medieval man had
in his bones a deep awareness of man's creatureliness;
it persisted, on the whole, even through the fiercest of his
rebellious moods, which were many. And it meant that
he regarded the first principles of thought, and the
existence of himself and his world, as things which in
principle you accepted, not as things which man's own
mental *virtù* must creatively establish out of chaos, like
the spirit of God working on the waters of the abyss.
Man was, and other things were, and man knew them
in his thought, and you could either take it or leave it,
when you got down to rock bottom. Certainly all of this
was rightly and justly subject to a process of rational

investigation whose analytical aspects might be pushed
to bewildering lengths. Yet the process had in its very
strenuousness an essential element of play in the sense
that it was at once taken perfectly seriously and also as
something which did not, from another viewpoint,
matter. The Middle Ages would have endorsed heartily
the famous dilemma of Aristotle: "You say that one
must philosophize. Then you must philosophize. You
say one should not philosophize. Then (to prove your
contention) you must philosophize. In any case, you must
philosophize." But they also held—even if implicitly
rather than explicitly—that the seriousness implied in
the "must" was the complement of a more fundamental
playfulness. Philosophizing might shake up into a
totally bewildering succession of kaleidoscopic complexities the simple pattern of common sense. But the
philosophical kaleidoscope was in essence a toy which
God had given his children to play with for their delight,
not a grimly utilitarian tool with which men must hack
their way out of lunacy toward omniscience.

When medieval man refused to let his critique of
sanity's intuitions run wild into statements like "The
Universe is merely a flaw in the purity of non-Being"[1]
he was doing exactly the same as the prep.-school cricket
captain who, on being bowled middle stump first ball,
conquers the uncivilized impulse to burst into tears and
says in trembling tones: "Jolly good ball!": he was
refusing to take himself too seriously, and turn a good
game into bad earnest. I suppose we must have laughed
our superior fill by now at the world of Sir Henry New-
bolt's "Play up, play up and play the game!", and
indeed the Anglo-Saxon world would have sadly lost its
sense of humour if it had been blind to the funny side
of the Pukka Sahib and the Old School Tie and the

[1] Paul Valéry, "L'Ébauche d'un Serpent".

84

White Man's Burden. Yet that seemingly barbaric and
near-pagan ethos of Victorian Protestantism had deeper
roots than its practitioners knew in the wisdom of
Catholic civilization. And when we look about us at the
indescribable horrors born out of serious mass refusal to
play the game of Christian civilization,[1] we may even
admit that a last laugh of a kind could be with Sir Henry,
Dear Old School, Dear Old Regiment, Dear Old Far-
Flung Empire and all. Perhaps he and his fellow champions of the stiff upper lip and the straight bat would
have been somewhat surprised had it been suggested that
there was a line of spiritual descent linking them to the
quarrelsome theologians of medieval Popery. But the
fact remains that medieval man, too, was "playing the
game", if in a more fundamental sense than Sir Henry,
when he remained unwavering in his consciousness that
all the bedazzlement of the philosophical kaleidoscope's
patterns were nothing more—or less—than fascinating
reflections and refractions of an enduring commonsense reality; the very recklessness of the dialectic that
ends up in nominalism reflects the sense of security of
men to whom the absurd, however brilliant, was still the
hedge about a playground and not the intolerable wall
around a prison.

There is thus a great deal of truth in what Bertrand
Russell felt, I think, to be rather a body-blow to medieval
philosophy when he remarked that St. Thomas Aquinas
could not be called a proper philosopher since all he did
was to find reasons for conclusions decided in advance.
But the joke is, appropriately, on Bertrand Russell; for

[1] I'm aware that the upholders of the ideal of "playing the game" could
be, and often were, appallingly innocent of applying their code outside
their own set—to the "lower orders" and the "wogs", for example, unless
these were prepared to accord them a loyalty as of admiring fag to school
prefect. But this wasn't a flaw in the ideal itself; it was a failure to realize
the ideal.

any intelligent child,[1] medieval or modern, could tell that obviously you can't start to think at all unless you know the answers about thinking, in some sense, before you start; and that it is silly (however brilliantly so) to start your philosophical career by asking whether anything can be known for certain—as Bertrand Russell did, according to one at least of his own accounts. St. Thomas Aquinas would have agreed with him that, where his—that is St. Thomas's—philosophy was concerned, the end was in the beginning, and that in a true sense all the answers were known in advance. It was a true game. In fact, the very form in which his greatest philosophical work was constructed is a highly formalized expression of play—the vigorous play of medieval disputation, a sort of chess of argument; the pattern of objection, solution and conclusion in the articles of the *Summa* reproduces in a highly abstract form the kind of serious and lively game which Socrates and his friends initiated in the dialogues recorded by Plato. Where St. Thomas would have differed from Bertrand Russell would have been on the conclusion that this playful kind of philosophizing, which you must put your whole heart into and which is yet in itself but "as straw", is not also "serious" philosophizing; and that serious philosophizing must consist in trying to establish by the power of man's own strong mental right arm the basis of the power of man's own strong mental right arm. Certainly, by the standards of judgement current since the great philosophical revolution of the seventeenth century, which created the world in which Bertrand Russell and his fellows live and move and have their being, the philosophy of the Middle Ages may not be considered "serious". But then, the thought of the Middle Ages would have maintained

---

[1] I do not intend this as a sneer; no *savant* need be ashamed of failing to preserve childhood's directness of insight.

that with all due deference to the titanic greatness of the modern revolutionaries, their revolution was, from one point of view, brilliantly silly. Really and truly brilliant; but really and truly silly—objectively, that is. To say this is not, of course, to indulge in cheap abuse of the makers of the modern philosophical revolution. One of the peculiarities of philosophy is that it can often be highly intelligent, and necessary, for a thinker to ask questions that are in themselves more or less absurd. A thinker's subjective greatness is often revealed to us only by the extent to which *he* reveals his *objective* foolishness.

I suppose that there are few places in which all this can be seen more fascinatingly than in the truly titanic yet ambiguously titanist figure of Descartes, the "father of modern philosophy". The "Cartesian revolution" of the seventeenth century is indeed an archetypal pattern of the development of the modern mind; from one aspect, at least, titanist to the core. There is the characteristic of absolute novelty; Descartes, despite all the criticisms which have been made of him by his successors, still, in some respects, appears to many modern thinkers now as he did then—as a Prometheus, *starting* true philosophy, laying in the depths of chaos, by the mastering power of his genius, the foundations of the kind of thinking which has created the modern world. And Descartes himself, of course, certainly saw the "incredibly ambitious" project of his "universal mathematics" as essentially the work of one man. Of course, it was not, even in this case, a question of individual genius alone; the Cartesian revolution was the work of the spirit of the age, just as had been the sterile degeneration of the great scholastic tradition, which set the stage for Descartes and did so much to substantiate the belief of those who saw in him a sort of pioneer of the Enlightenment, hacking a clearing for later deism and

rationalism out of the rank jungle of scholastic speculation and logic-chopping. And that spirit of the age was
the spirit of the Renaissance, summed up in a passionate
and dominative drive to self-assertion, with all this
implies of refusal to accept things as gifts and longing to
possess them masteringly by right of conquest.

If you want to sum up the way in which man's
dominative and submissive aspects pass from play to
war in Descartes, you can say that in him, in principle
and potentiality, the secondary vision of analysis and
criticism turns on the primary mothering vision of intuition and acceptance, and murders it. At first sight,
the dominative "masculine" attempt to provide an indestructible basis for philosophizing by philosophizing
may seem to be no more than the kind of thing Saint
Augustine was doing when he constructed his dilemma:
"You say that I am mistaken in thinking that I exist;
but if I am mistaken, I exist; therefore, I am not mistaken in thinking I exist." Arnauld thought so; and
Descartes got rather starchy over the suggestion. But
I've sometimes wondered whether there was not something more to Descartes' annoyance than suspicion that
he might be in the position which Chesterton so much
enjoyed—of making an epoch-making voyage of discovery to some truth which turned out to have been
the common property of all Christendom for hundreds
of years. Did he sense the enormous difference which
underlay the superficial similarity between his "I think,
therefore I am" and St. Augustine's "If I am mistaken,
I exist"? It is the difference between saying, "How
is it that I exist?" or "How is it that I know cardinals
and kangaroos?" and saying, "Do I exist?" and "Do I
know cardinals and kangaroos?" In the first place we
make an act of affirmation of our own creatureliness by
accepting as the starting point of life and thought

foundations which we cannot lay ourselves; in the second, unless we grasp more clearly than Descartes did, I think, the subtler implications of what we are doing, we challenge that condition fundamentally, if implicitly, by saying that we will not be—*saying*, be it noted—unless we can establish the fact of our own being, and will not think unless we can establish by thinking the basis for thinking. And this is very different from defending a basic axiom by a *reductio ad absurdum* of attacks on it.

It doesn't make sense, of course—unless, in a way which this book will try gradually to describe, we are *playing*. The clash between this fact and a superb genius for making sense of things, is of great significance, I think, with regard to the curious element of the ambiguous, the enigmatic, and the reserved, about which biographers of Descartes have theorised. As the logical positivists would (or would have?) put it, it is not seriously meaningful. Maybe the second half of it—the bit about setting up the basis for thinking by thinking—is more dangerous than the first. For you cannot contemplate the first statement—"I will not exist unless I can establish the fact of my own existence"—for two minutes with the childlike eye of sanity without seeing obviously that it is the product of a mental vision jarred brilliantly cross-eyed. Before you can even begin to say what you will or won't do about your existence, you have to exist—and whosesoever the terms may be on which you do that, they are certainly not your own; for they are already laid down, and have to be laid down, before you are in a position to talk terms about anything. Trying to draw up terms upon which you will accept, even for philosophical purposes only, the fact of your own existence, is objective silliness on a scale so grand as to acquire an eerie dignity of its own. You can get away with it, with yourself as with everybody else, only by seeing what you are doing in so fiercely cross-eyed a manner that everything gets jarred out of true with itself, and appears under the disguise of a twofold blur which is a caricature of sanity's rounded stereoscopy. The naked and even magnificent absurdity of an un-playful "Do I exist?" becomes acceptable by looking like the old, playful and sane: "How can I defend my certainty of my existence if some brilliant maniac challenges it?" But although it looks like the old question, it is really its very opposite: the brilliant maniac is now, if he isn't very careful, the thinker himself, and the answer to the question is no longer sanity's playful demonstration of how absurdity acts as a playground boundary. It is the desperately effortful attempt of a lucid lunacy to lift itself out of its own chaos by its own bootlaces; than which (to suit word to action) there are few things, which you can't do, more.

In comparison with all this the secondary Cartesian type of question about thinking—Bertrand Russell's question whether anything can be known for certain, for example—is a good deal less misleading, particularly when applied to the sense-experience world of shin-banging and the like. For there is enough of the obviously potentially misleading in the action of the senses to make a thorough questioning of their veracity by no means an obviously silly thing to do. But in the long run, the results can be just as wildly absurd as those produced by asking in the wrong tone of voice: "Do I exist?"—in fact, worse. For whereas in the first case you are producing the equivalent of sheer gibberish, in the second you are producing that persuasive kind of lucid unrealism which we find in persecution mania, for example. You can't possibly *prove* to the paranoiac that the perfectly innocent window-cleaner across the road isn't a foreign spy observing his movements

90

reflected in the window-panes; you can't possibly *prove*
to the determined solipsist that the ideas he has of other
people and things correspond to anything actually
existing outside his mind. And it is, if you take the thing
seriously, far more horrible to be inextricably imprisoned in a solitary confinement within one's own ideas
than to be hounded through the world by mysterious
persecutors who must at least exist to destroy your
isolation if they are to persecute at all.[1] The last end
of the less obvious non-sense is worse than the wild
beginning of the more obvious kind; but the more
obvious kind smashes up the essential mechanism of
sanity more thoroughly and immediately than the less
obvious kind does, and requires a more violent initial
squint if it is to be seen as possible at all. However, in
either case what is happening is the same. Things which
were once accepted as "dumb certainties of experience",
and analysed, only in playful "defence" of sanity
against the fantastic onslaughts of the absurd, are now
regarded as the first acts of creation by which can
and must be laid sanity's foundations in the very
vortex of chaos. The former game with the domesticated
monsters of the mind has become, in principle, a desperate war with them for possession of the mind itself.

It is, fundamentally, in the name of freedom that this
attempt is made to crash the absurdity barrier. To the
titanist, whether he be conscious or unconscious of his
titanism (and Descartes' whole fascination lies in the
extent to which he was unaware of his), it is an intolerable
servitude of dependence to accept the fact of existence
and the fact of knowledge, and a supreme proof of man's
godlike dominative power over himself and his world to

[1] Mr. John Custance, in his *Wisdom, Madness and Folly* (Gollancz,
1951), gives an interesting example, from personal experience, of how the
extreme depressive agony of a manic-depressive cycle expressed itself
for him in solipsist terms.

establish both. It is the essence of the Cartesian enigma that no one, I think—least of all Descartes, perhaps—can tell us for sure just how far the quest for the "new" philosophy, based on impregnably established foundations, was the titanism of the new age, and how far merely the necessary exploration of gaps left by previous philosophizing. But just because the Cartesian spirit turns good play into bad earnest in this way, the earnest, effortful and titanic struggle of the New Man to create his own mental world does, as it becomes more explicit and consciously affirmed, turn ironically into bad play, not unlike the bad joke which makes M. Sartre's *Huis Clos* end the world not in a bang but a chuckle. Ask whether you exist, playfully, and all is well; to the extent that you ask it seriously you simply smash up the language. You can talk as if your own existence, or your own power to think, were something that had to be established by your own efforts, but you cannot live as if they were. And once you jar what you say out of synchronization with what you can do, your developing gesture of total freedom from limitations becomes in fact a grim paralysis of total imprisonment within them. The hedge of absurdity gives you shelter for endless play as long as you accept it; insofar as you try to behave as if it were not there, it becomes the barbed wire of a one-man concentration camp. And with Descartes, and the element of objective absurdity so paradoxically entwined into the magnificence of his philosophical revolution, we see the Renaissance's assault on the absurdity barrier in all its baffling self-contradiction. "I think, therefore I am": when that proposition wavers from being part of the playful *reductio ad absurdum* of a foolish attack on common sense, towards being a laborious and uncommonly clever attempt to establish foundations of thinking by thinking, then the prideful upsurge of

Renaissance self-assertion has found its first ambiguous
self-awareness in a strictly philosophical formula.

"Ambiguous"—you have at once to round out the
picture with a complementary aspect. Descartes is a
true creature of the spirit of the age, but also other
things besides. He is a believing Catholic; a man who
goes so far counter to the spirit of Renaissance titanism
as to undertake the vow of pilgrimage to the Holy House
of Loreto, and meets his end, fortified by the sacraments
of the Church, in as edifying a manner as could be desired.
He is a child of the Church as well as being a child of his
age; it is God, he believes in all humility, who has chosen
him for the Promethean task of working out for the first
time, single-handed, the universal method for all sciences.
Like Shakespeare, though in a different way, he is a
Janus, a Mr. Facing-Both-Ways. As well as the "masculine" spirit of the new age, with its primacy of the
dominative element in man and consequent clash between
his critical and appreciative visions, there is in him also
the "feminine" spirit of the old age, with its primacy of
the submissive element in man and emphasis on his inescapable dependence. Indeed, as I have said, it's
impossible, for practical purposes, to disentangle in
Descartes the frank "feminine" need for mental security
and the proud "masculine" determination to win it by
force of the mental strong right arm. For they are
locked in a relation ambiguously on the turn from play
to war; a war which can only end, if fought to a finish,
in the atrophy of one aspect of man's mind and the running amok of the other. Either you will get, ultimately,
the kind of philosophy which analyses away the very
intuitive foundations on which philosophy rests. Or you
will get the kind which sacrifices all rationality in an intuitive cult of the blood and the loins, and with a ghastly
symbolism reduces any protesting philosophers to living

93

skeletons in its concentration camps, like the Valley of Dry Bones which was their philosophy.

It's true that in the thought of Descartes himself the old spirit and the new are still, to some extent, reconciled; when a serious, as opposed to playful, critique of our everyday experience seems to have destroyed all possibility of trust in our own senses, God is brought in as their ultimate Guarantor, to save us from the horrific possibility of being walled up all alone in a private universe of our own ideas. But, as Tchekov's student remarks, if you're going to mow everything down, why spare your own legs? The old demonstrations of the existence of God had begun with an assumption of the basic truthfulness of the senses: "It is evident to our senses," begins St. Thomas in his reassuring plain-bread-and-butter way, "that in the world some things are in motion." But once you have decided that you won't (or mustn't?) accept your knowledge of the world outside you unless you can establish its truth by your own efforts, then it begins to get pretty difficult, to put it mildly, to proceed to the invisible things from the things that are made. And so the followers of Descartes decline to call a halt to their critique when they get to the God of Descartes, and to accept his fortunate and sanity-saving deliverance of man from the prison of his own ideas. In so doing they verify the law which M. Etienne Gilson formulates when he says[1] that whenever a master in philosophy declines to follow the implications of his own premisses all the way, his disciples will do it for him. And they demonstrate how, despite all the sincerity of Descartes himself in this matter, and all his strange, enigmatic genius, the apparent integration of the old spirit and the new in his thought is in fact an appearance, concealing a fundamental split. For all his dominative on-

[1] *The Unity of Philosophical Experience*, London, 1955, p. 308.

slaught on the "lower world" of man's inarticulate metaphysical certainties and sense experiences, Descartes had
too much of the medieval sanities in his bones to accept,
or try to justify, a private universe[1] of the kind which
M. Sartre has affirmed with such grim and perverse
courage. His greatness appears not only in the extent
to which he attempted to crash the absurdity barrier,
but also in the degree to which he was too sensible to
grasp the full consequences of what he was doing. But
for all this manifestation of Christian instinct, he is still
none the less a "divided man", brilliantly and restlessly
driven by the inner conflict born of the breakup of the
play between the "left hand side" and "right hand side"
of the traditional mind of Christendom. And you can see
in his philosophical descendants how this his legacy
of interior conflict and disintegration increased and
multiplied.

This titanic overturning of the creaturely order, in
an attempt to replace accepted creaturely security by
achieved divine security, is something which is not, of
course, confined to the realm of pure thought. It is
something which shows itself very obviously in the
world of action—indeed, in that whole vast rapid
development of action at the expense of contemplation
which is so important a feature of the modern era. One
of the most obvious aspects of this process is the ever-
mounting crescendo of technological achievement which
accompanies, and is part of, the growth of the natural
sciences. Admittedly, this is not, any more than the
parallel philosophical development, something which
suddenly leaps into existence *ex nihilo* in the sixteenth
and seventeenth centuries. Ancient man and medieval
man had always found a place for the "masculine"
dominative element in their approaches to the natural

---

[1] Or should one say, a violated private universe?

world in ultimate dependence on which we all live; and the comparative crudity of these earlier steps in technology should not lead us to underestimate the achievement they constitute. It is a wonderful assertion of man's godlike rational power over the natural world when he harnesses beasts to his service, hoists a sail to the wind, or thinks out the three-field system of agriculture—just as it is every time a baby first takes a staggering step, or a small boy writes "cat". Yet the men on the earlier side of the Renaissance divide had always been aware that nature can never be wholly or even merely dominated. Here too the element of play comes in. Control over nature cannot be an absolute, but must be integrated with a more fundamental submission to her; the most brilliant feats of man's technological inventiveness must be worked out within the limits of a fundamental respect for the medium which they are achieved in. His power is unique, but it has its limitations. And indeed the men of ancient times, and of the Middle Ages too, were so acutely aware of this that often in matters of technology a superstitious wooing of supernatural powers took the place of rational enquiry and experiment.

The self-congratulations of the eighteenth-century Enlightenment are to a considerable extent justified, in that from the Renaissance onwards there was steady progress in substituting reasoned enquiry into the problems of the natural world for hit-or-miss intuitive speculation about them *a priori*. But unfortunately this wasn't the whole of the story; what was also happening was a drastic diminishing of the awareness of the limitations of man's power to dominate nature, and the fundamental acceptance of her conditions, within the framework of which alone this power to dominate her can be successfully exercised. Sir Francis Bacon was doubtless by no means the first man to say: "Know-ledge itself is power", and in any case it is quite true, of course, that knowledge *is* power. But that is not all there is to say about it, or even the most fundamental thing there is to say. And there's no doubt that with the coming of the New Learning, and its experimental, analytical critique of nature by scientific method, the control of nature really begins to be viewed as a dictator-ship rather than a constitutional rule based upon the consent of the governed—ill-informed and naïvely credulous though may have been the terms in which that consent was often previously conceived. It would be spoiling a good case, of course, to construct a para-doxical defence of, for example, the mentality which mumbles incomprehensible charms during ploughing as being the most important aspect of ensuring the success of the crop. Yet the superstitious abuse does at least contain elements of an awareness that nature cannot be simply bulldozed, which is absent from the ruthless and reckless mechanized exploitation that evokes the mute protest of "dust bowls" and the like. And in actual fact it is not, historically speaking, all that long before scientific and technological development, ever more speedily accelerating, begins to emerge as an attempt to play god to the natural world which is much like some modern philosophers' attempts to play god to the worlds of their own sense experience, thought and existence.

For that is what one aspect at least of the modern mind works out to (even though more or less implicitly in so many cases): a fantastic determination to achieve omnipotence, whether in establishing by its own power the foundations of its own power, or controlling utterly the earth on which it depends from day to day for its very life. Whether in the field of mind or matter, the project is, objectively and essentially, an absurd one,

97

and can in fact only be attempted by men held fast, to a greater or lesser extent, in the cross-eyed vertigo which seizes us at the point where the brilliant and the silly blur together.

To put it thus and leave the matter there would, of course, be to oversimplify. It is rare for titanism to work itself out to the bitter end, wholly into full consciousness. A large part of the internal conflict that gives titanists their restless dynamism is the clash between their titanism and their common sense. And there has been a good deal of excuse for men's dreaming in this way. To set out, as the modern philosophical revolution fundamentally did, to demonstrate that sense is sense and absurdity absurdity, is an undertaking so absurd in itself as to demand a considerable effort of historical imagination on our part if we are not to underestimate greatly the mental quality of the men who attempted it. You need a closer acquaintance with the mustiest aspects of decadent scholasticism than most of us would care to acquire if you are really going to understand why all Europe did not rise up as one man and ask Descartes why on earth he felt it necessary to prove that he existed before he felt able to begin thinking. The absurdity of the Cartesian enterprise is, from one aspect, so magnificently obvious that you are blinded with science as to its true nature, as was Descartes himself. But the application of Descartes' critique of experience in the field of natural science,[1] and its further applications in the field of technology, can produce very good sense indeed, and this not only on first glance but during the experience of generations.

Here at least the assertive drive towards a godlike

[1] This point has to be complemented, of course, by remembering also that from another standpoint it was the development of natural science itself that gave much of its impetus to the development of Descartes' philosophy.

absoluteness of control produces dazzling and genuine successes. The increasing inner confusion and unbalance in man as Locke dethrones Descartes, Hume dethrones Locke and Kant Hume, is counterbalanced in his outer world. Newton, Harvey, Vesalius, Kepler, Linnaeus, Huygens, Boyle, and all the rest of the growing army of experimental scientists, penetrate further and further into the secrets of the natural world, and the following army of technicians turn their knowledge to ever more breathtaking practical account. With the coming of the steam engine at the turn of the eighteenth century "Knowledge is power" becomes a word made iron flesh for all to see. The Industrial Revolution gives a definitive form to dominative technology. The factory becomes the focal point at which science passes from partnership with nature—well symbolized, however fantastically, in the work of the alchemists—to dictatorship over her. The mill changes from being that graceful partner of the winds which the Dutch developed to being that domineering monster which the visionary eye of Blake saw as plainly Satanic—not something half-growing out of the natural order, but something ruthlessly clamped down upon it, forcing it into a dark shape not its own. And human nature is subjected by the power of the machine, just as much as the air and the grass and the water. In the factory of the Industrial Revolution the oppression of the common man takes on a quality of dehumanization generally alien to the worst injustices of the Middle Ages but emerging already in the new Poor Laws of sixteenth-century capitalism. There, the machine passes from being an extension of the hand to being a substitute human being, capable of being kept at its inhumanly efficient pitch only at the cost of an increasing subhumanizing of its attendants. And it is only from about this point onwards that the dark under-

side of insecurity, anxiety and potential revolt begins to
show really clearly through the dazzling surface of
scientific and technical progress.

By the time that the natural sciences were reaching
the nineteenth-century heyday of their optimistic self-
confidence, there was a steadily growing body of thinkers
who, from men like Cobbett at one extreme to men like
the Pre-Raphaelites at the other, shared a growing awareness that man's tightening grip on nature was in danger
of becoming a stranglehold, and that the industrial
Promised Land of material progress could be a Waste
Land of spiritual impoverishment. This developing
spiritual sickness of the Railway Age is first chiefly
diagnosed by non-technicians—men like Blake, Matthew
Arnold or Baudelaire. And there begins to develop a
new danger of becoming negative-minded over science—
of losing sight of the vast positive achievement it has
to its credit. The two knockout blows dealt to nineteenth-century optimism by the first and second world
wars soon bring to the surface in the scientists and
technologists themselves an increasingly uneasy sense of
being the creators of a potential Frankenstein's monster—
a change of attitude encouraged, too, by the increasing
sense of mystery and humility brought into pure science
by Einstein's dethronement of classical physics, with all
that it had implied of knowing exactly where you were
and what was what. And by the time man's acquisition
of power moves into the breathtaking stage of the tap-
ping of nuclear energy it is no longer merely the mixed
bag of those hostile to technology who are struck with
fear. Even those who are most eager to develop it are
also filled with dread: not because of what they have
discovered in itself, but because of the contrast between
the potentialities of their new discoveries, and the moral
instability of the creatures who must control them.

This situation reveals a pattern which psychologists have made us familiar with in human behaviour at the individual level: that of an outer aggressiveness which is an attempt to compensate for an inner fear—the aggressivity here being, of course, of a highly formalized kind, but strongly marked with aggressivity's negative pattern of destructive dominativeness, for all that. And it is interesting to note that here, in the field of action—experimental science and technology—the pattern unfolds itself more or less in the opposite direction to that in which it unfolds in the contemplative sphere of philosophy strictly so called. The scientific aspect of the modern primacy of the "masculine" and dominative element in man doesn't begin by showing a fairly clear obverse of anxiety and insecurity, as does the age of the criticism of experience in philosophy. There, there is a half-explicit quality in the attempt to act as a god which automatically turns man's creaturely dependence into a mortal threat and an intolerable scandal, to be reacted against for dear life with effortful aggressivity. But in science, it's not so much that men are driven by any fearfully aggressive anxiety to master their world, as that they are more and more intoxicated by the unsuspected extent of their capacity for doing so. In philosophy, it is the growing sense of disintegration which stimulates the ever more grandiose and ever more unsuccessful attempts of the great system-makers, and ends in the maniacally brilliant and absurdly logical absolutism of some varieties of atheist existentialism, where the critique of the "mastering mind" has gnawed away the very branch on which the thinker sits to think.

This inside-out relationship is not surprising when you stop to think of the complementary relationship between philosophy and the natural sciences. It was things like the revolutionary empirical discoveries of Copernicus which set Descartes' mind moving towards his revolutionary criticism of experience; yet it is that very validity of sense experience which Descartes could not accept and felt compelled to establish, which needs to be assumed in order to make possible the observational discoveries of a Copernicus. As between the natural sciences and philosophy, the war in the modern mind is in fact one and the same, whichever the aspect of it which attracts our attention first. And its unresolvable clash between an impossibly absolute assertiveness and an impossibly partial submissiveness shows, in both manifestations, the dilemma in which man finds himself the moment he tries, consciously or unconsciously, to jump out of his creaturely skin. God is absolutely secure in his infinite self-sufficiency. But man fails in his titanic effort towards being a god. And then his own inescapable need for security turns his creaturely dependence into the occasion of a fear which, unlike that involved in recognition of the creaturely condition, is destructive; a gnawing anxiety which cannot be assuaged. Yet insofar as he *does* succeed in his thrust towards godhead, his own awareness of being unable to handle with godlike mastery the powers he has acquired fills him with exactly the same dread. Whichever end you look from, the pattern is the same.

It is because of this deep ambiguity that Descartes—who was, of course, a technician as well as a philosopher, very much so—is so subtly significant a symbol of the spirit of the new age. He is, as I've said, deeply akin to Shakespeare in being a Janus, a Mr. Facing-Both-Ways; both were veritable focal points for the self-awareness of the modern mind, and both also preserved striking continuities with the mind of the Middle Ages. But there is also a very interesting difference between them.

102

Descartes was a practising Catholic; he combined a most powerful but largely unconscious manifestation of the modern assertive and dominative impulses with a conscious exercise of the older acceptance. Descartes, like Shakespeare, is a titanist-who-wasn't. Titan though he was, he sincerely intended to be a Catholic titan, and it wasn't his fault that the project was fundamentally a contradiction in terms, or that because of the very form of his greatness he was unable to see at the time the implications which the next three centuries were to work out in detail. And it is this failure to work out the conflict at the conscious level which makes him a man at war within, a man brilliantly disintegrated, as were so many of the men and as was so much of the world that followed him.

Shakespeare, on the contrary, spends the whole of his middle period working out the implications of the clash between the old vision and the new with an insight and a courage which take him, in his insatiable quest for poetic truth, right to the last overhanging edge of sanity— the "mountains of the mind" of which Gerard Manley Hopkins spoke. Whether or not he, like Descartes, "dyed a Papist", as one tradition records, it is at least certain that his last plays reveal a mental world in which the old Catholic values are in principle re-expressed in terms of, and enriched by, the experience of the new humanism. As Mr. Wilfred Mellers has pointed out, there is a striking parallel between this process of development in the greatest poet of Elizabethan England, and that of her greatest composer. William Byrd's three Masses, which come towards the end of his life, combine a brilliant use of the linear individuality of parts typical of medieval vocal writing, and a feeling for the "vertical" pattern of chordal harmony typical of the later Renaissance. When you stop to consider how difficult it must have been to write music "horizontally"—that is, conceived primarily in terms of the individual melodic line—and still get it to sound as perfect in "vertical" harmonic balance as if that had been the composer's prime concern, you begin to see why this achievement of reconciling the old and the new did not—could not—form the foundation of a continuing tradition. The world of Byrd's Masses, like that of *The Tempest*, is of a tempered-steel delicacy producible only in the furnace of a genius outstanding even in an age of geniuses. Its repose is that of the still centre of the Renaissance Vortex; only a handful of men are capable of holding position in such a place, and the rest of the new artists and thinkers are flung off like so many dazzling sparks from this disintegrating catherine-wheel, moving away from the common centre and one another in glittering arcs of greater or lesser eccentricity.

Yet this transitory nature of the syntheses of Shakespeare and Byrd is not due to any destructive internal contradictions in the syntheses themselves. So prophetic a vision of the final consequences and implications of the processes only just begun was to take the common-or-garden great men of the modern era some five centuries to work out, step by laborious step. To be able to see the end of the new era in its beginning was an incredible feat of individual genius in a world explosive with individual genius, and in this men as supremely typical of their age as Shakespeare and Byrd suddenly emerge as also uniquely untypical of it. It was rarely indeed that Renaissance titans found their way back onto their creaturely knees by compressing into the vision of their instant all the coming five hundred years' implications of their titanism. And that is why Descartes, full of the restless dynamism of a conflict unresolved, is simply a typical Renaissance Janus, while Shakespeare is a typical

Renaissance Janus who is more—an archetypal figure of timeless synthesizing vision.

It is the "pure" titan, the "serious" titan who does not end by discovering that his titanism is a joke, who is the pattern figure for the modern age; and of this "seriousness" of titanism Descartes is a perfect symbol, as you may discover for yourself quickly enough, if you read what he has to say about laughter in his *Treatise of the Passions*. And if he is typically titanist to the extent of this unsmiling seriousness, he is equally titanically typical of the irreducible insecurity and anxiety which underlies the powerful self-assertion of modern humanism. In him the clash between overcompensating aggressivity and underlying anxiety is all the more clear because his spiritual instincts were sound enough to keep him a practising Catholic, and his Renaissance self-assertiveness was sufficiently checked by his good sense to make him, unlike some of his successors, determined to reach the old scholastic conclusions by his new way.

It is true that the same kind of tendency towards spiritual health which kept Descartes a Catholic continues to struggle, whatever the odds, to prevent men from making total fools of themselves, however brilliantly and however magnificently. But despite the fact that the majority of modern philosophers have retained sufficient of Descartes' instinct for humility and realism to refrain from following poor Nietzsche right into the lunatic asylum, the increasingly secularized thinking which developed from the Renaissance onwards is still fundamentally marked with the pattern of disintegration latent in Descartes' ambivalent greatness. Man's assertion and submission, his proper pride and reasonable humility, are no longer balanced in a fruitful "complex of opposites"; they are released in a great dazzling fireball. And this brilliant flowering of disintegrative

105

energies racks him by its destructive conflict into a condition of increasing split-mindedness, in which he zigzags between an absurdly optimistic dominativeness—when he tries to act as if he were a god—and an absurdly pessimistic submissiveness—when he despairingly renounces the privilege of acting like a man. It is a basic contradiction summed up in the evilly paradoxical struggle of man to achieve a godlike autonomy. For a genuine god would, by definition, already possess without effort and in rejoicing play that condition of self-sufficiency and utter repose which creaturedom can only partake of by accepting it as a gift, and struggles vainly and absurdly to win. The great age of philosophical criticism is in part at least the manifestation of an aggressivity which is a caricature of divine all-powerfulness, locked in interminable conflict with a fear-stricken insecurity which is a caricature of creaturely humility.

This process of dis-integration within the individual man is mirrored in a corresponding disintegration of society. The strength of a culture lies in the extent of its common assumptions; and in the eighteenth century, for example, the accepted humane values of European society were still a fuel solid enough to feed a most recklessly brilliant firework-display of analytical criticism. Yet even the most solid fuel is still ultimately consumed; and the uninterrupted onslaught of the singular geniuses of the modern era on the common assumptions of the common men of Christendom eventually began to bring about that state of affairs of which Yeats wrote:

Things fall apart: the centre cannot hold . . .

The common ideas of common sense—such as that we exist, and that other men exist too, and that God exists

106

—these are the assumptions that are so brilliantly challenged by the titanists. And the challenging of them is also a staking of the claim of innumerable individual geniuses to private control over the language—which, through a common acceptance of commonsense meaning, is the binding medium of the mental communion of men. The modern poet, for example, works in a world disembowelled of its natural symbolism, struggling to establish an adequate means of communication with a restricted circle of the initiated. It is a work-out in actual fact of the pattern initiated by Descartes when he demanded mathematical certainty from sense experience, and completed by his successors when they were driven to the logical conclusion that for all we can establish to the contrary we are all walled up in private worlds of our own sense experience. The private worlds of the philosophers' theories are worked out in practice in the plight of a situation in which poets struggle against private isolation from their public, scientific specialists struggle against private isolation from other scientific specialists, the intelligentsia struggles against private isolation from the common man; and all thinking men struggle against that lack of common agreement on the meaning of key words which makes discussion—mental communion—a frustrating tangle of cross-purposes instead of a coherent pattern of distinctions.

Granted, the destructive and sundering conflict is rarely, in practice, carried to its absolute conclusion. Despite all the damage done to the vital bond of European culture by the process of feeding upon itself which it began at the opening of the modern age, that culture, and the society which is its vehicle, obviously hasn't wholly disintegrated. As I have said, men's instinctive tendency to sanity—which is also a tendency to spiritual health—has kept them struggling, if only unconsciously, against the centrifugal force of their explicit titanist assumptions. They have not become wholly isolated from one another in a dreadful expanding universe of private individual worlds, insulated one from another by an ever-widening gulf of mutual unintelligibility. But this has been only in virtue of a war of their own nature against the whole dominant tendency of the conscious direction they have given to their civilization. And although the disintegratory process has thus not generally reached a Nietzschean or Sartrian or Beckettian state of absoluteness, the damage and strain of it has none the less constituted a mortal threat to the wellbeing of man and of society. Even the inanimate world of nature, buried under miles of concrete, hidden behind the mechanical rhythms of work that turns night into day, held at the length of a million mechanical arms, has shared in that state of alienation from man which leaves him haunted by the dread of being alone, and clutchingly possessive in his effort to re-establish contact with things other than himself. Here again society has gone a long way towards realizing in practice the implicit Cartesian vision of man as essentially shut off from direct communication with the world by an impenetrable maze of deceptive sense-impressions, which are all that is directly known.

The creature-created "new world" of the Renaissance is thus in principle an ever-expanding universe of "private worlds" in which ever more titanic "gods" proudly and brilliantly cut themselves off more and more from commonplace communion with each other and common men. And the scissors with which they do their cutting is the clash between the impulse to assert and the impulse to submit: the separation in war of what man's true nature demands shall be united in play.

The war of man's two complementary aspects against one another is, then, the clash of the shears that cut communication; that common fellowship of man with his fellow men, and with the natural world, which is the conscious reflection of his organic unity with them. This disintegration of man himself comes about when his dominative capacity for war is made primary, instead of his submissive capacity for play. And it is reflected in a disintegration of his society and his civilization.

In the order of history there is a successive reaction of man's assertive side against his submissive side. In the order of individual psychology there is a divisive reaction of the same kind. In the order of society and its culture there is a similar dis-integration of the "masculine" and "feminine" elements. And this is what I want to consider next.

The rhythm of this dis-integration is a vicious zigzag. You would think that when a split was made between these two sides of man each element would be isolated in its pure state; but the reverse is true. When the two are united in play each assumes its true form within the mould of the other's embrace; when they are disintegrated in war each becomes an exaggerated caricature of itself. The sharper the conflict, the more violent the caricature; the more violent the caricature, the more acute the antagonism.

If we want to get a picture of how this pattern works itself out in the field of culture, Descartes will again serve as a useful point of focus, to begin with at any rate. For the implicit titanism of Descartes emerges in nothing so clearly as in the fact that his revolution in the theory of human knowledge has in it elements of an attempt to

109

raise that knowledge to the level which the Middle Ages had considered to be that of the angels.

In the last analysis it has more than that, indeed, as we have seen: it has elements of the specifically titanist attempt to achieve the mental position of divinity. But this was an aim which was not explicit and conscious in Descartes; in fact, it is consciously entertained by few: systems of thought like Nietzsche's, and remarks like André Gide's "I am convinced that God is not, and that we must make him real", or Valéry's "Man thinks, therefore I am, says the universe", are (mercifully) exceptional. By bringing in God as Guarantor of those ideas which would otherwise form the prison walls of a solitary-confinement universe, Descartes made at least as effective an acknowledgement of the relation of creature to Creator as is implied in the self-knowledge of the angels. For these, according to the thought of the Middle Ages, derive even their kind of knowledge, vastly higher and more immediate than ours though it is, from concepts directly infused into their intelligences by God. Yet although it is something partly to veil the nakedness of pure titanism in elements of "angelism", the thing still remains an attempt to jump out of your creaturely skin. For we are not pure spirits, and cannot aspire to know as these do. We are a union of matter and spirit, and ultimately destined to remain so; to try to rise above the material element in our being, through which all our knowledge is filtered, is not to soar up towards man's ideal condition but to veer away from it. And it is precisely this futile attempt to play the pure spirit—to compensate by a mighty exercise of the mind's power for the repudiated limitations of matter—which is the key to Descartes' brilliant and in a way desperate quest for the total mental security of his famous "clear and distinct ideas"; the ideas which were to be freed altogether from the obscurities involved in man's experience as a spirit essentially "embodied". The distortedly "masculine" self-assertion implied in titanism involves, again implicitly, a rejection of all the "feminine" elements bound up in man's organic unity with Mother Earth and his sense experience. It is a head-on contradiction of everything implied in the bread-and-butter common sense of the scholastic dictum: "Nothing is in the intellect unless it is first in the senses."

This philosophical declaration of war on matter by mind, which has consumed so much mental energy in the attempt to solve so many subtle pseudo-problems, is, of course, paralleled in the social and cultural spheres by many similar declarations of war by the "father-god" side of man on his "mother-earth" side. Perhaps the most striking parallel is that whole aspect of the Protestant revolt against the Church which is summed up in the term "Puritanism", and in which a healthy revulsion from religious materialism and superstitious abuse is inextricably entangled with a wholly disastrous attempt to exalt spirit by despising matter. We only have to think back for a moment to the full process of the English Reformation to see how clearly this element emerges: the smashing of the stained glass, the destruction of the illuminated manuscripts, the breaking up of statues and carvings, the obliteration of painting and gilding, the abolishment of the complex dance of ritual gesture, the banning of incense and candles. In a word, a whole great onslaught on the material aspect of man's worship, aiming towards an ideal "worship in spirit and truth" in which the part played by man's body and senses becomes something inimical to the part played by his soul. It is true, of course, that we don't encounter the further extremes of this setting of spirit against matter until we get to the non-conforming Protestantism

111

of the later generations, in that very seventeenth century which saw the coming of Descartes. Then the idea of religious ritual itself is, in some cases, swept right away. But even though this extreme development is part of a later stage in Protestantism (and is not, of course, to be found universally in any case), the basic principle of the whole impulse can be seen clearly enough even in the early stages of the Reformation, in the attack on the Mass. For the whole concept of transubstantiation, and of the real presence of Christ under the appearances of bread and wine, is from one point of view, the very core of that whole union of spirit and matter which is the form of man. Just so, the Incarnation—of which the Blessed Sacrament is a perpetuation—meant the existence of a Man who was the very centre and norm of mankind, and thus the axis of all creation, from the mightiest of created pure spirits to the basic constituents of matter: "The firstborn of every creature", as the Bible puts it. The Mass, with its focal point in the consecrated Host, was not only the "point of intersection of the timeless with time"; it was also an archetypal wedding of spirit with matter. According to Catholic teaching, that utterly humble response to God which is the basis of true creatureliness opens to man—through God's love—the possibility of participating, eventually, in the very life of Divinity. In the Mass, that same Divinity at once shows that love concretely, and reminds man of his own lowliness, by coming to him, really and objectively, by way of matter; by way, that is, of that Mother Earth which bore the grapes of the wine and the wheat of the bread.

It is interesting to note here how the whole complex of ideas which groups organically round the Mass displays the pattern of the great related themes of matter, femininity and creaturely dependence. The concept of

112

God really present in the consecrated Host goes to the heart of man's tremendous need for the concrete and the homely, and in so doing also reminds him that there is built into his condition a lowliness of the same kind as that of bread and wine. The idea that this sacramental presence can be realized only through the ministration of a member of a divinely instituted priesthood makes it impossible for man to regard himself as basically independent in the matter of his religious relation to God. He needs other men; he needs other men as they are empowered to be by the Church, which he did not create and cannot do without. And that Church is, significantly, Mother Church.

You only have to stop to think for a moment of the utter dependence of a baby to realize why it is that the concept of motherhood is, inevitably and always, an implied reminder of our creaturely dependence. A grown-up philosopher can say that he won't accept even the fact of his own existence until he has established it for himself: a grown-up man of letters can say that God does not exist and we must create him; a grown-up Big Brother can say that he will create a new world or a new kind of man. But not even the most fanatically unrealistic superman can say that he bore himself, or that if a certain woman had not fed him and tucked him up in bed and changed his nappies and kept the room warm and all the rest of it he would have continued to exist for more than a few hours. Hence yet another reason for titanists of all kinds to use their "masculine" side to declare war on their "feminine" side with, and to carry that pattern of warfare into their relations with the world about them. Indeed, to the really out-and-out titanist the image of the mother is perhaps the most provocative of all possible manifestations of femininity; for it is the indestructible commonsense symbol of the futility and falsity of his aim. As long as man exists at all, he will never be able to destroy or argue away the Mother; and as long as he cannot do that he is confronted by inescapable evidence that dependence is an intrinsic element in his nature; and as long as he is playing the titan this will drive him raving. The very impossibility of getting rid of the Mother can act as a spur to his violence in his futile reaction against all that feminine side of nature which she sums up, and all that element of helplessness and dependence in the creaturely condition which is one side of the feminine's symbolic significance.

Hence it is not surprising that the opening of the modern era is marked by a comparatively sudden intensification of anti-feminism (especially in witch-mania); by a revolt against Mother Church; by a rejection of the devotion felt by the Middle Ages for Our Lady; by an atavistic regression to a domineering Old Testament patriarchy and a resurrection of its fierce and wrathful God, denuded of the new qualities of mercy and tenderness which the concept of him had developed as the Old Testament revelation moved to its conclusion, and which had been given definitive form in the Gospels. Here, it is true, we mustn't over-simplify; some of the early Fathers of the Church had been capable of an almost pathological anti-feminism, and the Middle Ages had its own forms of the same thing; the ideals of chivalry are not the only aspect of the medieval attitude to women. Yet we have to remember that the early Church did have a genuine and desperate battle to fight against the old pagan world in which the "feminine" powers of natural fertility, whether in nature herself, or in the field of sex, had been literally idolized. The ancient world died not of a poverty of natural vitality, but of a rank overgrowth of it which proliferated in a rotten and enervating lush-

ness. The end of nature-worship was not a D.H. Lawrence world of happy, uninhibited vitalists prancing
about clean-limbed in the sun, but one of flabby decadents trying to get a kick out of ritual orgies, and unpleasant rustic junketings of the kind most hygienically
handled in the dispassionate technicalities of the anthro-
pologist. Mother Nature had had things her own way in
the ancient Mediterranean world to an extent which (as
Dr. Jung has pointed out) we find it hard to realize, even
in the light of the seamiest of our contemporary feats of
immorality. And the degree of difficulty which we
experience in reconstructing the excesses of the ancient
world is the measure of the cleansing process which
hundreds of years of Christian standards have effected,
however widespread has been the failure to live up to
them. If the early Church handled Mother Nature a bit
roughly this was not, under the circumstances, altogether
surprising. And however savage may have been the
satires of men like Jean de Meung, and however great
the enthusiasm of the Middle Ages for wife-beating, the
fact remains that under the shadow of Our Lady medieval
woman achieved a status that was unprecedented. For
medieval civilization was shaped on the pattern of an
order of things in which a woman was placed at the head
of all purely human creatures. Eve's ancient title of
Mother of All the Living in the natural order was re-
affirmed, in the supernatural order, of that second Eve
who, it was claimed, had more than redeemed the curse
immemorially associated with womankind in the person
of the first. Figures like St. Catherine of Siena are there
in abundance to show that this status of medieval woman
was no merely theoretical one. And the tragic distortions
of femininity which in so many ways "masculinized"
the great feminist movement in the early years of this
century indicate just how grave a distortion had been

imposed on femininity itself—in England, at least—by the animal male grossness of the eighteenth century and the rigid male domination of the nineteenth.

I have already suggested that the combined aggressivity and insecurity of Renaissance titanism shows that pattern of ambivalence which has been so fruitful a concept in modern psychology. We shouldn't, therefore, find it surprising that a puritanical tradition of the under-valuing of matter grows up alongside the Renaissance humanist tradition of overvaluing it; or even that the two elements intermingle in one and the same channel, often enough. In one sense, the sixteenth century saw the start of an overwhelming swing of emphasis from the next world to this; in another, it saw the start of a catastrophic decline in respect for, and appreciation of, the part this world plays in serving the interests of the other. The graphic and plastic arts of the Middle Ages give, on the whole, an astonishing impression of fresh-ness, of the spring—because the very sensuous vividness that they display is translucent to the light of another world; a basically supernaturalized view of this earth makes the things of this earth particularly bright at the natural level. But the riper tones of the Renaissance are achieved because the natural world is becoming more opaque to human vision. That vision is arrested in it rather than refracted by it; and when the world of natural symbol thus ceases to lead beyond itself, the resultant idolatry is followed automatically by an even-tual iconoclasm. See the wonder of nature as the refracted wonder of God, and you become capable of full appreciation of nature at the purely natural level; see no further than the wonder of nature, and eventually it ceases even to be wonderful in itself. Insofar as the universe is emptied of supernatural life it is ultimately emptied of what illuminates it, and tends to become a dead end—just as much the walls of a prison to the spirit as the knowledge of the senses tended to become to the successors of Descartes.

The opulent lushness of the natural world as revealed to Renaissance creative vision was in part the product of a hidden decay whose end was to be the dust of the modern technological desert, where Brother Water is H_2O and no nonsense, and the stars are no longer God's jewellery but a graveyard of dead worlds. A zigzag to one extreme always involves, in one way or another, a zigzag to the other. The same grim Protestant extremism which tried, as far as possible, to purge man of his material element in his relations with God, is also the school of that materialism which—on an Old Testament model, again—makes success in business a confirmation of the favour of the Lord and poverty a moral disgrace. It is the idolization of the world of the senses which, imprisoning man's vision once more within the cycle of material change and decay, resurrects the ancient pagan sense of tears at the heart of things. More, indeed; by way of a sort of connoisseurship of death, it distils from a clotted richness of sensuous experience a bitter whey of the macabre.

On the surface there may seem to be a great resemblance between the fascinated dread of dissolution which underlay the encrusted material richness of late Renaissance and Baroque art, and the obsession with death which, in the face of the Black Death, the Hundred Years War, and the Great Schism, formed the obverse of a similarly sophisticated civilization in the later fifteenth century. Yet in fact the harsh realism of a Villon, for example, in this respect, is still only the other side of an intense savouring of natural life which is in its turn part of a more fundamental supernaturalism. As I have pointed out, it is the spring-rain glitter of the

117

Assumption which is the setting for the sombre and phosphorescent gleam of the Fair Armouress's picture of the ripening and decay of female beauty. In contrast, there is about the later work of a man like John Donne an element of funereal eroticism, a sensuous appetite for dissolution as the ultimate masochistic refinement of the pleasures of the flesh. And of course this decadent element, driven underground by the "good sense" of the eighteenth-century Enlightenment, emerges at full strength in the latter part of the Romantic period. The opposites which are openly copresent in the synthesis of play are still latently copresent in the "simplifying" analysis of war. The apparently successful war of man's secondary dominative side on his primary submissive side is in point of fact an inconclusive victory threatened by an underground movement. Man the god turns Mother Nature into a captive harlot; the inevitable revenge for the violation is the contagion of a disease and decay whose logical end is madness.

To consider this developing trend of disintegration and war in modern European culture is inevitably to consider it as manifested in the society which creates that culture. And the interconnection of the two things is seen nowhere more interestingly than in English literature. I have already glanced at the interesting fact that in the case of the poet—among others—the unfolding of the modern era has seen the working out, in the practice of social life, of the process of isolation which was the logical end of Descartes' philosophical view of the nature of our sense experience. The trend to make each individual a bad-joke "god", reigning in ironical omnipotence over a universe which is the solitary cell of his own mind, expressed itself also, I suggested, in terms of an onslaught by the singular genius on the assumptions of the common man. It expressed itself in an attempt by uncommon men to establish control over language, which had previously been an instrument of communion between men through their common acceptance of common meaning. In a world where the individual began to think it his business to decide what words should mean rather than to clarify what man meant by them, the tendency was for language to become opaque, as the natural world was doing to the artist. Instead of being windows through which one saw into the minds of other men, words became mirrors in which one studied the workings of one's own; an increasing number of increasingly private languages slowly began to wall off class from class, man from man, and artist from public. And this clash of war between man's two sides, which shears through the organic bonds of his natural communion, reveals in the social sphere that same tyranny of the "masculine" over the "feminine" as can be seen in the strictly cultural sphere. For the war of dominative, analytic thought on acceptant intuition is both cause and effect of a war of the intellectuals upon the common man; of the clerks upon the people.

Here, again, we mustn't talk as if the thing suddenly burst upon Europe out of the blue in the sixteenth century. The whole of medieval society had been based on a very clear-cut division between the three estates: the commons, who sowed and reaped, the nobility, who were to protect them by their skill-at-arms, and the clergy, who prayed and offered sacrifice for all. Because education of all kinds was a monopoly of the clergy, the clerk was, in fact, the cleric. And thus the medieval ecclesiastic encountered, as many an unedifying example shows, the full blast of that chronic resentment which the common man perennially feels against "them". It was the immemorial itch to have a go at lawyers, civil servants, schoolmasters, tax collectors, welfare workers, and in general all that great class of wielders of mysterious powers which the Army of World War II used to lump together, with genial ferocity, as "*educated bastards*": the mysterious "They" who always seem to be shoving one about, and always have The Law on their side. Medieval European civilization, like most civilizations, had always known a sharp distinction between clerks and people, and there had been more than enough of tension between them. Yet for all that it remains true that a definitive change takes place at the great sixteenth-century crisis. The distinction becomes dissociation; the tension explodes into disintegration; and both these things are new departures.

The remarkable tough and springy framework of medieval society had been just as capable of absorbing the tension between the intellectuals and the man in the street as it had been of absorbing the strains of endemic feudal gangsterdom, or roughhousing theological disputation, or the tug-of-war between Empire and Papacy. For all their emphasis on the aristocracy of intellect and physical prowess, the Middle Ages built their hierarchically structured society with the bricks of spiritual democracy. Perhaps part of the reason for the eerie zest which the later Middle Ages displayed for representations of the Dance of Death was its spiritual significance in the matter of equality:

> Sceptre and crown
> Must tumble down,
> And in the dust be equal made
> With the poor crooked scythe and spade.

It was the same kind of kick you got out of composing a poem which consigned plenty of eminent ecclesiastics to hell. This kind of idea of spiritual democracy is something which the modern era has inherited from the Middle Ages as a practically self-evident truth. But we have to remember that like so much else which we have been accustomed to think of as being in the very bones of the decent man, it is in fact an attitude of mind which, as far as we are concerned, is historically inseparable from the vast civilizing process imposed upon Europe by the acceptance of Christian dogma. The world of antiquity was quite at ease with the idea that by no means all men were equal in the sight of God.

This spiritual democracy did not apply only to the field of social relations. The medieval capacity for loving what was common, and seeing the spring-sunlight of the marvellous in the heart of it, extended too to the world of the intellect and the imagination. At the very opening of her career, when she had made her stand against the gnostics, the Church had overturned the whole ancient ideal of aristocratic wisdom, with its handful of enlightened men of leisure reaching up for spiritual riches from on the shoulders of the slaves who did the work for them. Knowledge of the supreme wisdom was no longer limited to an elite of intellectuals; it had become simple knowledge of the Man Jesus Christ and his message, and you did not have to be of the elite as far as natural endowments were concerned in order to reach it. It is true that the Church soon developed her own specialists in the life of the intellect and the life of prayer, and made it clear that she regarded their role as being of quite special importance. But her elites always retained their ultimate common ground with the common man. If the Church had no time for the man who decried the worthwhileness of applying the full power of the mind to the mysteries of faith, she also had no time for the professional theologian who took a superior attitude to the butcher, the baker

121

and the candlestick maker. She knew how to value one of the greatest bursts of intellectual activity which the world has ever seen; but she also knew that when a theologian saint and the village idiot kneel before the Blessed Sacrament at Mass there is scarcely the difference of St. Thomas's straw between the wisdom of the two, if you are relating it to the infinite mystery into which it plumbs. And in just the same sense as that in which you say that such-and-such is an honest bread-and-butter sort of job, or such-and-such a plain bread-and-butter way of putting something, you can say that the Catholic faith is a plain bread-and-wine sort of affair. Its mystery is not the mystery of the rarefied and the *recherché*, but the mystery of the ordinary; the unbelievably amazing character of all that we take for granted—birth, death, love, earth, bread, words, persons. Whatever the tensions or distinctions between the clerks and people, they are basically in communion in a common world of accepted common meanings and common experience. When one of the Church's greatest thinkers of all time wants to open for the human mind a way to the heart of the ultimate truth of things he doesn't begin with some sentence like "All existence is a stream of tendency detaching the self from its facticity in an effort to create a perfect vacuum of non-being." He says, "It is evident that some things are in a state of motion." That is the kind of world that Catholic intellectualism never, in principle, loses sight of. It is not the magnificent lunar landscape of titanism. It is the world of the common man.

We do not have to make the Middle Ages into the kind of historical Utopia that never was in order to say with truth that in it the visions of the people and the clerks respectively combined to give the general world-picture a stereoscopic roundedness. There are few things more "clerkly" than the subtle and sophisticated intellectual virtuosity of the medieval theologians; yet, as we have seen, its starting-point (and for the Middle Ages, remember, "my end is my beginning") is the homely bread-and-wine reality of the common man's commonsense world. And in homely and common recognition of their common creaturely status in relation to God, the Centre of the world, medieval men found unity, despite all the sharp differentiation, social and intellectual, of their hierarchical society. Indeed, the democracy of that common status and relationship provided the very principle of their hierarchy. For in it the concept of man's authority over man was formed in the image of God's sovereignty over his creatures. Medieval aristocracy is moulded in the embrace of medieval democracy; the community of men with one another rests upon their common communion with God. The centre of medieval civilization is the Catholic faith; and the centre of the Catholic faith is the sacrifice of the Mass; and the centre of the sacrifice of the Mass is the personal presence of the God-Man Christ in the consecrated Host. And the consecrated Host is the means of holy communion—not only of men with God, but of men with each other in God. Here God is possessed by anyone who has the ability to take and eat. The greatest clerk and the commonest clown are at one; and the radial pattern of unity formed about this staggeringly homely centre holds in a fundamental oneness the most sharply distinct extremes of brilliant clerkly mastery and obscure popular acceptance.

The period of the repudiation of this integration of the upper and lower worlds is also that of the dazzlingly novel flowering of Elizabethan poetry and drama. The specifically clerkly faction of the Elizabethan "University Wits", and their Jacobean successors, were able,

123

for a while, to exploit in their own brilliant clerkly interests an unparalleled wealth of commonly held assumptions throughout the range of the society in which their art was created. But this must not blind us to the fact that what they were doing was basically an exploitation, in the pejorative sense of the word. The vital resources of all future clerkly cultural activity were progressively impoverished. The increasingly un- and even anti-common world of the later Elizabethan and Jacobean dramatists, with its brilliant disintegrations of traditional values against the darkness brooding over the face of the new age, was a remarkable achievement; but, unlike the world of Chaucer and Langland, it wasn't one which the common people could live by. And in proportion as the common people cease to be able to live by a high art, that high art ceases to be able to draw upon the irreplaceable vitality which comes from the common world. When, as in the culture and literature of the late sixteenth and early seventeenth centuries in England, the aristocratic and clerkly elements in culture begin to grow apart from the common and popular elements,[1] then the synthesis of critique and acceptance has broken down. The profoundly comic irony which gives Chaucer's popular simplicity its depth of clerkly sophistication has disintegrated into a tragic challenge to things that cannot in fact be challenged. And we have set foot on the road which leads ultimately to the monstrous concept of the "intellectuals" as a social class on their own.

You can see the ultimate direction of this process quite clearly today. James Joyce was perhaps a supreme example of the secularized clerk, committed to the task of sustaining and revitalizing culture out of the

---

[1] This can be well seen in the growing apart of the popular and the courtly drama by the time of Charles I.

resources of culture alone; of the intellectual definitively isolated from the world of the common people, trying to provide out of clerkly resources alone the whole breadth of cultural vision by which the common people too are to live. In the effort to do it he was ultimately compelled—and this is highly significant—to try as it were to re-create the whole mental world of his public, working from his own mind outwards; to create a new private language which was to be the common language of himself and his readers. It was indeed a titanic feat to end all titanic feats, and none the less so because it was doomed from the start; apart from the fact that it just isn't possible for one man to create a new living language, the individual vision of one genius, however titanic, is not sufficient to provide a mental world for mankind to live in. Yet the attempt was made, and indeed by the logic of titanism it had to be made.

The innumerable more or less private languages of modern creative thinkers—philosophers, poets, musicians, painters and the rest—and the degree of sterile imprisonment these impose on their creators, are the price that the clerkly elite has paid for its aristocratic war upon the common people. And this is what I was referring to earlier in this book when I said that my original crude prejudice against modern poetry did have in it some elements at least of healthy criticism. For it isn't, in fact, a right or healthy state of affairs when common men are barred from communion with the elite of their culture by a poetic language which is that elite's more or less private creation. The separation of a superstructure of pure "culture" from its wider foundation in agriculture is a deed of violence, whose ultimate effect cannot but be destructive, however exciting its transitional creative achievements may be.

There is a striking resemblance between this cultural

dissociation of clerkly analysis from popular intuition, and the famous "dissociation of sensibility", of thought and feeling, which Mr. Eliot described as a major event in the cultural history of seventeenth-century England, and located more or less as from the date of John Donne. When he writes that to Donne a thought was an experience, and modified his sensibility, or refers to the split which exists for the ordinary man between the world in which he reads Spinoza and that in which he falls in love or sniffs the smell of cooking, he is talking about union between, and separation of, elements of a type with which we are now already familiar.[1] And when, both in his critical studies and his own poetic criticism of existence, Mr. Eliot pursues further the implications of this "dissociation of sensibility" in English poetic vision from Donne to the present day, he is also studying the social and cultural progress of the civil war between clerks and people.

In his early poems he portrays the interior war in modern man as splitting him up into either pure "clerk" —the sterilely self-critical J. Alfred Prufrock—or pure "clown"—the human animal "Apeneck Sweeney", with his brute world of pure sensation, and of eyes "assured of certain certainties".

> Sweeney shifts from ham to ham
> Stirring the water in his bath.
> The masters of the subtle schools
> Are controversial, polymath.

[1] I am aware, of course, that after achieving a status so influential as to have somewhat surprised even its author, Mr. Eliot's theory is now a good deal less widely accepted, and more generally qualified. But I think it acquires permanent validity if we avoid treating the famous "dissociation" as something overwhelmingly novel, and view it rather as an identifiable intensification of tendencies perennially present; and it is, of course, such a revised interpretation which Mr. Eliot himself suggested in his Milton Lecture of 1947.

Between Sweeney and the self-destructive critique creating the intellectuals' ever-more-private worlds there is indeed a great gulf fixed; the gulf of the change into war of the play between the right and left hand sides of the mind. And because the war is an evil caricature of the love-play which should be the true relation between the two, the combatants' condition of defiant "pure" isolation from one another is a condition of caricature; a condition of Prufrockery and Sweeney-ishness.

When Mr. Eliot first came to grips with the whole problem of reanimating the English poetic tradition, largely gone to seed in the late Romantic hothouse, he nowhere displayed a more uncanny acumen in diagnosis than when, in the very same essay which produced the concept of dissociated sensibility, he put his finger on Milton as a central watershed of this great divide. Milton, he said elsewhere, built a Chinese wall about the English language; and again, "his celestial and infernal regions are large but insufficiently furnished apartments filled by heavy conversation". The two phrases hit off, with the accuracy of true poetic intuition, the subtle interrelation of two facts whose connection isn't immediately apparent.

The Miltonic universe was indeed no longer a natural and supernatural home of man, his organic setting. For Dante, with all his sinewy intellectualism and god-like creativeness, the universe, however complexly conceived, had remained the house of man's Father, in which he lived securely by acceptant inheritance. But for the new titans of the Reformation and the Renaissance the universe was in principle bare till it was equipped with whatever supernatural furniture one chose to use. However little it may have been grasped explicitly at the time, this was the position, for earnest Puritans

127

like Milton just as much as for later sardonic agnostico-deists like Voltaire, or whole-hogging human gods like Nietzsche and Comte. For all their apparent likeness to the metaphysical scenery which medieval man found already there in his world-vision, the Miltonic heaven and hell are in reality quite different, because they are there for a different reason; they are not found put there by some objective revelational authority, but are brought there by the selection of the individual man from the traditional Christian data. In principle, man is now the potential god, asserting an absolutely funda-mental right to criticize and choose for himself; and this is not altered in the least by the fact that he may happen to choose many of the things which his medieval predecessor accepted as given, in the course of an overall acceptance of an objective religious authority. When Nietzsche proclaimed that God was dead and that the Superman must take his place, or André Gide said that he was convinced that God was not, and that it was man's job to make him real, they were only working out the logical conclusions contained in the Bible Protestan-tism of men like Milton—though Milton would have been sincerely horrified to hear it. Hence the sense of loneli-ness and artificiality which haunts and chills Milton's great panorama. We are not in homely communion with a world genuinely outside us in all its otherness—as in the case of Dante, for all his greatness of stature; we are looking at wonderful pictures with which an in-dividual mind walls itself in, just as we are, ultimately, according to Cartesian theory. And however animated and fascinating the pictures are, we still feel the funda-mental chill of that isolation. It is again the mental world of the Christian titan, camping out in a blank universe with whatever he can provide out of his own resources to make himself feel at home in it; and the basic sense of dispossession involved in that experience is admirably summed up in Mr. Eliot's phrase "furnished apartments".

So much for the "furnished apartments", then; what of its connection with the "Chinese wall"?

The absence of what can only be called cosmic homeliness is something which stands out at once very clearly if you contrast the intense concreteness of Dante's poetic imagery with the abstractness and generalizedness which are the essential condition of the "Miltonic sublime". And if you let the comparison shift from Milton back to Dante and then forward to Shakespeare again, and remember how Shakespeare is *par excellence* the master of the richly concrete poetic image, you can see at once how it was that Milton's titanic effort to rebuild man's supernatural home in the universe mirrored in the actual development of its language exactly the same championship of spirit against matter as had branded the Mass as idolatry. Milton's sublimity is a purging of poetic language of its popular element, as something incompatible with its clerkly one; it is the development of a concept of "loftiness" in man as something to be isolated in a "pure" state from his lowliness —as opposed to being something inextricably connected with it. Milton substitutes superb clerkly abstractions, squeezed out of experience by the typically dominative analysis of the "intellectual", for the homely earthiness of Shakespearean popular imagery. And this marks a distinctive establishment, in modern English literature, of a "literary" language dis-integrated from the popular one, and a kind of culture whose very essence is to be separated from the homely world of agriculture. In Milton, deeply sincere Christian though he was, the dominative "father-god" in the Renaissance titan declares implicit war on the "mother-earth" of the

129

common people, with its "idolatry" and "superstition" and obscure, intuitive, confused symbolic thinking. All that is incompatible with the new intelligentsia's dis-infected world of "clear and distinct ideas"; with every-thing which the following eighteenth century was to regard as "enlightened". In Milton, as Mr. Eliot so clearly saw, there decisively fly apart the two elements whose incipient dis-integration gives to the work of Donne its brilliant, dangerous and slightly decadent attraction, and its suggestive possibilities to any poetic thinker trying to put the movement of dis-integration into reverse.

The thing which it is most important to note in this connection, at this particular stage in our exploration, is the link which exists between this aristocratic civil war of the uncommon man against the world of the common man, and that civil war within the individual man which consists in exalting the spiritual element in him at the expense of the material; in maintaining that worship in spirit and in truth is incompatible with wor-ship via the material appearance of bread and wine. The technological war of man against Mother Earth, the cultural war of the intellectuals on the common man, the war of concept against symbol, analysis against intuition and criticism against appreciation—all these different manifestations of the disruption of the loving play between man's masculine and feminine sides are of the same pattern with the dictatorship of his spirit over his body and the matter of which his body is made.

It is significant that when, not so very long after Milton, an explicit attempt is made by the cultural elite to resume creative contact with the speech of the people, it is made not in the interests of poetic vision but of scientific description; the Royal Society's concern with the language of "Artizans, Countrymen, and Merchants" is very different from that of Shakespeare, or of John Synge, when he lay with his ear to the floorboards, listening to the talk of the servants in the kitchen below. By that time English poetry had already begun to acquire what Dr. F. R. Leavis so nicely thumbnailed as "the vulgar lilt of the Restoration lyric". Indeed, it is one of the symptoms of the destructive split between the aristocratic and the common that in the modern world of professed democracy and covert tyranny the products of the clerkly elite can develop a seamy side which has a nasty taste almost unknown to the medieval world of overt authoritarianism and spiritual democracy. You see it, certainly, in the eighteenth century—for example, in the near-pathological, lavatory-wall section of Swift's poetic output; there is a world of difference between this clammy cloacal underside to a world of self-styled "enlightenment", and the well-sunned manure-heap of medieval bawdy. It is instructive to compare the kind of vision of the grotesque—that is, the clownish—which is achieved by Hogarth or Rowlandson, with that of the medieval sculptors. In this "enlightened" world of pure reason the "lower orders"—social, physical, psychological —have no place and develop a monstrousness quite different from that which was once admitted into the shrines of the incarnate God. On top there is Queen Anne furniture and polite conversation, but underneath there are Gin Lane, Bedlam and Bridewell; and these are what they are precisely because, in a world where there is supposed to be no more Original Sin and no more devil, they have no real business to be in existence at all. Men like Dr. Johnson and William Blake, who nearly split themselves in two in the mighty feat of keeping a foot still in both the clerkly and the popular camps, feel and show at its acutest the rending contrast between the false alternative worlds of "enlightenment" and "en-

thusiasm". And indeed, by the end of the century the
neglected and repressed world of "enthusiasm" explodes
thunderously in Jacobinism—the popular underworld's
own synthesizing and apocalyptic experiment in titanism,
and protest against the critical, aristocratic titanism of
the modern world's first stage. But in English literature
this threatening split expresses itself for the most part in
nothing more violent than parallel strains of sceptical
irony and sentimentalism; and it is not till the very end
of the century that the development of the Gothick novel
of horrific and highly un-reasonable adventure heralds
the great emotional upheavals of the Romantic movement. And this, during the nineteenth century, accen-
tuates the split-mindedness, setting the technician fairly
and squarely in opposition to the aesthete.

Nothing is more significant, in the work of the later
generations of Romantics and the "decadents" who
followed them, than the extent to which their work has
to be created out of a specifically "poetic" world not
only distinct from that of the society in which they live,
but often enough deriving its very form precisely from
being everything which that society is not. When
Chaucer draws upon the siege of Troy or Shakespeare
upon Plutarch for his raw material, this is because such
legendary or historical matter is seen primarily in terms
of the society of the day, and is regarded as being in one
way or another organically one with and relevant to it.
The Trojans are, as it were, medieval Europeans seen at
greater depth in the mirror of ancient tradition, and
ancient Rome provides a focusing lens for seeing deeper
into the men of Renaissance England with. But when
Tennyson turns to Malory it is not as a mirror in which
to see more deeply into the heart of Victorian industrial-
ized England. It is as an escape world of fancy dress in
which the poet can take refuge from the real world

which four hundred years of titanist exploitation seem
to have eroded of all spiritual fertility. The world of the
ivory tower is one in which poetry, reduced to feeding on
itself instead of on life, rapidly approaches death from
self-consumption; the creative language of the clerkly
elite, increasingly uprooted from the experience of the
common people, goes to seed, and retains its power to
communicate only at the cost of communicating nothing
much more than echoes of the creative visions of the
past.

This was the situation which confronted Mr. Eliot when
he began to make his contribution to English literature,
as poet and critic. And for our present purposes, the
first important point to grasp about what he did is, I
think, conveyed, balanced on the razor edge of a Lear-ish
nonsense that might be not quite so funny, in his "Lines
for Cuscuscaraway and Mirza Murad Ali Beg":[1]

> How unpleasant to meet Mr. Eliot!
> With his features of clerical cut,
> And his brow so grim
> And his mouth so prim
> And his conversation, so nicely
> Restricted to What Precisely
> And If and Perhaps and But . . .

"The masters of the subtle schools Are controversial,
polymath". . . . In a world divided up into the domains
of Sweeney and Prufrock, Mr. Eliot's portion is with
Prufrock; he is nothing if not the product of that particular species of aristocracy which was created when
the secularized clerks of the Renaissance shed the
implicit spiritual democracy of their forbears and set up
a new hierarchy of "enlightenment". His background

[1] I must admit I have not the remotest idea why the poem is so called.

133

is that of the university and the comparatively leisured upper class which formulated the concept of culture as something basically dissociated from agri-culture and the whole common business of "eating reg'lar". The unchangeably "clerical cut" of the features of his work, whether in its early purgative stage or its later illuminative one, is marked by the action of all the forces which, during the past five hundred years, have turned into a dissociation the distinction medieval Christendom had always marked between clerk and clown. You might indeed say that *The Waste Land*, in which his earlier vision of the world first, perhaps, found definitive formulation,[1] is, as far as English literature is concerned, the final logical conclusion of the whole titanist critique which grew out of the Renaissance-Reformation crisis. It is a vast surrealistic panorama, focused into a small compass, of the "dust bowl" of a culture apparently worked out. Here was the definitive application of critical response to the work of that titanic tradition of critical response which had eroded European man's spiritual landscape down to bare bones of dust and rock, a lunar world of cold nightmare in which "one can neither stand nor lie nor sit".

This element of aristocratic critique is of absolutely vital importance if you are to understand the nature of Mr. Eliot's greatness and the way in which he realized it in terms of the very difficulties which faced any man trying to achieve greatness at that particular point in the history of English literature. It's part of the growing self-consciousness which is an integral part of titanism, that poets should increasingly tend to become practising literary critics too. But in Mr. Eliot the critic not only achieves an almost unprecedented balance with the poet; he takes an unprecedented share in forming the poet.

[1] Its final formulation quite clearly appears to be *The Hollow Men*.

Whereas in the past the critical theory of poets had grown largely out of their practice, in the case of Mr. Eliot the poetic practice was in many ways evolved to meet the needs revealed by the application of the critical theory. Even the creative act itself is here the product of a highly deliberate, reflexive, self-conscious analysis of what the poetic creative act is and why it should be so difficult in the early years of the twentieth century. You can say, in fact, that here, probably for the first time, someone is making poetry out of the difficulty of making poetry;[1] and this procedure—unprecedentedly desperate from the cultural standpoint—is also an indication of the high degree of intelligent sensitivity with which Mr. Eliot was attuned to the tone of the times.

The peculiar quality of the critical element here lies in the fact that the ruthless analysis of the destructiveness of the modern analysis expresses itself, almost against its own will, in a kind of trend towards synthesis. This is something which perhaps appears in Mr. Eliot's technical preoccupations as a poet earlier than it does in the world-picture out of which the poetry is built, and which is, of course, realized largely through the creating of the poetry. Out of the ultimate critique of the critical tradition an attempt at poetic synthesis grew in spite of itself. And its great problem was how to by-pass the Shakespearean terminus and the Miltonic blind alley, and resume organic contact with that culture of unified sensibility which both these achievements, in their different ways, mark limits of. Here it's extremely interesting to mark the course Mr. Eliot followed. Unlike Gerard Manley Hopkins, he did not grope instinctively towards that native tradition of alliterative verse

---

[1] I owe this phrase to the late Mr. A. P. Rossiter, whose untimely death recently robbed English studies of a fascinating mind and a good man. May he rest in peace.

which lies, on the other side of the great divide, in the Early and Middle English poets. As far as the English tradition was concerned, his most stimulating study appears to have been John Donne. And the interesting thing about Donne, in this connection, is that he exhibits the condition of unified sensibility so clearly just because he exhibits equally clearly the intensity of the strain under which it is being held together. He is already decisively an inhabitant of the new, basically disintegrated world; the overripe fruit which is rich with the beginnings of rottenness—all the magnificently decadent in the Baroque. If, in him, the language of the people is still being united with the insight of the clerkly elite, this is no longer in essence a condition naturally occurring, but rather one created by the intensely self-conscious and deliberate dominative mastery which is typical of the Renaissance titan. A realization of the condition of unified sensibility so laborious in principle was naturally of special significance for a man like Mr. Eliot, making so profoundly unspontaneous an effort to regain spontaneity. And the deliberation of Donne is mirrored with redoubled complexity in the highly deliberate use here made of him.

Mr. Eliot's use of traditional English material is in fact for the most part concentrated on writers in whom the world of integrated culture and sensibility is just on the turn in this way. The later Elizabethan and Jacobean dramatists are prominent, as is Donne; Chaucer, Langland and the Anglo-Saxons are conspicuous by their absence. When he does make use of a poet writing directly out of the integrated culture of the Middle Ages, it is not to the English tradition he goes, but to Dante. And when you recall that it was very much in terms of a latinization of the English language that Milton began the severance of lofty abstraction from earthy concrete-

ness, it strikes you with something of a shock that in the
selection of the ingredients Mr. Eliot assembled for
revitalizing English poetry with he is—to twist for a
moment Blake's insight into Milton's titanism—of the
devil's party without knowing it. However sincerely he
has deplored the disintegration of culture and poetic
sensibility marked by the Miltonic development following Donne, the particular kind of use he has made of the
Latin tradition has been Miltonic rather than Shakespearean. You have only to think for a moment how
deeply English is the assimilated classicism of Shakespeare, and then to look at the attempted "popular"
sections in Mr. Eliot's early religious pageant drama *The
Rock*, to see that in his handling of the "vulgar" elements
in English culture Mr. Eliot is worlds apart from Chaucer,
Shakespeare or Dickens. Where popular material is used
effectively (as in the closing-time pub conversation that
closes one section of *The Waste Land*) it is so used because
"placed" from above; the world of culture is looking
down aristocratically on that of agri-culture. To realize
just how much this is so all you need to do is to
compare instances such as those I have mentioned with
the use made of the speech of the common soldier in
the fine war epic, *In Parenthesis*, written by Mr. Eliot's
contemporary, Mr. David Jones. The deeply moving
echoes of liturgy and epic there conjured out of the
Army speech of World War I are made possible by a
deeply humble and compassionate acceptance of the
world of "knaves that smell of sweat"—based, in this
case of course, on a painfully lived self-identification
with it. For Mr. Eliot, the world of the people is con-
sistently "known apart, in otherness". Insofar as it *is*
known, Mr. Eliot's eye is on Donne. But Donne, as I
said, is already a poet who has to hold the worlds of
people and clerk together by force; he is that far from

137

Shakespeare, although he overlaps Shakespeare in time. And in the degree of the otherness and apartness in which that world is known Mr. Eliot is even closer to the Milton against whom he rebelled than the Donne whom he learnt from.

What we are looking at is a pattern we have met before —that of the "Janus". It was a situation of disintegration—literary disintegration mirroring a profounder crumbling of the worlds of culture and religion—which presented Mr. Eliot with both a tremendous problem and a challenging opportunity. The critical revolution of self-consciousness and dominative mastery in the European mind had issued in a five-centuries' exploitation of the rich loam of unifying symbolism reclaimed by the Christian centuries from the overgrown jungle of late antiquity. But this reckless forced cultivation had ultimately left a wilderness where there was

> . . . no water but only rock
> Rock and no water and the sandy road . . .

In that desert Mr. Eliot turned the modern critique of existence upon itself to produce a Huis Clos of "paralysed force, gesture without motion"; the kind of frustrated violence and impotent rebellion against all that is which makes of the human situation something intolerable to be in though impossible to escape from. All this is firmly and fully in the tradition of titanist clerkliness; an integral part of the dissociation of culture from agriculture, and the reflexive, self-conscious creativeness of the cultivated few from the contemplative and spontaneous creativeness of the simple many. It is, as in the case of M. Sartre, a *reductio ad absurdum* of the tragic combination of the sweet and bitter wonders.

But—and this is where the Janus-pattern emerges—

138

this nightmare world, which is indeed the end of a world in a whimper, doesn't maintain itself determinedly in its anguish, as in the case (so far) of Mr. Samuel Beckett. Here, the very integrity of the poet—that integrity which is at once the nobility and the fatal weakness of titanism —demanded that he should not make of his loyalty to the titanist tradition a justification for digging in in Rats' Alley. The final analysis of Rats' Alley for what it is was to lead him to turn right around and walk out of it in the name of life—following the titanist track backwards into a new through-the-looking-glass world of humility. This following of titanist integrity to the ultimate conclusion of its own self-destruction is again a *reductio ad absurdum*—but the absurd seen for what it is, an avoidable hell, not a serious dead end. Consequently the crucial "flash-point" of extinction becomes a redemptive death leading to a rebirth. The hellish conclusion of the titanist drive towards total mastery becomes, no longer a hell, but a liberating purgatory; it is an example of what Heraclitus called *enantiodromia*— the process by which something passes over into its opposite. For assertion, submission; the retreat from Rats' Alley is a reversal of modern man's titanic attempt to scale the heights of heaven. In view of so definite a turning inside-out of the process which fissionized the medieval world in the modern explosion, it's hardly surprising that it was in explicitly Catholic terms that Mr. Eliot created his new "garden in the desert". In all this, the rupture with the immediate past is revolutionary and profound.

But (and this is where the second face of the Janus-pattern becomes visible) there is continuity as well as rupture. You cannot, obviously, put a mechanism into reverse gear unless the mechanism itself remains there to be reversed. It is important to grasp how completely

Mr. Eliot *did* reverse the mechanism of the titanist critique in order to carry himself out of Rats' Alley. But it is equally important to recognize that it was the same mechanism which carried him out as carried him in.

This can be seen most immediately if you shift attention back again for a moment from the spiritual world-picture out of which the poetry is born to the more technical aspects of the creation of the poetry itself. *The Waste Land's* spiritual paralysis had been of the same kind as that which overtook the centipede in the fable when the fly asked him how he kept in step, and he began to think about it; self-awareness carried to a nightmare pitch of self-hypnosis. Mr. Eliot realized that in the very name of life itself we had to get out of this Waste Land into the garden of spontaneity:

> As I am forgotten
> And would be forgotten, so I would forget
> Thus devoted, concentrated in purpose.

But was there ever a world of spontaneity put together with such agonized deliberateness?

"If you want [tradition]", he had written in "Tradition and the Individual Talent", "you must obtain it by great labour"; and the profoundly laborious, profoundly un-playful[1] character of his poetic creativity persists in the second, Christian stage of his work just as it had marked the first, secular stage.

It is true that by the time we get to the *Four Quartets* we have gone a considerable way beyond the collage technique of *The Waste Land*, where a great part of the essence of the poetic creation was the forceful assemblage of disintegrated fragments of past culture—"These frag-

---

[1] I'm not forgetting about *Old Possum's Book of Practical Cats*. But see the comments on the "comedies", further on.

ments have I shored against my ruins". In the *Quartets* we are no longer being presented with the picture of a whole civilization's collapse. The powers of destruction and disintegration, summed up (as in Shakespeare's sonnets) in "devouring time", are here taken up in an intensely personal vision of painful redemption. "The point of intersection of the timeless with time" is the healing "still point of the dance" round which all four poems revolve. Instead of a vision of analysis, we have one of synthesis. And there has been a corresponding blossoming of "the garden in the desert"; the "dry bones" of *Ash-Wednesday*—the world of nature and agri-culture, and the world of culture—have to some extent regained the sap of a living intrinsic significance. Burnt Norton and Little Gidding, both as places in the world of nature and places in the world of culture, have regained the kind of symbolic significance which could only be imposed on the fragmentary bits-and-pieces of *The Waste Land* by an intensely deliberate use of two essentially analytical studies—Frazer's *The Golden Bough* and Jessie L. Weston's *From Ritual to Romance*. In the earlier poem the very pattern of a culture's disintegration had been caught as in a flashlight photograph by setting it against a critical evaluation of the meaning which that culture's symbols once had for earlier peoples. But the very fact that both *The Golden Bough* and *From Ritual to Romance* were thus analyses of things thought once but now thought no longer made of the brilliant snapshot which they framed something which could not be perpetuated. They suggested a pattern for presenting the disintegrated fragments of past culture in. But that very scientific detachment with which they analysed what had once been life-giving symbols emphasized the fact that the symbols were no longer alive, and that the pattern they presented for analysis was making, in the

141

museum-form of a technical study, positively its last appearance.

When, in *The Waste Land*, Mr. Eliot writes

> . . . While I was fishing in the dull canal
> On a winter evening round behind the gashouse
> Musing upon the king my brother's wreck
> And on the king my father's death before him

the symbolism, the pointing-of-things-beyond-themselves, is created by the highly deliberate fusion of the analysis of the significance of the myth of the Fisher King with the ordinary image of ugly desolation and deadness evoked by gasworks and dirty canals. The deftness of poetic intelligence is only equalled by the fundamental laboriousness with which the separated elements are assembled in the pattern of the constructed whole. Compare this with the opening of *Little Gidding*:

> . . . When the short day is brightest, with frost and fire,
> The brief sun flames the ice, on pond and ditches,
> Reflecting in a watery mirror
> A glare that is blindness in the early afternoon.
> And glow more intense than blaze of branch, or
>   brazier,
> Stirs the dumb spirit: no wind, but pentecostal fire
> In the dark time of the year. Between melting and
>   freezing
> The soul's sap quivers. There is no earth smell
> Or smell of living thing. This is the spring time
> But not in time's covenant. Now the hedgerow
> Is blanched for an hour with transitory blossom
> Of snow, a bloom more sudden
> Than that of summer, neither budding nor fading,
> Not in the scheme of generation.

Undoubtedly, the dry bones have come alive. The village landscape at the winter solstice is realized for us, despite the comparative generalizedness of the imagery, as that of one particular historic site. Both the particular place and the whole world of nature for which it is the focus have regained symbolic significance in their own right, and not in virtue of the impress of some analytical study of symbolism. Yet suppose you cast your mind back for a moment to the kind of vision which D. H. Lawrence conveys of the worlds of nature and agriculture.

In the inner dark she saw a handsome bay horse with his clean ears pricked like daggers from his naked head as he swung handsomely round to stare at the open doorway. He had big, black, brilliant eyes, with a sharp questioning glint, and that air of tense, alert quietness which betrays an animal that can be dangerous.

"Is he quiet?" Lou asked.

"Why—yes—my lady! He's quiet, with those that know how to handle him. *Cup! my boy! Cup my beauty! Cup then! St. Mawr!*"

Loquacious even with the animals, he went softly forward and laid his hand on the horse's shoulder, soft and quiet as a fly settling. Lou saw the brilliant skin of the horse crinkle a little in apprehensive anticipation, like the shadow of the descending hand on a bright red-gold liquid. But then the animal relaxed again.

It strikes you at once, in contrast, how profoundly unspontaneous, how deeply deliberate and self-aware and consciously synthesized, is this Eliotian manipulation of the poetic kaleidoscope. In this connection there's a certain point, though less than justice, in the scene in Lawrence's *Women in Love* where the school-teacher

143

Birkin rounds upon a type-figure of clerkly elite culture, the society hostess Hermione Roddice, with a typically savage criticism:

"Spontaneous!" he cried. "You and spontaneity! You, the most deliberate thing that ever walked or crawled! You'd be verily deliberately spontaneous— that's you. Because you want to have everything in your own volition, your deliberate voluntary consciousness. You want it all in that loathsome little skull of yours, that ought to be cracked like a nut. For you'll be the same till it *is* cracked, like an insect in its skin."

Lawrence's criticism of the clerkly culture which is "committed to consciousness" is not the whole story or the last word—let alone the kindest—particularly in this present connection. Yet there is no doubt at all that from the skilful collages of bits from St. John of the Cross and Julian of Norwich to the tightly-planned plot construction and character creation of the later comedies, the element of deliberate dominativeness is just as profoundly characteristic of Mr. Eliot's later Christian synthetic phase as it is of his earlier secular analytical one, though less obviously. In theory, the poet's anti-titanist submission to his own need for the supernatural has recharged the tiered worlds of nature, agri-culture and culture with just that sap of symbolic significance which had been all but squeezed out of them. And in actual practice, as we have seen, this recharging is evident to some considerable extent. Yet nonetheless, if you consider D. H. Lawrence's vision of this threefold reality, in all its directness—in *Women in Love* or *St. Mawr*, for example—you can't help being struck by the fact that in Mr. Eliot's case all three are seen as it were refracted through the literary medium. The poetry remains, to a surprising extent, one built up out of literature, and out of the direct experience of common living only as refracted through it; from the secondary world of minority culture, as opposed to the primary world of popular agri-culture.

This doesn't mean that there is anything here like the fancy-dress world of last-gasp Romanticism, where a "poetic" vision of life is equated with the manipulation of a set of literary props. This later poetry, just as much as the earlier, is obviously built out of real experience, of a high intensity; yet that experience is curiously "distanced" by having come to the poet in the same way as it leaves him in communication—via the elaborate filter of intense self-consciousness; the mechanism, in synthetic reverse as in analytic advance, of the mastering titanist mind. And the curious tenseness and academic self-consciousness with which Mr. Eliot has continued to use the English language (thrown into sharp emphasis if we contrast it with Lawrence's almost Shakespearean ear for natural rhythms and the potentialities of colloquial speech) is, naturally, merely the audible manifestation of a complementary unspontaneousness of thought. Experiencing is here a complicated and laborious matter, like the centipede's keeping in step. We have a sort of fascinatingly and beautifully distorted reflection of reality, as in one of those convex mirrors. It is as if the starting-point of the creative action was not things and events themselves, but the concepts of them—a perpetuation, on the other side of the end of the titanist experiment, of the Cartesian private world of the mind in which it began.[1]

[1] We may think back to the lines of *The Waste Land*:

> . . . I have heard the key
> Turn in the door once and turn once only

What we are seeing is, in fact, this. The dominative power of the mind is being used to hold into symbolic significance, by a titanically laborious Christian effort, natural "bits and pieces" which are still seen as being, in themselves, the sterile things the earlier analysis had left them. In theory, the world is recognized once again as godly; a refracted mirroring of God. In practice, it is still seen as ungodly; still a waste land of disintegrated fragments, which has to be shaken up by main titanic force in a Christian kaleidoscope if it is to show that supernatural pattern which is the basis of all significance in the purely natural order:

> . . . And the weak spirit quickens to rebel
> For the bent golden-rod and the lost sea smell. . . .

The integrated world of the resurrected Christian vision is not seen as something rooted in the very nature of the order of being, but as something to be laboriously created against the inertia of the spiritual blindness of "the people" and the inertia of the natural order itself. Again and again in the *Four Quartets* there recurs the note of dogged effortfulness, the laborious and resigned struggle to master what cannot be mastered. The "lower world" of man's experience, whether of inanimate nature or society, remains, in general, the alien thing, the

---

> We think of the key, each in his prison
> Thinking of the key, each confirms a prison . . .

and the note appended to those lines from F. H. Bradley's *Appearance and Reality*:

> My external sensations are no less private to myself than are my thoughts or my feelings. In either case my experience falls within my own circle, a circle closed on the outside; and, with all its elements alike, every sphere is opaque to the others which surround it . . . In brief, regarded as an existence which appears in a soul, the whole world for each is peculiar and private to that soul.

146

enemy to be dominated by the higher elements in his being—though these higher elements, and their war on the lower, are now conceived in explicitly Christian terms.

In this painfully humble attempt of rebaptized dominative clerkliness to master the intuitive wisdom of the common people the basic ambivalence of the Eliotian Janus pattern crystallizes. For if the making of any such an attempt is an affirmation that the popular and clerkly worlds are complementary, the *way* in which this particular attempt is made is an implicit affirmation that they are still mutually alien. This internal tension persists right through even into *The Elder Statesman* (of which more later, however). "The lesson of ignorance, of incurable diseases" has remained, overall, the secret of the kind of people who "ride ten in a compartment to a football match in Swansea". And the element of aristocratic disgust on the part of an elite for the mass of the philistines has proved none the less persistent for being translated into terms that have more than an echo of New England Puritanism. Mr. Eliot is a child of the age before ours in thinking the world in need of redeeming, or attempting to help redeem it; yet he is in nothing more completely a child of the modern age than in attempting to carry out that redemption as from above:

O weariness of men who turn from GOD
To the grandeur of your mind and the glory of your
    action,
To arts and inventions and daring enterprises,
To schemes of human greatness thoroughly discredited,
Binding the earth and water to your service,
Exploiting the seas and developing the mountains,
Dividing the stars into common and preferred,

Engaged in devising the perfect refrigerator,
Engaged in working out a rational morality,
Engaged in printing as many books as possible,
Plotting of happiness and flinging empty bottles,
Turning from vacancy to fevered enthusiasm,
For nation or race or what you call humanity . . .

It is still very much the voice of the uncommon man, profoundly in continuity with the titanists of the past under the immediate surface of his violent rejection of them.

There is, of course, a different kind of approach toward "the world". That great Christian humanist St. Francis de Sales, for instance, was once talking to a priest who was inveighing against the pathetic worldliness of come-down-in-the-world nobility, who were always going on about their illustrious ancestors and relations. St. Francis took him to task in turn. "How can you have the heart", he said, "to begrudge these poor people one of the few little things which help them to cheer themselves up in their misfortunes?" Such a capacity to identify oneself with all that is positive in "the world" and to refuse to regard the Christian's mission of redemption in terms of any kind of spiritual slumming has, admittedly, been absent in many men of outstanding sanctity. But objectively speaking it is of the essence of Catholic Christianity, for it lies at the very heart of the Incarnation, in which God, who is our Father, did not undertake a sort of social-worker's mission among us, but became our Brother. At the level of poetic vision, it permeates through and through the work of Mr. David Jones, for example. Indeed, the work of this last contemporary of Mr. Eliot's provides, against his, a contrast of quite unusual interest. For, as I have indicated earlier, its whole source of inspiration is the world of "all common and hidden men and the secret princes"—as Chesterton put it, "the people of England, that never have spoken yet". It is the "lower world" of those who plot of happiness and fling empty bottles, but seen from another angle, as intrinsically "charged with the grandeur of God", and hence known not "apart, in otherness", but from within. I do not think it is ever, in principle, known in that way by Mr. Eliot, despite the genuine increased status which Monica Claverton-Ferry and Charles Hemington are given, in *The Elder Statesman*, in comparison with, say, the Chamberlaynes, in *The Cocktail Party*. For Mr. David Jones, the function of the poet has been, in part at least, to recognize and utilize the creative sap running all through the common world of private soldiers, merchant seamen, artisans and labourers, of "all trades, their gear and tackle and trim"—with their slang and their "mysteries"; to Mr. Eliot it has been to "purify the dialect of the tribe", who I think, do really remain in the last analysis the kind of people who ride ten to a carriage to a football match in Swansea and haven't read Lancelot Andrewes. Hence there was some justification in the attitude of the Marxist critic who wrote of Mr. Eliot's work as "the end of bourgeois poetry". For although it is quite certainly not that, it does seem that you could scarcely carry any further the self-conscious creation of culture out of the self-concious criticism of culture. Just as Mr. Eliot ambiguously perpetuates in his new world of Christian humility the laborious dominativeness of the titanism which it repudiates, so in his later variations on the theme that "the poetry does not matter" he perpetuates much of the mentality to which poetry matters more than religion. In attempting to revivify the sub-cultural Waste Land by intensifying the growth of that elite culture which has exhausted it,

149

he perpetuates a basic tenet of Matthew Arnold, whose view that culture is the successor of religion he has so decisively repudiated.

This profoundly serious and un-playful labour of culturally redeeming from above the world of bottle-flinging and ten-to-a-carriage-riding is still organically one with the quasi-religious extension of the artist's function which took place during the later nineteenth century. A swarm of criticizing titanists, from the Darwinians and Comte to Nietzsche, were then thought to be analysing away irrevocably that binding medium of religious belief which had hitherto held the world together in some kind of symbolic significance. And it was the view of the clerkly elite as a sort of new secularized priesthood, mediating spiritual vitality to the masses, which was summed up by Arnold's estimate of the place of the poet and the critic in society. Paradoxically enough, Mr. Eliot forms his later message—that culture isn't enough—in terms of a more intensive effort to redeem elite culture out of its own resources than has, perhaps, ever been made before. The elaborately constructed spontaneity of the later plays shows distinct signs of being a more complicated permutation-and-combination of extreme deliberation and self-consciousness than any of the more obviously self-conscious earlier poetry. And you can see this fascinatingly ambiguous continuity-in-revolution more clearly than ever if you consider in more detail the mental attitudes from which some of the early and the later poetry are, respectively, created.

The Waste Land was a highly condensed "epic of dis-integration"; a vision conceived in terms of a whole culture, a whole civilization. But this same theme had already been worked out earlier in individual terms in poems such as "The Love Song of J. Alfred Prufrock"

150

and the "Portrait of a Lady". In these two works the existence of a typical secularized "clerk", with its overpowering note of paralysed-centipede self-awareness, is "formulated, sprawling on a pin" of piercing self-disgust —the devouring critique of the age of enlightenment turned universal wolf and preying on its own product. Prufrock's love-song is, ironically, the song of a man who has never quite been able to get under way as a lover or anything else. It conveys the futility and isolation of an "emancipated" intellectual community where there is no communion in the common sanities but only an arid determination on the part of each individual to establish the private world of his own singularity in triumphant opposition to those of all the others:

> And I have known the eyes already, known them all—
> The eyes that fix you in a formulated phrase,
> And when I am formulated, sprawling on a pin,
> When I am pinned and wriggling on the wall,
> Then how should I begin
> To spit out all the butt-ends of my days and ways?
> And how should I presume?

Here there is intellectual activity in plenty[1]—

> In the room the women come and go
> Talking of Michelangelo . . .

but it creates nothing; it merely serves to erode yet further what little substance of meaning is still left in existence, and the "overwhelming question" with which Prufrock longs to "disturb the universe" is never asked, for if it were

---

[1] A little reminiscent of Yeats's dream vision of Shaw as a "sewing machine that clicked and shone" but "smiled, smiled perpetually".

... would it have been worth it, after all,
After the cups, the marmalade, the tea,
Among the porcelain, some talk of you and me,
Would it have been worth while
To have bitten off the matter with a smile,
To have squeezed the universe into a ball
To roll it toward some overwhelming question,
To say: 'I am Lazarus come from the dead,
Come back to tell you all, I shall tell you all'—
If one, settling a pillow by her head,
Should say: 'That is not what I meant at all.
That is not it, at all.'

It is sufficiently clear that the paralysed-centipede
frustration of Prufrock in his self-consuming world of
secular clerkly culture—a world where it is precisely the
endless analytical "talk about Michelangelo" that has
made the air "thoroughly small and dry"—and his
loneliness amid its constellated "private worlds", are
closely bound up with his inability to achieve, with
regard to any member of the opposite sex, the

... awful daring of a moment's surrender
Which an age of prudence can never retract.

Here, as in the sphere of intellectual communion, Prufrock
cannot—will not—break out of the private world of
mirrors created by his agonizingly intensified self-awareness; there is always "time to turn back and to descend
the stair". And it's the very stair mounted on an October
night by the hero of "Portrait of a Lady", where the
sexual aspect of the problem of clerkly self-consciousness
and self-isolation is studied in itself and at a greater
intensity. The visitor of the Lady has, in a sense, got
a lot further than poor Prufrock, who would never have
managed to take anyone to

. . . hear the latest Pole
Transmit the Preludes, through his hair and finger-tips,

still less have gone back with her afterwards to

An atmosphere of Juliet's tomb
Prepared for all the things to be said, or left unsaid.

But none the less, the essential atmosphere is basically
just as much one of frustration as is that of Prufrock—a
frustration reflected in the ambiguous status of the
"lady". At some points in the poem the atmosphere
is, on the surface at least, highly Platonic:

But what have I, but what have I, my friend,
To give you, what can you receive from me?
Only the friendship and the sympathy
Of one about to reach her journey's end.

Yet the epigraph to the poem quotes bluntly

Thou hast committed—
Fornication . . .

and the general context of the poem, summed up perhaps in the tart

Well! and what if she *should* die some afternoon[1]

indicates pretty clearly, I think, that we are to regard
all this talk of journeys' ends as not more than the
rhetoric of the *femme de trente ans*—taking that category
in its wider sense.

[1] Italics mine; I believe that this is the emphasis with which the line
is intended to be read—though the italic overstates it, of course.

But in fact the studied ambivalence of the situation, from the sexual point of view, is, I think, symbolic of a situation of self-defeat as total as that of Prufrock. If the set-up were truly Platonic, the Lady's admirer would have no problem; if it were bluntly and simply the reverse, like that of Mr. Eliot's Sweeney, who

> . . . addressed to shave
> Broadbottomed, pink from nape to base,
> Knows the female temperament
> And wipes the suds around his face

there would be no problem either. As it is, the relation uniting Lady and admirer is a sort of sensuality of the mind, which of its very nature is at once a nagging stimulus and perpetual frustration of desire. It is something which arouses the desire for, and prevents all possibility of, real communion and union in either the sphere of the body or that of the mind. There remains possible only a sort of playing on the nerves, a savouring of the situation's destructive tension in the very exploration of its frustrations:

> You do not know how much they mean to me, my friends,
> And how, how rare and strange it is, to find
> In a life composed so much, so much of odds and ends,
> [For indeed I do not love it . . . you knew? You are not blind!
> How keen you are!]
> To find a friend who has these qualities,
> Who has, and gives
> Those qualities upon which friendship lives . . .

It is, in fact, a case of

Here we go round the prickly pear
Prickly pear prickly pear
Here we go round the prickly pear
At five o'clock in the morning.

Both these poems are permeated with irony. But as we have seen, Mr. Eliot was not prepared, in the interest of comfort or convenience, to call any arbitrary halt to the destructive critique of existence which this irony implied. The cynical sophistication of the "Portrait" was not permitted to halt its corrosive action either at the Lady or even at the Lady's visitor himself; it was to go on till it consumed itself, and with itself the poet's old self:

Lady, three white leopards sat under a juniper-tree
In the cool of the day, having fed to satiety
On my legs my heart my liver and that which had been
 contained
In the hollow round of my skull. And God said
Shall these bones live?

You might say that the earlier poems to which we have referred show an ambivalent combination of a certain disgust with the human condition, as shown in the writer himself and those whom he depicts, and a certain pleasure in the critique by which that disgust is expressed. And a matching ambivalence marks the new poetic vision which emerged from the other side of the despair of *The Waste Land* and *The Hollow Men,* and even in the process of death and resurrection by which it arose.

You could quote from the *Collected Essays,* or *The Idea of a Christian Society,* or *Notes Towards a Definition of Culture* in support of this; but some of the most striking evidence is to be found, I think, precisely in the

155

first of Eliot's works to seek deliberately—and how
deliberately!—a more popular audience for its message:
The Cocktail Party.

The whole point of *The Cocktail Party* is that it com-
plements the intensity of the earlier religious poems'
height and depth with a greater breadth of Christian
experience. In the *Quartets*, the emphasis is concentrated
on that intensity of Christian contemplation which is
"an occupation for the saint", and the rest of us

are only undefeated
Because we have gone on trying.[1]

The "only" gives common-or-garden life a depreciatory
qualification paralleled in *The Idea of a Christian Society*'s
"Whatever reform or revolution we carry out, the result
will always be a sordid travesty of what human society
should be—though the world is never left wholly without glory",[2] or in *Notes Towards a Definition of Culture*'s

[1] It is interesting, here, to compare the way in which Chesterton approaches a similar theme in *The Ballad of the White Horse*:

> Away in the waste of White Horse Down
> An idle child alone
> Played some small game through hours that pass,
> And patiently would pluck the grass
> Patiently push the stone.
>
> Through the long infant hours like days
> He built one tower in vain—
> Piled up small stones to make a town,
> And evermore the stones fell down,
> And he piled them up again . . .
>
> And this was the might of Alfred,
> At the ending of the Way;
> That of such smiters, wise or wild,
> He was least distant from the child
> Piling the stones all day.

[2] I am aware, of course, that the context of this phrase is the perfectly
balanced view that "we have to remember that the kingdom of Christ
on earth will never be realized, and also that it is always being realized".
But here, as throughout the Christian work of Mr. Eliot, the interesting

instruction to the reader that he is to "abstain from deriding" politicians like Mr. Attlee or "the late re-gretted Miss Wilkinson". The elite mentality persists explicitly. But in his later plays Mr. Eliot has made a characteristically intelligent, self-conscious and deliberate effort to develop in his poetic vision that "humanist" breadth of scope which Catholic tradition insists upon just as much as the height and depth of the experience of a spiritual elite. And we shall be right to admire the soundness of the instinct which urged the attempt, and the characteristic skill, sensitivity and intelligence with which it has been made. But you only have to think for a moment of, say, even the starkest of Gerard Manley Hopkins's poetry—to say nothing of his pieces that affirm the wonder of existence—to realize how limited is its success. The isolation of the clerk from the popular world is not nearly as crudely obvious as in *The Rock*; yet there persists the later Puritan-ascetic transformation of the original distaste for the vulgar world of the people; significantly enough, in that very relation of the play's "spirituals" to its "ordinary people", which is the heart of this new stage in Mr. Eliot's development of his Christian theme.

Alex, Lady Julia and Sir Henry Harcourt-Reilly are certainly a lot more concerned with the possibilities of Christian living available to "ordinary people" than were the *Four Quartets*. Yet in a sense the mere fact that they can be described as "interested in ordinary people" gives the whole game away. For anyone who is concerned to help ordinary people, as a class distinct from himself, hasn't really begun to be in a position

---

thing, for our purposes, is, in the main, the contrast and conflict between *what* is being said and as it were the *tone of voice* in which it is being said. From this viewpoint the choice of phrase I have here given in example is, I think, significant.

from which he is truly entitled to help. Abbot Chapman, whose spiritual letters were only collected and published after his death, and who remarks in one of them, "I do not profess to be a 'director'!", defines the spiritual director's job simply as enabling the penitent to walk on his own; and in fact the most skilled spiritual direction consists precisely in directing as little as possible. This is rather different from the popular picture of the spiritual director as a benevolently condescending *guru* giving less advanced souls the benefit of his having achieved a superior plane to most in matters spiritual.

But there are not a few details here and there which make one feel that that kind of attitude, however sincerely held, is in fact exactly the attitude which the spiritual elite in *The Cocktail Party* adopt towards one another and those whose lives they so benevolently manipulate. And though there have always been and will always be plenty of Catholics who firmly identify the business of spiritual direction with this kind of benevolent psychological imperialism, that isn't in fact the genuine Catholic tradition. When Lady Julia says to the psychiatrist Harcourt-Reilly "You must accept your limitations", you can't help noticing the difference of pronoun from, for example, St. Francis de Sales's "We shall be lucky if we get free of sins of weakness a quarter of an hour before our death". Or again, when Sir Henry says to Celia "Go in peace, my daughter, and work out your salvation with diligence", one recalls at once the words which Catholics hear so often from the other side of the confessional grille: "Now God bless you; go in peace and say a prayer for me sometimes." And it is significant, I think, that despite the positive affirmation given by the "spirituals" to the life of marriage, Harcourt-Reilly has to speak of "breeding" children. Spirit is still not wedded to flesh, but takes a sort of holy revenge for the subjection of the historic past by exercising a benevolent despotism over it.

A certain qualification must undoubtedly be made here with reference to *The Elder Statesman*. The "spiritual" protagonist, Lord Claverton, has a very much more humble relation to the "ordinary-life" characters, his daughter and her lover; indeed, the division into the categories of "spirituals" and "ordinaries" has been very much modified. And when the Elder Statesman finally finds redemption from the falsehoods of his past in death, his passing leaves upon the lovers a kind of benediction that implies a far more wholehearted affirmation of the value of the natural world than anything we have had in Mr. Eliot before. It is quite a way from

> And no future life is even conceivable
> In which we should not be conscious of each other
> And conscious of our loving

back to the very qualified approval of the married life which is the best that Harcourt-Reilly can offer Celia in *The Cocktail Party*. Here there is an endorsement of the goodness of the "lower world" which is not merely a naked act of the will.

You might say, indeed, that just as the destructive critique of existence in *The Waste Land* worked itself through its own death to the kind of more positive approach I have quoted from the *Quartets*, so again the titanist-puritan critique of the new Christian phase has, to a certain extent, worked itself to a standstill too; to a new positiveness, parallel to that which emerged from the first death-into-life crisis. And this would, I think, be partly true, though the workout has not, perhaps, been wholly due to the potentialities of the "middle period" Christian attitude taken in itself alone.

159

But I pointed out earlier on that despite the indisputably new element of greater spontaneity exemplified in the opening of "Little Gidding", the change is striking only within the context of the general extremely cerebral deliberation of Mr. Eliot's poetry; and that if we pause to look for a moment at an artist in whom more abundant poetic life really bubbles over—a Lawrence or a Dylan Thomas—we are at once forcibly reminded how painfully self-conscious even this more spontaneous poetry is. And this still holds good, I think, of the change which *The Elder Statesman* marks in comparison with its predecessors. A new approval of the "lower world" is there, and to be applauded. Indeed, where the development of so intelligent a man as Mr. Eliot is concerned, it would have been rather surprising if it had not finally emerged. But it is perhaps just *because* it is so logical a conclusion, and the development has been so remorselessly intellectual, that from another point of view nothing has really changed very much—as again, we might perhaps have expected. The internal conflict and tension, between the strained dominativeness of the singular titan and the acceptant play of the common Christian, persist. The highly deliberate effort initiated in *The Cocktail Party* to broaden the scope of Christian vision has worked out to its logical conclusion; and the new naturalness which is that conclusion has been translated, still, into the painfully deliberate terms of the whole preceding development. The contrivedness of plot, character and language is perhaps more evident than ever before; more evident in particular, perhaps, the extraordinary remoteness of the characters from the ordinary human being of flesh and blood. We have a lovingly constructed mechanical model of more abundant life rather than the thing itself. It is much that the model should have been constructed at all; but it remains a model for all that. And although the main theme of the play is redemption, yet the redemption remains in many ways of a distinctively pessimistic kind—as becomes clear if you consider in contrast the handling of a similar theme in the last plays of Shakespeare. The *Oedipus at Colonus* does, after all, occupy the background place in *The Elder Statesman* which is occupied by the Catholic theology of grace and repentance "and a clean life ensuing" in *The Winter's Tale* and *The Tempest*. The weight of the play is not with the lovers, but with the Elder Statesman, who only "becomes himself" in "becoming nothing", and there is none of the paradisal freshness of "new heaven and new earth" that pervades the atmosphere of Shakespeare's last manner. And indeed, barring a quite extraordinary transformation of personality and temperament in Mr. Eliot at this stage in his career, we should hardly expect this finally achieved contact with spontaneity to be anything else but—however genuine and sincere—translated into terms of the tense, titanic deliberateness which has, in one form or another, been the persistent characteristic of his whole work.

It might, indeed, be argued that a real and genuine peace has here at last been achieved between the forces of nature and those of titanist supernaturalism, precisely at the cost of the near-exhaustion of both sides. That ambivalent situation would in fact form an adequate pattern for the whole complex of persistent internal tension and contradiction which we have just been discussing. A critic shrewdly described *The Elder Statesman* as "written by Prospero without his book"; and indeed it seems, as far as I can judge at the time of writing, to lend some further support to those critics who have argued that in Mr. Eliot the developing serenity of the Christian has been the progressive impoverishment of the poet. Perhaps Mr. Eliot himself, who in his most recent volume of essays described himself as having "a Catholic mind, a Puritan temperament and a Calvinist heritage", may have given us the best line on the puzzle he presents when he spoke of the artist, in "Tradition and the Individual Talent", as "the man who suffers".[1] As I shall try to show in discussing the element of conflict in Chesterton, I do not think such a description anything like an adequate picture of the poet, and rather particularly the Christian poet. But if in fact it is a profound insight into the kind of poet Mr. Eliot is, then we have, maybe, some solid ground for our suspicion that it is the earlier rather than the later Eliot who will have the most lasting effect upon the mind of English literary tradition. It is perhaps just because there seems so deliberate a parallel between the three comedies of Mr. Eliot and the last plays of Shakespeare that the parallel fails so signally—more than can be accounted for by the mere impossibility of competing with Shakespeare. Even where finally accepted, the common world of the natural is still seen and presented as if in a mirror —the mirror of the irremediably distinguished mind.

Here the comparison with Donne again becomes most fruitful—Donne the archetypal figure of the modern clerkly consciousness, anxiety-ridden, self-conscious and head-splittingly cerebral. The most interesting thing about him in this particular connection is the extent to which the development of his main poetic themes parallels that of Mr. Eliot's, both in its change of emphasis and in the persisting attitude which underlies that change.

Both poets open by depicting the world of the "great visitor of ladies"; an essentially "worldly" world of

[1] See the comments in F. O. Matthiessen's *The Achievement of T. S. Eliot*, Oxford, 1947, pp. 102–6.

intense sophistication, both sexual and cultural, in which the personal relationship of love between the sexes is conceived in non-Christian terms. The intensely cerebral analysis and exploration of this first "worldly" world is, of course, in both cases (though in different ways) a playing on the contrast between its non-Christian fruits and Christian subsoil. That gains in piquancy, if anything, through an acid awareness of its inherent limitations, and the frustration which underlies all the satisfactions it can offer. And both poets progress from this to a poetic vision created out of an equally passionate and intellectualized revulsion against their first world of "the flesh", and championship of the world of the spirit against it.

These substantial similarities are complemented by important accidental differences. To begin with, in the case of Mr. Eliot the world where the women come and go, talking of Michelangelo, and the Lady dispenses tea to friends, is far more deeply permeated with frustration than that of the early Donne. Donne's I-taught-my-silks-their-rustling-to-forbear period, though already ferociously self-conscious and introspective, and thus a whole stage onwards from that of medieval courtly love,[1] still has about it a full-blooded elementality absent from the poetic world of *Prufrock and Other Observations*. To Donne, the "olde daunce" of relationships between the sexes still has plenty of kick in it; for he is exploiting the rich soil laid down for him by fifteen hundred years in which Catholic moral order had channelled the savage vitality of Europe's barbarian stocks into ideals concerning marriage and virginity which gave the women of Christendom a place unique in the world. By the early twentieth century the breaking down of the

---

[1] Even in so sophisticated a version as that of Chaucer's *Troilus and Criseyde*.

traditional standards had gone so far that the "olde daunce" of truly profane love had left in it little sacrilegious spice to disguise the bitter taste of its basic frustrations. Hence the world of the early Eliot poems more or less begins from that condition of "sorrowing dulness in the soul" which was for Donne the lees of a cup which was pleasant draining. The elemental sensuality and intense self-consciousness which were one in Donne are here split apart, before we start, into the ironic and self-defeated Prufrock and Sweeney, the human orang-outang. The thoroughly popular zest with which Donne carried out his clerkly logistic of the war of the sexes is, in the early Eliotian poetic world, already turned somewhat thin and bitter. And this is of course not just something to be accounted for by the difference between the backgrounds provided respectively by the Cadiz Expedition, and Harvard and Boston. It is a part of the change in the mind and heart of England which we have been looking at in terms of the disintegration of play between man's two aspects into war, and which formed a staple subject of Mr. Eliot's own literary criticism. And the greater full-bloodedness of the early Donne is paralleled by the greater full-bloodedness of the later. Whether Donne is making a daring conceit of the spirit's control of the flesh as a rape of man by divine love, or making of the physical event of death a sarabande of austerely macabre images, his violent spirituality expresses itself as before from bowels and head at once with a savorous intensity not inferior to that of his earlier libertinism. And this despite the fact that force is already needed to maintain the synthesis. The new Donne is simply the old one stood on his head—or (to prefer an image whose dire and complicatedly macabre implications perhaps come nearer to fitting a true Fantastick), turned inside out. But although in the case of Mr. Eliot's poetry it is a certain self-conscious *ennui* of the flesh which is paralleled by a certain later bleakness of the spirit, the pattern of strong continuity underlying violent change is the same. The early distaste of the Lady's visitor for the world of Sweeney, and the later benevolent superiority of Julia, Alex and Harcourt-Reilly towards the world of the Chamberlaynes—these are cast in the same mould: the enmity between the divided higher and lower elements in man, and the dominative mastery of the first over the second. Even Lord Claverton retains a sort of Harcourt-Reillyish predominance in importance over his daughter and her fiancé.

In the poetry of both Mr. Eliot and Donne, then, we have a powerful swing from an early world of "the flesh" over to a later one of "the spirit"; a dialectic of extremes, worked out in terms of an unchangingly deliberate, self-conscious and highly cerebral experience of existence. And this pendulum swing between extremes is, in the case of Mr. Eliot, something which concerns not merely his attitude to and handling of his own individual talent, but also his attitude to and handling of the tradition which he has taken such enormous pains to relate it to. It remains Donne—and Baudelaire behind him—who really give us the key to the nature of the Eliotian vision of the Christian universe. The seedbed of all his later poetry is the world of Dante reassembled after the manner of Donne.

All this means that in the work of Mr. Eliot you have a subtle and fascinating combination: a very deep grasp of certain essentials of the Catholic world-picture, together with other elements which are profoundly un-Catholic. This absolute rule of higher over lower in man is at the opposite pole from that constitutional monarchy of wedlock in which Catholicism unites them

165

in a creative interplay of opposites. And this is none the less true because medieval civilization can exhibit many fierce aberrations from that central Catholic norm, as well as many adherences to it, from the vivid material beauty of its art to the sociological foundations of all later humanism and humanitarianism. Mr. Eliot's world-picture is, in essence, profoundly un-Catholic—all the more so for often appearing, like Jansenism, to be super-Catholic; yet it is formulated in profoundly Catholic terms. As such, it is a testimony to the enormous obstacles which he has had to contend with in the spiritual pilgrimage which has lain behind the epic of his creative work. Yet it is precisely because he has so much to offer to all who value the Christian creative tradition that it is all the more necessary for his admirers, whether Christian or no, to be aware of the ambivalences which are part of the very weave of his creative achievement.

There is a connection, I think, between this capacity for expressing basically un-Catholic attitudes in intensely Catholic terms, and those influences which Mr. Eliot at one time viewed—in Milton especially—as foreign to the central tradition of English poetic creation. In this connection his later change of views concerning Milton might profitably receive an attention which I cannot here digress to give it. For whether, in reviewing the main influences in Mr. Eliot's poetry, you think of the inverted Jansenism of Baudelaire, or the Puritan traditions of Mr. Eliot's ancestral New England, or the nihilistic strand in the Indian philosophies which were his early study, or the inherent schizophrenia of a cerebral sensualist-turned-ascetic like Donne, you are all the time dealing with variations on one basic theme: the more or less violent domination of spirit over matter. And it is precisely this phenomenon of the oppression of man's "popular" bowels and loins by a "clerkly" intellect and

166

will which does in fact find classical expression in the great Miltonic divide.

Mr. Eliot is in fact a Janus of the same basic type as Descartes; in both of them we see a similar complex conflict between the Christian and the desperately serious, dominative and anxiety-ridden Renaissance titan. Descartes is fiercely anxious to preserve the old Catholic certainties and sanities, but is at the same time determined to do this in the new Renaissance style. Mr. Eliot is, in his later work, explicitly committed to a new Christian vision of the natural world as godly in its own being; yet he cannot help affirming this basic goodness of the common world with all the self-contradictory dominative tension of the old post-Renaissance titanism.

V : THE TWO LOBES IN THE BRAIN
OF A PLOUGHMAN

The two faces of all effortful conflict, resolved play and unresolved earnest—that is the point, under the sign of Janus, to which we return, glancing back at all that has been said about the nature of tragedy and comedy, when we turn from Mr. Eliot to the second focal point of our enquiry, G. K. Chesterton.

The nature of the relation between the two men and between all that they respectively sum up and stand for, will emerge a good deal more clearly, I think, if we use a third man as a sort of mirror in which to reflect them. "Mirror" is an apt image here, because of its implications of direct opposition and reversal; for D. H. Lawrence, who is our mirror in this case, stands in many ways at exactly the opposite pole to Mr. Eliot.

This opposition between the two men is a sort of summing-up in little of that whole "dissociation of sensibility", and disintegration of clerkly head and popular bowels, the process of which we have explored already in several of its ramifications. The backgrounds of the two men speak for themselves. First, Mr. Eliot, the product of an aristocratic strand in Puritan New England culture, with his leisured progress through Harvard and the Sorbonne, his minor academic post, his time in the City and basically alien position with regard to that English society into which he has inserted his roots with such skill, patience and intelligence. Then, Lawrence; the miner's son, with his council-school education, scholarship, surgical-goods-factory job, attendance at Redbrick University, and final passage, with increasing disgust, through Bloomsbury—a man who ran the gamut of the strata of English society, from its most fundamental "popular" depths to the heights of its clerkly cultural elite. Despite all his own scaldingly caustic qualifications of the "democratic" elements in the world-picture which inspired him, Lawrence remains in a very real sense a voice for "the people of England, that never have spoken yet". He is very much an expression of the opposition of the popular depths of English culture to its disembodied clerkly upper crust, and a protest of the "lower", intuitive, elemental and earth-rooted aspects of English creativeness against the "higher" aspects—analytical, sophisticated, and agonizedly cerebral—which have exercised over them five hundred years or so of increasingly violent and frustrating oppression.

> Thought, I love thought,
> But not the jaggling and twisting of already existent ideas.
> I despise that self-important game.
> Thought is the welling up of unknown life into consciousness.
> Thought is the testing of statements on the touchstone of the conscience.
> Thought is gazing on to the face of life and reading what can be read.
> Thought is pondering over experience, and coming to conclusion.
> Thought is not a trick, or an exercise, or a set of dodges.
> Thought is man in his wholeness wholly attending.[1]

There are times when Lawrenc 's vision of the popular world as that of the mob seems to be almost a wildly demonic version of Mr. Eliot's well-bred distaste. And his affirmation of the uniqueness of artistic vision is post-Renaissance to the bone in its emphasis on singularity

---

[1] A description, this last line, which St. Thomas Aquinas would, I think, have much appreciated.

169

and uncommonness. But he is still a man rooted in the popular world, as Mr. Eliot has never been. And for all his setting up of creative distinction against the world of vulgarity, he is no more a titanist in the Miltonic style than was Blake. His clerkly power of individualized articulateness was, for all his rages against "working men . . . living like lice on poor money", used to proclaim a belief in the under-world of common people and war to the death on any kind of clerkly aristoculture which was split off from it. Any rage against the vulgarity of the popular under-world was, for Lawrence, not provoked by a vision of that world as of its nature vulgar, as Sweeneyish. It was provoked by a vision of it as rich, rather, in more abundant life, but denatured into squalor by the results of that increasingly agonizing modern process of tense, reflexive, dominative living which Lawrence summed up when he said: "Before Plato came along with his damned ideas men went slimly like fishes and didn't care." When he rages against England's people it is because he believes they have been alienated from their true selves. And it is because Lawrence saw his clerkly genius as making articulate just such a "lower world" of "true selves" and not of a world of cultural supermen alone, that he is, for all his clear-cut status as a professional literary man, a common man first and last; a voice from English culture's popular depths.

This pulls him continually towards a far more central view of human existence than Mr. Eliot's. He is an aboriginal inhabitant of the natural subsoil of Christian supernaturalism. His instinctive attitude to the natural world is as positive as Mr. Eliot's is negative; and this is so because his essential "popularity" means he's in organic continuity with the pre-sixteenth-century tradition of creaturely acceptance of being. His starting-point is off the narrow line of the titanist's *via dolorosa*; he doesn't experience any need to hold together by tense supernaturalism a natural world which remains in essence waste and disintegrated: to put into reverse gear the laborious machinery of the modern critique. For he stands outside the whole process of which Mr. Eliot has been so tormented a final product. He comes from a line of social development which has by-passed the "clerklification" of English culture, and is rooted in that world of common breadwinning which is the seedbed of natural religious awareness. And consequently, as you would expect, not only is the inner nature of his world-picture at the opposite pole from that of Mr. Eliot, but he makes an approach to tackling the contemporary problems of English culture which is diametrically opposite to Mr. Eliot's. The latter has revived the tradition of creative English writing by a brilliantly academic manipulation and mastery of its disintegrated elements; Lawrence revived it by re-creating directly out of the world of common agriculture which all high culture is built out of. Disregarding the whole long tradition which had interposed between man and what was not himself a growing labyrinth of self-conscious reflexion, he looked at the world with the direct vision of a child. And the value of this is not fundamentally affected by the fact that in his case the child was all too often an abominably spoilt and ill-mannered one. He simply looked at all that had been made, and saw that it was very good. The aberrations that there are in Lawrence's championship of the natural world are in principle the excess exuberance of a deep, if in some ways confused, sense of the goodness of being and the holiness of all that is. And this is in itself the irreplacable subsoil of Christianity.

It would be a poor sort of compliment to the genius

of Lawrence, however, to overlook the fact that his
"natural theology" exhibits to a greater or less degree
the usual aberrations which have characterized natural
theology in the concrete, whether outside, or previous to,
the Christian revelation. The concern for vitality itself,
which is so valuable a test for all formal profession of
religion, can, and does in Lawrence's case, produce its
own threat to dehumanize. We are justified up to the
hilt in backing him when he revolts against the ethical
and doctrinal complacency of decadent Christianity. But
we are also justified in refusing to be imposed upon
when he develops in its place his own kind of existentialist self-righteousness, which can be every bit as unpleasant. It is one thing to applaud vitality; it is another to sneer at the lack of it, and it is into such a sneer
that Lawrence's paean of praise sometimes shrilly develops. Yet all this, together with the more unattractive
aspects of Lawrence's own character and conduct, doesn't
alter the fact that as far as the achieved poetic vision
is concerned Lawrence is implanted in the natural subsoil
of Christian supernaturalism as Mr. Eliot is not. In
fact he has—ironically enough—stronger contact with
the organically unified world of medieval Christendom
than his strenuously traditionalist contemporary. Where
the rigorously explicit Christianity of Mr. Eliot remains
deeply akin to the world-picture of the de-Christianized
centuries that preceded it, the overtly anti-Christian
spirituality of Lawrence has, in spite of itself, much in
common with that creaturely acceptance of the gift of
being which was the bedrock of the medieval mind.

Yet the fact that in Lawrence's case it is the anti-
Christianity which is explicit and the Christianity which
is implicit makes him none the less of a Janus than Mr.
Eliot, in whom this situation is more or less reversed.
Mr. Eliot's titanism is none the less real for being a

suppressed contradiction of his Christianity; Lawrence's is none the less real because it is in conflict with the side of him which is implicitly *naturaliter Christiana.* It is often when Lawrence is talking at the top of his voice about God and humility and spiritual health that he is giving rein with the greatest gusto to the complacent arrogance inevitably potential in any vitalist naturalism cultivated in a "pure" state, apart from its supernatural complement. Against this, Mr. Eliot's painful effort towards the Christianization of his thought and work, and all the tense and effortful dominativeness of his attitude, show themselves in a new light. Such a strenuous effort to subject the personality to an outside discipline is signally lacking in Lawrence; just as Lawrence's most "un-modern" intuitive grasp of the goodness of being's gratuitous gift, with all its spontaneousness and immediacy, is a thing seriously deficient in Mr. Eliot. In both cases the dis-integration within the poetic vision is the symbol of opposites linked in a pattern of war, not play. There is a deep ambivalence here, because there is an unresolved tension between revolt against all that stands for modern mastering man, and a persistence, either explicit or implicit, of attitudes which are still really the same as his.

The similarity between Lawrence's overt titanism and that which so subtly remoulds Mr. Eliot's Christianity from within can be seen in the fact that for all his awareness of the godliness of the created universe, Lawrence's attitude to existence was still basically critical. In him the bitter wonder runs neck and neck with the sweet; his awareness that it is good to be often balances just about evenly with his indignant wonder that it is not better. And this critical modification of his existentialist affirmations shows itself in that streak of tremendous arrogance which we have already noted.

His sensitivity to sheer vitality, pure intensity and power of being, becomes something that can make him throw on one side, like a spoilt child, all the riches the created world can offer, because they are still, in the last analysis, inadequate. But this is, of course, vitalism's back-handed recognition of the Christian truth that God alone can satisfy us totally. And the element of submissiveness, the simple capacity to say "yes" to life, straight away, for what it is, the fundamental acceptance of the creaturely condition—this is in fact the deepest reality in Lawrence the writer, as his kinship with the dominative tradition against which he rebels is the most significant element in Mr. Eliot. And that, I think, is why Lawrence is in the last count the greater artist, the more universal. He is more central in his position than Mr. Eliot because the world of agriculture, and the creativeness born of direct vision, are more central to human experience than aristoculture and the creativeness stimulated by indirect vision via the arts. The world of Harvard and the Sorbonne and the study of Sanskrit is less central to human experience than that of the mining village and the council school and the first job in your 'teens—even when this is overlaid later by the world of the old Café Royal.

It is in this centrality, and the degree of wholeness within the whole man which it implies, that Lawrence and Chesterton stand on common ground. The extent to which they do so appears (to a degree which may slightly startle some admirers of Chesterton) if you compare some of Lawrence's more "theological" poems with some of the early jottings of Chesterton in his notebook.[1] Indeed, the essence of the marvellously

[1] For example:

Chesterton:
You say grace before meals
All right.

174

direct evocations of natural life which fill the work of Lawrence might be summed up in Chesterton's remark: "I think there is no man alive who takes a fiercer pleasure in things' being themselves than I do." Neither man needs to make any journey from the place at which he starts in order to know that place for the first time; they do not need to establish that the world is good, or that it is good to be, any more than they need to establish, Descartes-fashion, that the world exists, or that they exist. Indeed, one of the darkest crises, if not the darkest, in Chesterton's whole spiritual development, consisted in an appalled encounter with, and passionate revulsion from, the doctrine of solipsism in its full and real implications—as with Mr. John Custance. The immediate, intuitive and vivid apprehension of the goodness of natural being was basically, in the case of both men, an assertion of wholeness and centrality; wholeness in man himself as between his senses and mind, his spirit and body; wholeness of unity as between man

---

But I say grace before the play and the opera,
And grace before the concert and the pantomime,
And grace before I open a book
And grace before sketching, painting,
Swimming, fencing, boxing, walking, playing, dancing;
And grace before I dip the pen in the ink.

Lawrence:
    . . . Even if it is a woman making an apple dumpling, or a
        man a stool,
    if life goes into the pudding, good is the pudding
    good is the stool,
    content is the woman, with fresh life rippling into her,
    content is the man.

    Give, and it shall be given unto you
    is still the truth about life.
    But giving life is not so easy.
    It doesn't mean handing it out to some mean fool, or let-
        ting the living dead eat you up.
    It means kindling the life-quality where it was not,
    even if it's only in the whiteness of a washed pocket-
        handkerchief.

175

and a world in which he is organically implanted, because he accepts it instead of seeking to dominate it, either for himself or for God. Their protest against the tradition which led up to *The Waste Land* was thus very different in kind from that of Mr. Eliot. Where he diagnosed a deviation of the age in one direction and prescribed a violent swing into the other, both Lawrence and Chesterton were looking for the central norm from which the age had strayed. Each did this in his own way, and if the similarity between them is sufficiently ill-recognized to be worth emphasizing, the differences are sufficiently obvious to need no cataloguing in detail.

The root of them can be seen in Chesterton's effortful element of self-discipline[1] and submission, like that which we have noted in Mr. Eliot. Chesterton balanced the Lawrentian capacity for spontaneity and immediacy by an Eliotian moral effortfulness; he was capable of the commonplace effort which dwarfs all the most singular exploits of the titanists—the effort to be pleasant. In addition to the intense capacity for sheer savouring of life which he shared with Lawrence, he had what Lawrence lacked overwhelmingly—a capacity for practical humility and charity in the humdrum sense. It is when Lawrence's scalding existentialist diagnoses become a shrill scream of contempt for deficiency in being that it becomes a wry joke that Lawrence was himself anything but a glorious animal of a man. And this is where his titanist element, with all the frustration and futility which is titanism's ironic underside, emerges so clearly in comparison with Chesterton. For Chesterton, too, though in a very different way, was not far off a grotesque divergence from the ideal norm of a man,

---

[1] His indisciplined aspect, the where-am-I-supposed-to-be-going, please-tie-my-tie side, is well known. His capacity for self-sacrifice and hard work is a good deal less immediately obvious, but, I think, the far deeper reality.

with his immense and rather flabby size, his squeaky voice and general tendency to be unable to do up his own bootlaces. Yet his "fierce pleasure in things' being themselves" never strikes us as being in any way conditioned by revolt against personal inadequacies. He has none of the implicit sneer at the deficiencies of self which manifests itself in the explicit sneer at the deficiencies of others. His powerful "vitalist" sense of being's vividness expresses itself in a mercifully sharp eye for the good there is even in what is worst or most sick or shoddy or twisted; Lawrence's, all too often, in a savagely sharp eye for the most serious thing wrong with the best that can be produced. Lawrence had a strong gift for diagnostic sarcasm and wit, but was, I think, totally without a sense of humour; he was, for all his undoubted "popularity" as contrasted with Mr. Eliot, as titanistically serious a man as ever lived. Chesterton, without in any way abating his childlike and elemental pleasure in perfections of being, was able to accept his own inadequacies with the utmost good humour; and this was because a tremendous practical gratitude for being at all outweighed in him awareness of the deficiencies of being in himself and others.

That secondary awareness was none the less intense in itself, and again and again forms the starting point of his thought, particularly with reference to the doctrine of the Fall and original sin. Yet his most violent shudder at that privation of being which is evil, is always contained within his amazement that there should marvellously be anything in existence at all, in the first place, to be deficient in being, in the second. There is in him a perpetual wondering repetition of the child's question: "Why is there something and not nothing?" This capacity for accepting the gratuitous gift of being not only without fundamental criticism but with great

177

joy is in fact a recognition of and assent to the creaturely condition; Chesterton's gratitude is quite inseparable from his absolute and unconditioned humility.

It is this fundamental commonness, diametrically opposed to the permutations and combinations worked on the titanist theme by Mr. Eliot and by Lawrence, which sets Chesterton in a world apart from either, just because he combines elements from both. Mr. Eliot has Christian supernaturalism; but it is formed in the mould of the old secular aristocratic contempt of the enlightened philosopher for the common lower world of sweat and bread-getting and inarticulateness and elemental fecundity. Lawrence has awareness of the essential godliness of all that is natural; but in his defence of it against the kind of supernaturalist tradition which Mr. Eliot nobly represents, he deviates back towards the old pagan aberration of idolatry—that clouding of the translucence of the natural order which ends ultimately in the opacity and deadness of the spiritual world of late Antiquity. Chesterton knows nothing of either supernaturalism or naturalism in these "pure" states—that is, as cultivated either at the expense of the other (a virginity which is indeed a thing of deficiency, and no virtue). Instead, he combines them in a marriage in which each finds its true nature in the arms of the other. And this is why, I think, most fervent admirers of Mr. Eliot or Lawrence find it a wholly unfamiliar mental exercise to take him seriously. Both the other men's art derives its power from the restless war between opposites which is the basic pattern of the modern world. Chesterton's peasant art and thought has the childlike repose of energetic play; and so impressed are we (despite the later Shakespeare) with the achievements of titanism's strenuous anguish that for most of us it is a considerable effort to conceive that there could be deep insight and profound spiritual maturity in the nursery world of the children of God—even if we do accept "Unless ye become as little children . . ."

If we ask why Chesterton should be able to combine the positive elements in the attitudes of Mr. Eliot and Lawrence the answer is, I think, clear and comparatively simple. In his reaction against the post-Renaissance world there's no conflict between rejection of it and persistence of the attitudes which it has fostered. His reaction is not a critique of the criticism of existence; it consists in appreciating existence rather than criticizing it. Chesterton not only stood outside the post-Renaissance world—as did Lawrence—but also outside the traditional human attitudes which it accustomed men to—as Lawrence, the type figure of the demonic Bohemian, did not. Mr. Eliot has the will of a Christian and the instincts of a titanist; Lawrence had the instincts of a Christian and the will of a titanist. But Chesterton had both the instincts and the will of a Christian and consequently displays a kind of serenity and simplicity which catches somewhat on the wrong foot anyone whose mind is largely attuned to the brilliant and restless anguish of the modern age. In him there is no conflict such as is so dangerous and so fruitful in the other two. There is, indeed, the tremendous *resolved* conflict of the serenity of play, as we shall see; but this is something of a wholly different kind.

Now, to say that Chesterton has in some way a deeper spiritual insight and a surer grasp of reality than Mr. Eliot or Lawrence—to say that he is, in some sense at least, a greater man than either—is to fly almost *solus* in the teeth of a howling gale of contemporary disagreement. Many would, no doubt, consider the opinion so eccentric as to be not worth the trouble of refuting. But those who were prepared to go even so far as to discuss the matter would probably feel that the quickest way to dispose of the claim would be this: "If what is spiritually most sound[1] in Mr. Eliot and Lawrence is indeed combined in Chesterton, then surely it is reasonable to suppose that he must be a greater artist than either. Do you seriously propose to maintain that?"

My answer is, of course, that no man in his senses would maintain it for a moment; or even maintain that in this respect he was in the same class as these two men. No; his superiority is of a different kind. And yet to consider it, and the lessons to be learnt from its relation to his artistic inferiority, is to learn something of great value to us in that purely cultural field where considerations of literary artistry lie.

We have already seen that despite their reaction against the world born at the Renaissance, both Mr. Eliot and Lawrence remain profoundly at one with that world. And this we see all over again in the surprising extent to which both men continue the high Romantic tradition of the Great Artist and his role.

The Romantics made of the community of great artists something not unlike what the early Christian epoch made of the Desert Fathers—an elite of spiritual supermen in which the spiritual vitality of a whole society was held to be focused with quite special intensity. As soon as you begin to get men like Shelley talking about poets as the "unacknowledged legislators of the world" you are getting an explicit saddling of the artist, in an increasingly secularized era, with that mission of concentrating civilization's spiritual vitality which, in the Christian centuries, had been entrusted to the ascetic and the mystic. And despite all their reaction against the condition of culture which endorsed this viewpoint,

---

[1] Be it remembered, we have argued to its soundness from humanistic grounds rather than with reference to the criteria supplied by revelation.

both Mr. Eliot and Lawrence remain "of the devil's party without knowing it". The culture of modern Europe was, in its origin, a by-product of Christianity; it made a gigantic attempt to achieve autonomous freedom from its religious roots; and it has followed that attempt by trying to remedy the resulting sickness by recreating out of the resources of culture alone that religious substructure which is in fact culture's prior basis. The task remains one of the self-redemption of civilization as concentrated in a leisure culture divorced from the business of agri-culture. And it expresses its essence in the utterances and responses of a small elite world of mental aristocracy.

Here again, Chesterton proves puzzling to the mental habits of our age by standing wholly outside the framework of this cultural situation. Mr. Eliot and Lawrence are children of the modern age, even though rebellious children; Chesterton is not. Nor is he, as he is often thought to be, an illegitimate child of the Middle Ages. He is a child of the timelessly reposeful vision which gave to the Middle Ages, for all their violence, an underlying balance and serenity. And this enormous difference is perfectly summed up in the way in which Chesterton decisively identifies himself with the "vulgar", in opposition to the fierce "distinction" of the other two writers. To the discriminating vision, "knowing good and evil", which the titanist makes his tragic judgement on existence out of, he opposes head-on a childlike "lack of taste" and capacity for indiscriminate enjoyment. It is a vision which, like that of the inarticulate common man, looks at things with a puzzled love which is none the less loving for the intensity of its puzzlement; with the deep, almost animal patience of the humble who seek blindly for life through the strangest aberrations which lack of reflexive clerkly discrimination can lead to.

181

It has, in fact, the "noble vulgarity" which Chesterton ascribed to life itself. As such, it stands condemned out of hand by the critical standards developed by the tragic civilization of secularised humanism. Yet if the assumptions of that attitude be regarded as challengeable —and I have argued that on humanist grounds alone they not only are challengeable but must be challenged— another view must be taken of it, as something which calls in question the basic standards of a whole epoch.

The shift of meaning in the word "vulgar" which took place in the middle of the seventeenth century is a symbol in little of the change in the attitude toward the common people which separates medieval kings (however oppressive) washing the feet of ten poor men before dinner from Puritan captains of commerce (however upright) coining the concept of "the *deserving* poor". It is a change which is organically one with Milton's developing the poetic sublime at the expense of common speech, and the whole "dissociation of sensibility". Mr. Eliot tackled that split from the aristocratic camp, and in so doing helped to perpetuate the reality of the division; Chesterton identified himself with the vulgar elements in the split in such a way as to challenge the validity of the whole Eliotian approach. He is firmly rooted in a world often regarded as particularly lacking in cultural distinction—the bourgeois world of the late Victorian age. In that world greatness, in the post-Renaissance sense of particularized individual cultural *virtù*, is conspicuous by its absence. It is a world of commonplace activities and commonplace opinions, commonplace virtues and vices, commonplace tastes and aims such as the taste for immortality and the aim of salvation. Its sins and deficiencies have been catalogued *ad nauseam* by every fourpenny Prometheus who ever arrogated to himself the right to despise his

182

fellow-men. And indeed the world of the common man
at the opening of the twentieth century exhibits glaringly
all the deficiencies of taste which have been inflicted
upon it by the generations upon generations of uncommon men who have broken up the common sense of
the first Christendom as fuel for brilliant bonfires of
blazing insanity.

But Chesterton embraces without reserve the noble
vulgarity of life. He affirms, in direct opposition to Mr.
Eliot, that when all that is clerkly is disintegrated from
all that is popular we must look to the popular element
for the power to heal the split. He locates the springs
of creativity in creaturely commonplaceness as opposed
to titanic singularity; and in so doing he sidesteps all
the endless complexities which continually frustrate all
attempts of elite culture to redeem its civilization from
the top. His grasp of the godliness of common being
(*vis-à-vis* Mr. Eliot) and lack of resentment at its un-
godliness (*vis-à-vis* Lawrence) enable him both to make
an instinctive diagnosis of the real nature of the dissociation of sensibility which has uprooted Europe's
clerkly flowering from its popular seedbed, and to
counteract it not by reversing it but by stepping right
outside its results.

In the world of artistry in the strict sense—the world
of elite culture—he has thus very little to teach us indeed, compared with Mr. Eliot and with Lawrence. But
in the wider and more fundamental world of mere creativeness—or mere making, whether it be of a baby or a
pudding or a rabbit-hutch or a newspaper article—he
has things to teach us which must be learnt if the
world of artistry is to keep its health. The value and
order of his world was not something masteringly established from above in the tension of constant anxiety, by
the action of a cultivated minority which forms the

G   183

"conscious point of the race in time". It was, rather, something received from the humble, the common—particularly, the common man. To him it is that very "vulgar herd", always being denigrated by the intellectual aristocracy, who, in and through the most gaudy manifestations of their vulgarity, are still the seedbed of elemental vitality without which high sophistication becomes decadently self-consuming. Everything that makes the common man despised by the cultured titanist, from his love of bright colour to his love of the silly joke and the happy ending, Chesterton makes his own, just as St. Thérèse made her own everything in the way of Saint-Sulpicerie which made bourgeois religion seem unstomachable even to a man with such painfully strong Christian instincts as Baudelaire. He is the Charlie Chaplin of theology and the Walt Disney of the religious parable. And this vision of supernatural depths beneath the natural commonsense of common men is in itself both his motive for desiring communion with them so passionately and the basis of his means for getting it. For it is the great commonplaces of human experience which are incarnate in platitude and proverb, and the very poetry of colloquial speech which provides, in the marrow of language itself, the symbolic means of intellectual communion. However crudely it be possessed, this means remains something which the shrinking elite of clerks has come to lack increasingly—both among themselves, and even more as between themselves and the society in which they live. To Chesterton, the anguishes and despairs of that cultural elite could not be anything else but a gross overestimate of their own importance and a gross underestimate of the simple man's spiritual reserves.

His whole importance then, is that in an artistic and philosophical world of titanism running riot—a world in which it had become almost axiomatic that greatness is achieved in terms of the singular—it fell to his lot to be the champion of the wonder of the ordinary. He turned to artistic and philosophical account once more such things as the fact that an external world really exists, just as it seems to do, and that men have free will and yet cannot choose whether or not they will be born. In a world which had poured untold genius into the cultivation of an increasingly dazzling insanity, his was the curious distinction of hymning the thrill of being sane.

He is great, then, precisely because he is *not* a great man in the lonely titanist sense of the word current since the sixteenth-century crisis. In an expanding universe of ever more isolated singular geniuses he exemplifies the scandalizing yet healing concept of man as great in another way; great in realistic creaturely humility, in what he has in common with all men, in his power to be sane; great in his grateful acceptance from God of the gratuitous marvel of mere being, and in seeing within the setting of that simple primal appreciation all the marvellous things he can do. It is in this basic acceptance, shown intellectually in the championship of common sense and morally in the glad recognition of man's creatureliness, that Chesterton is revealed as a manifestation of the "feminine" mother earth of English society and an incarnate contradiction of its uprooted "masculine" clerkly elite. His way of seeing and creating is quite other than that of the high culture of his day because it is comic and contemplative, as opposed to tragic and critical.

To appreciate the full implications of the deceptive simplicity and even crudity of Chesterton's thought and art, it's important to realise that his criticism is very unlike what we are accustomed to. For it consists largely

in searching out whatever it is—however little—which
he can applaud and praise in minds of every kind,
including those diametrically opposed to his own.
Where the critical appraisal of Mr. Eliot or Lawrence
would see in the world that produces the "penny
dreadful" and the Technicolor epic little else but
cultural degradation, Chesterton's vision is more akin
to that of the sympathetic comparative-religionist. He
sees in such a world, groping blindly and with a twisted
humility, the great elemental thirst for more abundant
life, and in consequence the forms, however blurred
and confused, of primary religious vision. Where in a
wide-screen epic about highgrade executives, penthouse
flats, night-clubs and huge cars, Mr. Eliot would, I
think, chiefly see degrading enslavement to The World,
like that deplorable football match in Swansea, and
Lawrence would have seen a degrading wallow in unreality, Chesterton would have seen something very
different. He would have seen the expression, however
distorted, of a healthy desire to live largely, richly and
colourfully, a life of big deeds and heroic gestures. He
would have been as critical as Mr. Eliot of the actual
terms in which such a life was there conceived, and as
critical as Lawrence of the mechanical and vicarious
elements in the vision. But that critical reaction would
have been secondary to the primary appreciative vision
—that the pasty-faced youth and flashily dressed little
girl, who clasp clammy palms and chew gum while they
watch the panorama of skyscrapers and twelve-foot
wide kisses and glittering limousines, are seeking, however blindly, a greater fullness and richness of existence.
He would have sympathized with the crudest features of
their ritual which elite culture could despise; for he
would have seen them as fumbling gestures of worship
toward the Unknown God. Rooted as he was in a world

which had none of the cultural elite's self-destructive discipline of critical taste, and placed as he was in a world which was increasingly one of "mass civilization and minority culture", Chesterton worked with such materials as he had, and did it not with resignation but with joy. He took the common vision, with all its gaudiness and crudity, and made it the vehicle for a communication of truth which lay right outside the restrictions and complications of all primarily cultural redemption of civilization. Thus, his vision was intelligible to the widest possible audience, to the clown every bit as much as to the clerk; a picture of reality painted in those strong and simple colours common to peasant art, medieval illumination and the Wild West film.

But Hilaire Belloc was not indulging in idle flattery when he said that Chesterton's style reminded him of St. Augustine's. In him, as in Augustine, childlike simplicity, and a curiously unsophisticated profundity and subtlety, coexist in a fashion disconcerting to those accustomed to the soup-down-your-tie tradition of academic philosophy, and to extreme abstruseness and unprecedentedness as the hallmarks of distinction in thought. Chesterton's ideas, and the symbols in which he brings them alive, are neither complicated nor abstruse. But they are paradoxically profound in their very simplicity. His crudities are never the product of woolly thinking. And it is because of this, and because it took genius to see, in his own day, the need for a new simplicity of vision, that his severe limitations at the purely cultural level can be viewed not negatively but positively, as a sort of transitional cultural asceticism. It is true that this asceticism came naturally to him; but the value of his achievement is not diminished by the fact that he reached it through being true to his own nature.

This, then, is the key to the peculiar kind of importance of Chesterton's "Christian barbarism" for the healing of a secularized culture severed from its religious roots, and a clerklified culture severed from its popular roots. His capacity to find creative potentialities in the vulgar world is based on his recognition of the profound metaphysical and spiritual mysteries which underlie the world of common living, common speech and common sense. He is able to relate the world of Notting Hill to that of the clerks; to relate it not because he thinks there ought to be a connection between the two if we are to have a healthy culture, but because he sees the two things as being organically united in actual fact. It was a truly clerkly capacity to reason, reflect and discriminate which made Chesterton both aware of the fatal inadequacies of the purely clerkly mind and able to recognize the missing elemental vitality and sanity in the crude yet deep vision of common men and the common world. Although his creative vision is communicated in essentially popular terms, it is as clerkly as it is possible to be, in the depths of subtlety which underlie its sharp, bright colours and simple shapes.

Thus his identification—surely reasonable—of the popular world with humility and the clerkly world with pride does not imply championship of the one at the expense of the other. For man has in fact a proper pride (since he is made in the image of God) as well as a proper humility (since he is made out of nothing). And his proper health and balance lie not in being all swagger and no grovel or all grovel and no swagger but in knowing, as Chesterton said, where to swagger and where to grovel; in combining in himself, as in his culture, the full height of clerkly aspiration with the full depth of popular acceptance.

VI : JOY AT WAR

Chesterton was confronted with a task which most of the great religious teachers of earlier Christendom had not had to tackle—that of reawakening in men a taste for life itself. He lived in a civilization undergoing that kind of crisis which Gilbert Murray described as a "loss of nerve"; a loss, not only of the sense of the value of the supernatural, but also of the natural. He had to try to restore the capacity for delight in the withering world of culture by reawakening a capacity for that delight in the mere existence of things which precedes it and is its indispensable basis. In championing the heritage of Christendom he defends the cause of culture against men like Lawrence, who see it primarily as something condemned to a hopeless task of self-redemption and self-renewal, and consequently tend to be drawn towards despair of culture through their very sense of its value. In championing the world of nature—of mere common existence —he defends the rights of the world and the flesh (for all their dangers and aberrations) against revengeful angelist spiritualism of the Eliotian type. To him, the lower vision of humanism and the natural world was precious beyond words, and to be most jealously defended. But this could be done only insofar as they continued to make sense within themselves; and this they could only do, in the long run, framed in the higher vision of Christian supernaturalism.

In nothing do you see more clearly this reconciliation of the modern age's warring opposites than in the total reversal which Chesterton's natural and supernatural good news makes of the evaluation of life summed up in the vision of Sartre's *Huis Clos*. It is not primarily one based on the claims of revelation. It is first and

189

foremost a humanist, rationalist challenge: one based
on the claim that Sartre's beyond-tragic concept of
human maturity implies an absurd attitude toward the
absurd. The *Huis Clos* situation is all one with that
which Army folklore describes in the tale of the olley-
olley bird's flight round and round the desert in ever-
decreasing circles, and its final surrealist, rude and startlingly logical disappearance. Provided you talk your
nonsense in the same frame of mind as produced the
sad tale of the olley-olley bird, you're all right; but if
not, you are in a bad, bad way.

It is precisely here that, as Chesterton points out,
the supernaturalist Christian vision comes in to reinforce
pure human reason with such power and accuracy that
it is hardly surprising if men who are worried when
things seem to work out all right conclude it must be a
case of wish fulfilment. For the Christian says that the
whole reason for the conditions which give rise to this
tragic critique of existence, and the absurd attitude
towards the absurd in which it ends, lies in an event at
the beginning of all human history which is also an
example of the absurd attitude towards the absurd.
The impossible attempt of man to be God has as its
archetype the primal sin of the archetypal man. And
behind *that* sin lies another, yet more fundamental: that
of the first created being who staged a titanist revolt.

The devil, said Chesterton, fell through taking himself
too seriously—"through force of gravity". The remark
is interesting not only in what it says but also in how
it says it. It is the kind of *jeu d'esprit* which the clerkly
intellectual could well dismiss as an embarrassing piece
of jolly-good-show-chaps Christianity, but in fact it
embodies in its very humour a deep seriousness—like all
good jokes. In fact, it is a living embodiment—as was
Chesterton himself—of the truth that knowing how to

laugh—a precious capacity, and of absolutely primary importance in the Christian life—is the reverse side of knowing what to take seriously. The fall of Satan was in fact the simple consequence of breaking up the loving play that holds these two visions in unity, and setting them at war—clashing them one against the other like the blades of shears that cut one's connection with reality. The idea that a created being, of its very nature utterly dependent on its Creator, should use its most godlike gift—free will—in an attempt to assert a divine independence—this was, of course, is, and always will be, the very essence of absurdity. Serious recognition of it as such would have brought the gratuitous reward of a heavenly laughter. For the loyal angels, it did bring it. Heaven is not an eternal Third Programme. To the dwellers in Paradise the very idea of a titanist Luciferan revolt was, and is, seen as the joke of all eternity. The laughter of heaven sets the absurd in its proper place; the negative boundary of that playground of reality on which man enjoys, in perfect freedom, the eternal game of serious fulfilment, before the smiling face of God. Thus it is the reconciling archetype of both the discriminating "knowledge of good and evil" which is the tragic element in rebellious self-assertion, and the joyful assent to being which is the key element in comic acceptance and contemplation. Man's fall out of the hand of God thus begins when a perfectly good joke is taken seriously; the seriousness of that absurd enterprise ends, if carried to its ultimate conclusion, in a perfectly bad joke—the kind of ironically evil "comedy" summed up in *Huis Clos*. And sanity is thus held in shape, you might say, by lunacy harnessed. The shape of realism is determined by laughter. It may be the laughter of heavenly rejoicing in the creaturely condition. It may be the laughter of that earthy humour which glorifies

191

man's dignity and rationality by reminding us that their reality is in no way diminished by their fragility: which strengthens our sanity by enabling us to see without panic and with exhilaration that it is only by the grace of God that we don't all sink without trace in the abyss of irrational chaos. But in any case, the sanity which comes from heaven has lunacy tamed and in its right place as the negative limit which reveals our proper creaturely shape, while diabolical anti-sanity is engaged in a perpetually futile attempt to make sanity its prisoner. In the first case Caliban is where Shakespeare depicts him—horrific enough in his absurd way, yet firmly under the control of a merciful laughter. In the second case Caliban is, as it were, perpetually, absurdly and futilely trying to step out of *The Tempest* independently of the conditions laid down for his existence by the mind of Shakespeare, and to reorganize the play—to say nothing of the play's author and the actors and audience—in accordance with his "own" ideas.

What has happened is that the game has been allowed to lead the player "a bit past himself", as the Nanny of my nursery days, God rest her loving soul, used to put it with a wealth of instinctive metaphysical wisdom. The devil, and Adam after him, got well and truly past themselves. The play of their freedom was to be stretched beyond its human limits towards the divine. Thus it lost its heavenly self-sufficiency and its whole playful nature; like Adam's tending of the earth, it became utilitarian, directed outside itself in an anxiety-ridden and desperately dominative purposefulness, which was also futile. And the whole dominative critique of existence formed in the image of this archetypal revolt is a similar unplayful war of man on his environment; work in its curse aspect. Once Adam had refused to accept his own being as gift, he was committed to trying to achieve possession of it as a right. The whole enterprise made, of course, no sense whatsoever; for any being who possesses his own existence as of right must always have done so and cannot possibly have achieved that position from the starting-point of some lower status. Indeed, the very effort which Adam had to make in order to retain his hold on life at all was part of the very process which inevitably led him in the end to lose his hold on it. His life of holy play was turned to one of work; and yet the very element of "seriousness" which is the stamp of the transition is not truly serious. The work cannot achieve the end which it cannot help trying to attain. And in death Adam gives, whether he likes it or not, the decisive proof of the absurd incompatibility between creaturely participation in life and divine possession of it. Man's tragic attempt to jump out of his creaturely skin ends in realism, however unwilling; the moment when he chooses to try to earn by right the gratuitous gift of his being is the moment that decrees his mortality.

Realism thus breaks in brutally enough, you might say, on the absurd pipe-dream of titanist man. Yet if realism will, by the nature of things, keep breaking brutally in—you aim to be as gods and in fact you die the death—this can none the less be the opportunity for cheerfulness—the lost joy of heaven—to break in again too. Death was the symbol of man's attempt, and failure, to break through the absurdity barrier—the limits formed by his own very shape; yet God could also make it an instrument of redemption. You might say that here man's involuntary realism (for no man chooses to die, though he can choose how and where, if he so wishes) opened for him a way through which it was possible for God to get inside his private world of unreality and set him free from it. As long as the

honesty and integrity of the tragic critique retains the
power of self-criticism—that is, holds back from the
absolute absurdity of total pride—the absurd continues
to be faced and rejected, faced again and rejected again,
over and over. The very thing which keeps it from
shutting itself up for good in the bad joke of *Huis Clos*
is the thing which renews both its anguish and the inarticulate hope on which that anguish must live, para-
sitically, if it is to live at all.

This is something you can see clearly in Greek tragedy,
and to see it is both to see how strongly the Hellenic
questions shape toward the Semitic answers, and yet how
inevitably shut out they were from the unique dimension
in which those answers are given. Any developed consciousness of the problem of man's suffering implies some
kind of awareness that he is not himself; but this is not
at all the same thing as the concept of the Fall. Any
attempt to resolve that problem, at whatever level,
implies some kind of awareness that good is more real
than evil, and consequently that a profounder comedy
is essential as the background against which alone
tragedy can be, and be tragic; an attempt to resolve the
problem at all implies a gesture of faith in the meaningfulness of existence. But that isn't the same thing as the
amazing Semitic expectation; the increasingly concrete
mental outreaching of the Jews towards a Messiah who
was somehow to fit life's baffling evil and even more
baffling goodness into some pattern inconceivable to
man on his own. Outside the Jewish-Christian tradition,
in the realm of purely natural theology, the tragic
question has to be asked without receiving the unparalleled answer of the Cross. Yet it was one of the
Roman inheritors of the Greek culture who—perhaps—
came nearest to formulating (whether consciously or
unconsciously doesn't matter) the potential depths of

meaning just behind the apparent meaninglessness of this answer that the tragic question could not be answered by man, who could not help asking it. Virgil's vision included, beside the lucid *Sunt lacrimae rerum*, the mysterious Prophetic Eclogue, in which the remorselessly questioning voice of the Hellenic tradition suddenly seems to speak, almost like a medium in a trance, the first broken words of the prophetic Semitic synthesis. The persistence of the Hellenic rationality in the face of the apparent absurdity at the heart of things set the stage, in the very humility of its pessimism, for the incredible answer to the impossible question. In the Incarnate Word of the Jews God answered man's tragic question in a whole concrete life, "making peace through the blood of his cross."

For Christ was in fact the perfect tragic hero whom the Greek stage had tried to provide. Behind the Greek actor and his mask lay the mythical heroes of the legendary past; behind them lay the dying god Dionysos; and behind Dionysos lay the yet more shadowy figures of the dying vegetation and animal gods of the Middle East, and the whole concept of renewed life through sacrificial death which they embodied. All these Christ came not to destroy but to fulfil. And his sufferings and death do in fact work out in concrete historical reality the archetypal patterns of redemption confusedly and imperfectly prefigured in pagan art and ritual. The whole significance of the redeeming sacrifice of Calvary—for our purposes here—lies in this fact that it is the unique effective sacrifice of the tragic hero; that the symbol of Christ's Person, life, and death, like that of the consecrated Host in the Mass, *is* what it signifies. It is, I think, only in the light of this fact that the enigmas and ambiguities of tragic drama ever reveal their secret.

195

The archaic culture of the Middle East had, as we know, its divine kings and royal deities, whose ritual deaths were the life-bringing death of the old season, and liberated those who shared in their fruits to another round of the seasonal cycle, the closed circle of time. Through the worship of the dying god Dionysos, and the ritual dance and song connected with it, Greek tragedy transposed this fundamentally this-worldly death and resurrection into terms at once more human and more transcendent. They were more human in that the protagonist of the tragic drama was now not a god pure and simple but a legendary human hero; they were more transcendent in that the liberation aimed at was not merely from the death of the year, but from that whole oppression of suffering through time, of which death is the focal point. Now the tragic hero is no longer actually sacrificed, as the archaic god-kings were actually put to death. He has shifted from the serious level of work to that of play; he plays at dying and rising again. He pretends to endure that tragic destruction which is in fact experience of the tensions of our fallen condition at their highest peak of disintegrating power, mental and physical—madness and death. Because this supreme sacrifice is successfully played, the audience, who participate in the experience in unity with the actor, can in some shadowy way achieve a temporary "redemption" from man's fallen condition— the *catharsis*, the purging of our pity and terror of which Aristotle spoke in the *Poetics*. They can in some sense endure the utmost that the fallen world can inflict, and survive that experience.

But in actual fact the many gods of the refracted pagan vision are not God; and mere humans can't really both endure and survive, of their own power, that ultimate experience of the destructive tensions sin let loose in the world. Thus both the ancient sacrificial deaths of the vegetation gods and the ritual play of later tragic drama cannot help but fail to achieve what they cannot help attempting. The deaths of Osiris and Dionysos, and of all their human counterparts, originally aim at "redemption" only within that closed circle of birth and death in which the Fall shut us out from immortal life; the later concepts of immortality these traditions come to imply are basically identifications with the cosmic forces and the cosmic cycle. Spring follows on winter; but winter follows again upon spring, and on the final winter which is death there follows a future existence as shadowy as the gods themselves in their legendary past—shadowy in that way just because it is a perpetuation of the world of time. And this is equally true of the mournful Homeric underworld and the more cheerful paradise of the Egyptians. It is precisely because the religious ritual is so very serious (particularly in its early human-sacrifice stage) that it makes so clear a confession of its own limitations. In contrast, the sacrifice of the tragic hero does indeed offer a kind of experience of escape, in the concrete, from suffering, in the concrete. But it is able to offer this just because it does so only in play. Play and earnest are here inextricably connected—as indeed they always are—but the wrong way round. The serious sacrifice is at bottom no more than play, and the playful one all too impotently serious.

Perhaps it was necessary for us to undergo the tragic crisis of the sixteenth century in the European mind if we were ever to be in a position to grasp at full depth the absolutely genuine, commonplace joyfulness and playfulness of the Christian comedy. Because of that crisis it becomes possible to see—perhaps even more sharply than the men of the Middle Ages saw it—how the

redeeming sacrifice of Calvary, and the world of hope
which is recreated under its sign, reverses that wrong
relation between play and earnest.

Christ is a unique tragic hero, as I said. Admitted,
there is perhaps no feature of the Christian redemption
for which you can't find some kind of parallel in one or
other of the extra-Christian dying-god cults; as you
would expect, if Christ did in fact fulfil the archetypal
gropings of the human soul throughout space and time.
But the pagan cults never manage to assemble *all* the
features of the Christian one; they always gain on the
roundabouts at the cost of a loss on the swings. For
example, even in so striking a saviour cult as the later
one of Osiris, the distanced, legendary and shadowy
nature of the god remains most marked; and it was that
very element of the mythical which, under the growing
pressure of Greek rationality, revealed the pagan "re-
demptions" as ever more unsatisfactory. It is the growing dissatisfaction with the gods which both elucidates
in the Greek mind a worthier conception of divinity and
confronts it with a *human* tragic question growing ever
sharper. And this again is a gain on the swings at the
cost of a loss on the roundabouts. The mythical extravagance and remoteness of the mystery cults is progressively eliminated; but so is most of their consolation.

It is as the symbol—the holding-together—of *all* these
apparently incompatible elements in full redemption,
that Christ shakes up the old components of ritual and
drama, kaleidoscope-like, into a new pattern. He is a
dying God in the pattern of all the earlier dying gods;
indeed, he is put to death at that very time of the year
when the vegetation deities of the Middle East under-
went that *agon* which preceded, and was identified with,
the resurrection of nature's life in the spring. But
instead of offering a renewal of life within the cosmic

cycle and the cosmic limits, he claims that his death
provides a way out of that closed circle, and all that
cycle of eternal return which underlaid with a certain
quiet steady horror the more obvious and violent
manifestations of Greek pessimism. The redemptive
death of Christ doesn't pretend either to abolish death
or man's natural and healthy revulsion from it. But it
does claim to rob death of its ultimate sting and the
grave of its ultimate victory, even within the context
of man's own immediate experience, here and now in
this life. It claims to take the focal point and summing-
up of the consequences of sin, just as it is, and to make
of it a breach in the closed-in world that these consequences build around man (in all of which there is, of
course, strong contrast to the death-as-misfortune which
overtakes Osiris, again). In Christ, man makes an assent
to death's involuntary and unavoidable admission of the
absurd unrealism of man's archetypal titanist revolt—an
assent which he could never make apart from Christ.
Christian redemption aims at a real break-out, here and
now, from the treadmill circle of the natural left to its
own devices and its own resources, a break-out into the
infinite playground of divine life itself. In this respect,
not only is the death of Christ real and serious, as were
the deaths of the old god-king victims; but also the
liberation it brings is serious.

But Christ was not only a dying God; he was a dying
Man too, a human as well as divine Hero, joining together in his very existence the two spheres which man
had put asunder. Indeed, he was a much more human
hero than the usual run of those who, either by virtue
of a peculiar place in some mythological system or
through the mere accretion of legend, are thought by
men to have a foot in both the divine and the human
spheres—men like Hercules, or the "culture-heroes"

of so many primitive mythologies. For there is nothing shadowy about Christ or the age in which he lived. He is not supposed to have existed "once upon a time", he doesn't fight primeval monsters with wonder-working weapons forged by fairies, or win through to mysterious treasure-hoards with the aid of magic herbs. He is and remains a carpenter's son from a certain not-very-well-reputed village, born under a certain Caesar and executed by a certain provincial official. This does not, of course, mean that the marvellous and extraordinary elements always associated with the divine hero are not present too—quite the contrary. The remarkable feature is the both-and aspect of him; all the archetypal patterns are there, but translated into the concrete everyday terms of his own day and all time. He enacts his tragic drama not in the cloudy terms of legendary epic but in the prosaic terms of common life. The labyrinth he traverses on his way to the supreme contest and treasure is not a legendary maze like that of the Minotaur, but the narrow, twisting streets of the Via Dolorosa in historical Jerusalem. The monster he goes to fight is not some fabulous dragon but ordinary death itself, at its most sordid in capital punishment. His betrayal is no crafty use of some magic secret by a jealous minor deity but a squalid cash transaction carried out by a petty thief for a recorded informer's fee. The "kingship" made the occasion of his death is no magico-ritual office, but a thing of straightforward political implications; the lesser monsters he contends with on his way to the supreme prize are no fabulous beasts or semi-human beings but the commonplace bogies of extreme fear, loneliness and physical weakness. Although he is more godlike in his claims than the very gods themselves, his epic and tragic story has about it a greater and simpler humanity than any of the human tragic heroes of ancient legend. And here again he is reversing the inside-out combination of the wrong kind of play and the wrong kind of earnest which was the best that the utmost integrity of his precursors could achieve. Christ translates the tragic conflict of mortality into its proper human terms and super-cyclical implications, *without* being forced into the dimension of false play. His tragic *agon* is absolutely real, and the endurance and survival of it are also absolutely real, both in themselves and in their effect on the human situation.

I have said that Christ's death on Calvary reverses the false relations of play to earnest which inevitably marked all the earlier prefigurings of the redemptive act. But so far I have only spoken of the aspect in which false play is replaced by real earnest; and it may seem as if this transition from play to earnest is indeed the whole of the new Christian pattern, so that the first demand of the Christian world-vision is indeed that we should wipe off our faces any lingering traces of a smile that happen to have survived there, and settle into the condition of redemption with a fundamental grimness.

But this is quite false. It is, in fact, only when we have grasped just how very much in earnest the whole Christian tragedy is that we first become able to see the full role of play in the new pattern, and the meaning of divine comedy.

Both the world of antiquity, and the world of the Renaissance, which in so many ways resurrected it, suffered the condition which makes man cry out for liberation in a way which ultimately drove them to the impotently serious play of a purely human attempt to achieve it. The explicitly Christian world that lay between these two suffered that same condition within the transforming context of a belief in the Christian redemption. God, it held, had, like the tragic heroes of

the ancient stage, endured that condition's utmost
tensions, in such a way that those who participated in
his *agon* were enabled to survive and triumph over that
experience. Only he didn't merely play at doing it; he
did it. And the participation of those who believed in
him was not the played participation of the theatre
audience, but a real incorporation, through Christ's
mystical body, the Church, in the actual Person of the
dramatic protagonist. And the liberation was not the
transient release of the tragic *catharsis*, but immediate
release into a new and hitherto inconceivable dimension
of hope. It was a permanent *catharsis*, yet dynamic and
not static; the new order of the fallen and redeemed
world derived its repose from a resolution of enduring
tensions—a "resolution of forces" of which the physical
pattern of crucifixion itself is a fittingly concrete embodiment. The architectonic forces of the paradisal
repose, destructively released in the atomic fission of
humanity's ironic "experiment in divinity", are thus
re-harnessed to structure the matter of a new world.
It is a world new not in the sense of mere unprecedentedness, but rather in the sense of repossession of the freshness that was in the beginning and is always in eternity,
from which the progress of the time-ridden world of
mortality estranges us. The very latest thing is in the
next second the dated thing; but the common thing,
seen with the eye of wonder, is a fresh discovery every
moment. And it is the vision of wonder, of appreciation,
which is made possible as soon as the war of the sweet
and bitter wonders is resolved in play. That play is one
with the play which Adam spoiled by stretching it
beyond the limits which gave it its freedom. The first
Christendom found our lost centre of gravity again
when it made Calvary, and Calvary's perpetuation in
the Mass, the axis of its cosmic dance; and in so doing

it found too that the centre of gravity was even more fundamentally a centre of hilarity.

For it is the "seriousness" of evil, suffering and death —a seriousness one with that which could see nothing funny in the idea of a creature's becoming God—which strikes at the pure playfulness at the root of joy. On Calvary that utter laughterlessness which lies under all evil is, by a sort of divine judo, made to provide of itself the full proof of its own absurdity. The full seriousness of evil as we know it in this world—death—is allowed to be in the grimmest earnest it could desire; to fasten its grip on the Creator himself. The idea, of course, that death could make its destructive power effective on God himself, is utterly absurd—the next best joke since the original one the devil refused to see. But once he had made the original sacrifice of his sense of humour—another word for his sense of reality—he could hardly be expected to see the point of any subsequent joke whatever. As before Eden he took the absurd seriously, so he did again on Calvary; the monster death was allowed to close its jaws upon the hero Christ, and of course it burst asunder, teeth, jaws and all, with the party-balloon bang of Daniel's dragon.

This is the pattern on which sheer game and sheer earnest are wedded. Christians are bound to put everything they have got into the business of self-redemption by their own lives, as seriously as ever did any titanist who levelled his unavoidable tragic critique against the impenetrable wall of the fallen condition. But it is also true that in the final analysis the "serious" part of the work, which they can in fact only play at, is done by God. So that without abandoning one iota of the seriousness of their war, they can also see it as already the joyful, strenuous and exhilarating play of the children of God.

203

You get a deeper insight into the nature of this curious Christian release into the happiness of the second childhood, which from one aspect changes nothing and from another changes everything, if you stop to consider for a moment the plain physical significance of the cross pattern.

For the Catholic the pattern of Christendom centres, as we have seen, about the Mass; and for him, as we have also seen, the symbolism of the Mass is the supreme example of that which effects what it signifies. To stop to think about this is to find your spiritual stereoscopy becoming so intensified that the depth of the picture becomes dizzying.

The whole point of any symbolism is that it binds together, as the original Greek word indicates, elements which are apparently separate, holding in paradoxical unity things apparently disparate. For that reason any kind of symbolic vision has this stereoscopic element; multiple viewpoints combining to give a picture in the round. And since the whole pattern of Christian comedy is a complex of opposites, a resolution of forces, it is wholly fitting that the root of the whole Christian faith and Church should be the redemptive sacrifice of Christ effectively symbolized in the breaking of bread. But the curious thing about the symbolism of the Mass is that it reconciles a pair of opposites unique in the list of elements held together in symbolic systems.

Any symbol has two opposite poles to it, as it were. It has to be itself before it can be symbolic of anything else. Bread can be a symbol of life—"Give us bread!" —but it can be so only insofar as it is true to itself. If it is mouldy it won't do as a symbol of life; it can't point beyond itself effectively, because it is not itself. On the other hand, the whole point of a symbol's being itself is precisely that it *should* point beyond that self; the element of deeper reality is contributed by the thing symbolized, the thing which is what the symbol is not.

The whole point about the symbolism of the Mass is that these two aspects of symbolism itself are held together in the consecrated Host. The bread—from one aspect—is itself; unchanged in size, shape, colour, texture and all else that pertains to the senses' grip on the material world which is the *sine qua non* of any symbol. Yet the bread is also "beyond itself"; it is really the body of Christ, and in it Christ is really present. The symbol *is* what it signifies.

Precisely because symbol and reality here coincide, the fundamental point about Christ's presence in the Host is that the Host should be eaten; not meditated on, or conceptually analysed, but eaten. In coming down from heaven, God comes up to us through the lowliest depths of materiality. In eating God, we eat heaven; heaven, and all its divine comedy, comes in reality into the here-and-now of our conflict-ridden human condition. The dazing of our vision which occurs when the focus of its symbolic stereoscopy becomes infinite is a sign that here our "intellectual knowing" is to give place to a deeper union with God—a holy communion, in fact—of which the "knowledge" of the marriage union is an image; a "knowing by the whole person". In the redemptive sacrifice of Christ, the "here-and-now" element and the "beyond" element thus come blindingly together. And just because of that the whole vast complex of symbolic vision which radiates out from the centre of Catholic life shows all the more clearly the distinction that separates these two elements, and makes symbolism in the ordinary sense a straightforward binding-together in organic unity of things whose identities do not coincide.

This is obviously very important because of the fact

that though "all shall be well", as the Christian may
put it, all is not well as yet. If justice is to be done to
both truths, there has to be a firm grasp of the dynamic
pointing-beyond element in Christian symbolic thought,
as well as the static here-and-now element. And the
very central point for grasping this is the symbolism
of the Cross.

For the Cross is, literally, the physical pattern made
by a resolution of opposing forces: the starting-point of
a whole series of equations which can be fascinatingly
and beautifully worked out in the mathematical and
geometrical patterns of the science of mechanics. If you
believe that the human condition is patterned by that
complex of mutually opposed drives which we call the
Fall, you won't of course, find it anything but appropriate that the redemptive resolution of these forces
should be effected in such a way as to embody the
spiritual reality concerned in a material pattern of the
same kind. The Cross was from the beginning a natural
geometrical symbol of repose achieved through the harnessing of destructive dynamism. What more natural
than that it should be made the supernatural symbol of
a redemption achieved through turning to account the
ultimate destructive consequences of sin itself? And this
was something which, I think, Chesterton, with his almost
uncannily intuitive mind, sensed from the beginning.
His instinctive revulsion from the circular symbols of
fatalistic and cyclical philosophies, and the sense of
liberation stressed in his early vision of the Cross as a
"signpost for free travellers", show how deeply he sensed
the philosophical implications of the Cross symbol long
before he believed in the effective symbolism of the Mass.

But it is, of course, precisely the transposing of the
Cross symbolism from the philosophical to the specifically
Christian plane which gives it its "pointing-beyond"

quality *par excellence* and hence its dynamism. To the
Christian the symbolism, the pointing-beyondness, of
the Cross, is of just as much importance as the fact of
the Cross; and this balance is a most important one.
There is a vast and essential difference between the
Cross's being the centre of Christianity and being the
central symbol of Christianity. Christians do not worship the Cross. They worship the Man who made of
that focal point of the Fall's conflict an instrument of
joy's redemptive reconquest. Once it carries Christ, the
cross of human suffering opens to us again in terms of
hope the vision of paradise, for paradise is the reality
of things. It is brutally true that the Christian revelation
and redemption doesn't do away with suffering. But it
is also true—bafflingly true, you sometimes feel, in
face of the sudden sheer nightmare which this world can
spring upon you—that it does genuinely make present
to us again the fundamental goodness and joyfulness of
being. The coexistence in one world picture of these two
apparent incompatibles is the resolution of forces of the
incredible historical Cross. Through its centre runs the
axis of the Christian hope (which, properly understood,
becomes all the stronger the more hopeless things appear).
It offers, weirdly and inexplicably yet undeniably, a real
foretaste of the joy of paradise coexisting with those very
sorrows which are—and feel as if they are—the offspring
of the hatred of hell.

Thus the acceptance of this reconciliation—what St.
Paul meant when he spoke of Christ's "making peace
through the blood of his cross"—is not an absolute and
unconditional acceptance of suffering, with all which
this would imply of violation of our nature and denial
of our deepest longings. It was, says St. Paul again,
"having joy set before him", that Christ endured the
crucifixion. The alternative to the lost paradise of

unclouded joy, which one can still see in small children, is not a grimly courageous total acceptance of suffering, but a conditional acceptance of it as the way back into the earlier world which we need not pretend ever to have stopped desiring. And by virtue of that breakthrough of hope there is a place in the Christian mentality for a persistent element of unshadowed childish hilarity; something which would seem, in theory, to be quite incompatible with that most sober awareness of evil which any kind of maturity, Christian, ex-Christian or pagan, inevitably implies. A playground is provided for the polarized forces of assertion and submission whose civil war constitutes the whole conflict which rends the fallen world.

The influence of this Catholic idea can persist with surprising strength (or is it so surprising?) even when Catholicism itself is explicitly rejected. The cheerfully maniacal violence and surrealism of some modern Anglo-Saxon humour is as inconceivable as some of the ferocious pessimisms of the Middle Ages save against the background of a universe in which the play of joy is the fundamental thing (even if only just). Perhaps it would be an exaggeration to say that humour is a Christian invention. But at least it would be the kind of exaggeration that magnifies an essential truth. And the crazy humour of modern Britain and America often shows in a particularly lucid way the pattern of destructive conflict turned to play.

The devil, says St. John, is a murderer from the beginning, a liar and the father of liars. Reduce the lie to its basic element of falsity, and hence unreality, and you have the lunacy and violence which, in the worlds of mind and matter respectively, are the essence of that disintegration into formlessness which underlies all evil. And it is just those two elements of lunacy and

violence which are so conspicuously tamed and harnessed
to recreative purpose in so much modern Anglo-Saxon
humour, as when Mr. Thurber involves us in the *Wal-
purgisnacht* on which the Bed Fell or the Ghost Got In,
or Mr. Bob Hope finds himself terrifyingly embroiled
with pirates, gangsters, redskins and international spies.
Perhaps the best example of all, at the time of writing,
is still the phenomenal Goon Show, to English radio
audiences of the past half-dozen years or so the centre
of a growing cult, of an intensity almost to rival that
of Thurber addicts. Space alone forbids me (even were
it possible) to attempt to depict, for those suffering from
Goon deficiency, this surrealist development of Alice-in-
Wonderland doctrine in terms of steam radio: the
strange weekly saraband of Eccles, Henry Crun, Neddie
Seagoon, Colonel Bloodnok, Hercules Gritpipe-Thynne
and the rest, with their individual rituals, like the characters of the *Commedia dell' Arte*, and their weirdly epic
adventures (such as stealing from the Louvre the piano
which Napoleon played at the Battle of Waterloo, or
constructing a dry canal across Africa for the use of
aeroplanes without lifeboats). The interesting point
about the Goons is that their Dali-plus universe is very
much the "tough" Sartrian one stood clown-like on its
head—you might almost inscribe over the portal of the
Sartrian *théâtre des situations* Gritpipe-Thynne's hos-
pitable invitation: "Have a grenade." The Goon
sound-effect symphony of deafening splashes, thunderous
explosions, wild howls and stampedes is again a *Wal-
purgisnacht* played backwards to break, not cast, an
evil spell; the forces of destruction have been coaxed
back into performing the kind of entertaining games
that should have been the essence of that great joke
which the devil refused to see. And the game they play
is of the same kind as that which sent the apoplectic

209

Herod of the medieval mystery plays rampaging off the travelling stage into the delighted crowd; more important still, is of the same kind as that which gave Herod's master, the devil, despite his fearful reality, a genuine kinship, in the same plays, with the pantomime Demon King of a later age. There really is, despite all our revulsion from the pious platitudes of the preachers, a genuine Christian childlike laughter, which has very little indeed to do with wit, and whose carefree playfulness comes straight through the heart of the Cross. There is a real link between every clown who ever blessed our lives with laughter, and the outrageous God of Israel whose act of love seemed clownery to the pessimistic maturity of the Greek mind; the God who seemed a Charlie Chaplin among the gods to the cultural elite whose minds had been formed on the dignity of the pagan tragic critique. It is an act of great courage and integrity to accept the sorrow and horror of life. But it is also an act of great courage and integrity to accept its more fundamental beauty and joy.

The Cross is thus the Alice-in-Wonderland keyhole through which we repossess that springtime vision of wondering regard which every baby shares with Aristotle, the Master of Them that Know. But that wonderful vision, rightly and peacefully inherited as God's free gift, is only retained by unceasing, hopeful and chivalrous war, the play *à outrance* of the hatredless warrior. Here again assertion and submission are wedded. The playful element in the deeply serious creative warfare of the Christian derives partly from the fact that in a very important sense he refuses to take evil seriously. Of course, few types of men should be less likely than he to make light of evil's reality and consequences; of the enmity of the devil, the horror and danger of hell, the plain appallingness of suffering in all its forms.

210

Yet none the less, when evil is tracked down to its root cause—the self-assertion of the creature against its Creator—the Christian cannot help but not take it seriously, in the sense that he cannot conceive of the absurdity of this attempt as anything else but absurd. There is thus no contradiction, for the Christian, in having a profoundly serious and responsible attitude to evil, yet at the same time being able to see the personal attitude that is its root as matter for a mysterious yet real and normal laughter. Julian of Norwich laughs so uninhibitedly at the discomfiture of the devil that all those present start laughing too; St. Thomas More mounts the steps of the scaffold with a final genial wise-crack; Bishop Ullathorne's dying words are: "The devil is a jackass!" It is only when we can see quite clearly the full horrific element in Caliban that we can see equally clearly the element of absurdity in the demonic pretensions of Iago.

I think it is very much worth pondering upon, that the effective opening of the Anglo-Saxon tradition of crazy humour coincides with the first really explicit formulations, on the Continent, of philosophies of the absurd, as with Nietzsche. That line in philosophy, which comes to its ultimate point, I think, in some of the positions of canonized non-sense held with such brilliant ingenuity by M. Sartre, is the development, via Kant and Hegel, of the chain-reaction of fission initiated in the brilliant split mind of Descartes. And the whole point of that tradition, as we have seen, is that in it what Chesterton called the "huge helplessness about all complete conviction" is not galvanized by our analysis and critiques into creative play, but held down by them in an ever-tightening stranglehold. The only possible result is, on the one hand, a nightmare paralysis which is a caricature of reposeful submission, and, on the other, a feverish restlessness which is a caricature of dynamic assertion. It is civil war in the mind of Europe between two monstrosities.

A distinctive feature of this mental condition is, as we have seen, the tendency to try to establish by the strong right arm of rational discourse the foundations that make rational discourse possible.[1] And as the tradition accelerates towards its weird apocalypse in the present century you find this futility of trying to establish the bases of proof demonstrated with the utmost clarity in terms both of life-giving laughter and deadly earnest.

Here you get down to a very elemental level of the mind. If it doesn't strike you that laughter, and not seriousness, is the appropriate reaction to absurdity, then one thing is certain: that no amount of masterfully serious philosophizing will do you the least bit of good. If you really cannot see *any* funny aspect whatsoever to the world of *Les Deux Magots*, or André Gide's little-boy determination to be just as bad as bad can be,[2] then there is nothing for it but prayer or a reading of, say, Mr. Thurber on his friendship with D. H. Lawrence or the career of Eliot Vereker. And the two things are not so unconnected as they might seem. When men try to burst through the impregnable walls of absurdity that protect creaturely sanity the way to avoid being swept out with them in their disintegration is to play at the same attempt, so that the funniness of its absurdity can appear. And this is comic, as opposed to tragic, irony.

We have been somewhat conditioned to think that if we want adult thought and adult politics and adult everything else it is to the whole-hogging Continentals that we must go, and that the incurably childish and

---

[1] I do not, of course, suggest they must be uncritically accepted.

[2] I'm not denying, of course, that these things do have a very unfunny side.

amateurish Anglo-Saxons, with their games and their
sense of humour and their pragmatism and obstinate
distrust of logical conclusions, may have a curious
knack of muddling through successfully in practical
matters, but are not very much more than a pleasant
joke in the world of the mind and the spirit. This, I
think, is in a way quite true; but it means something
quite different from what it is normally taken to mean;
because there is nothing more profoundly and life-
givingly serious in the world (if you come down to rock
bottom) than a pleasant joke. If all God's creatures had
seen the point of the pleasantest joke ever made, the
whole history of the world would have been different.

It is only on the surface that men like Hegel and
Nietzsche and Comte and M. Sartre (none of whom I
have the least intention of patronizing) seem the really
serious men, and men like Lewis Carroll and Edward
Lear and Mark Twain and Mr. Paul Jennings and Mr.
James Thurber seem the frivolous ones. It is not true
that *Alice in Wonderland* and *Alice Through the Looking-
Glass* are clever childish caricatures of the themes which
were in fact to be debated in the future by serious
thinkers in deadly earnest. It is Lewis Carroll who is the
serious thinker: serious because sane, and sane because
able to see the true comic nature of the absurd.[1] When
the Viennese logical positivist Schlick met a violent end
at the hands of a student, those who disagreed with
the view that ethical statements are meaningless might
well have quoted it as the argument *ad hominem* to
silence all others. The *crime gratuit* is only "Have a
grenade" in true continental earnest; an unsmilingly
logical workout of the through-the-looking-glass mad-
hattery which Humpty Dumpty expounded to Alice
in his philosophy of language: "When I use a word

---

[1] I am, of course, thinking of his work here, rather than his own life.

it means just what I choose it to mean . . . The
question is, which is to be master." But Lewis Carroll
puts linguistic-analysis titanism in its true place—a
large smiling egg perched complacently on a high wall.
The unfortunate Nietzsche was no more—and no less—
than a truly Teutonically earnest incarnation of Mr.
James Thurber's Walter Mitty. The despairing and
futile violence of the efforts made by the hero of M.
Sartre's *Les Mains Sales* to get himself taken seriously
are the obverse of the panorama of howling redskins,
roaring pirates and glowering gangsters against which
Mr. Bob Hope, equally and superbly shameless in his
abject cowardice and the boasts with which he so un-
successfully covers it, secures for our own fundamental
weakness the merciful redemption of being taken playfully. What France follows with grimly wrinkled brows
in the writings of MM. Sartre and Gide, England and
America laugh at in the Goon Show or the drawings of
Charles Adams.[1] The nightmare world which atheist
existentialists of the strict observance cuddle obscenely
to themselves like a time-bomb set for eternity provides
for the devotees of Goonery and the like an explosion of
cathartic hilarity. And in all this baroque extravagance
of redemptive lunacy there is nothing more Goonish
than the reflection we may make upon it—that this
riotous chaos is funny precisely because it is a vision of
sanity which you get when you stand on your head. The
surrealist logic of Goonery is, if you like, a therapeutic
harnessing of the energy in the big bang with which the
Renaissance split the atomic structure of the medieval
order; the modern world's disintegrating insanity turned
into a trick to make men laugh—and implicitly, by

---

[1] I know, of course, that Mr. Adams skates on an even thinner edge
between the absurd and the horrific than do the Goons or Mr. Thurber.
The fact remains that his drawings are funny—all the more so because
they are very nearly horrible.

laughing at the sheer oddity of things, wake out of the
nightmare *ennui* of despairing titanism and see the point
of their creaturely condition. By that judo trick, the
maniacal "order" symbolized in the paralysed systems
of atheist existentialism is joyfully shattered in a releasing bang, and the suffocating hothouse world of *Huis
Clos*, where the air is indeed "thoroughly small and dry",
goes up in a thousand absurdly tinkling fragments
against the wide outer blue of sanity.

This is the healing violence of laughter, that strange
and cataclysmic convulsion which surely comes nearer
than anything else to the old pagan idea of sudden
possession by a god. The Anglo-Saxon achievement in
play, from the invention of cricket down to the Model
Oddlies of Mr. Paul Jennings, or Mr. Perelman's "with
a blow I sent him grovelling. In ten minutes he was back
with a basket of appetizing freshly-picked grovels"—all
this is a much greater cultural achievement than any
of us, with our solemn titanist habits of evaluation, find
it easy to appreciate. Man's bitter realization that he
cannot be God (which is, from one aspect, all human
history since the Fall) is made sweet again, however
astringently so, as the material of a saturnalian ritual
of holy play. That play of humour continually shows
forth in its pattern man's true condition: at once great
and small, made in God's image yet made of nothing.
Every true enjoyment of comic irony is, precisely, a glad
recognition of this paradoxical condition; and because
of that, the reverse side of a straightforward act of
worship. When we laugh at ourselves in the persons
of the great clowns, our laughter has its proper delightful
meaning because it is the reverse side of the seriousness
of sanity. If there is no serious positive standard of
heroism against which to set Mr. Bob Hope's attempt to
hide behind the heroine's crinoline during the battle

with the pirate ship, or no positive standard of wisdom against which to set Mr. Tony Hancock's swindlings at the hands of Mr. Sydney James, then these things are no longer funny. But if there were no mercy for cowards and no divine affection for fools, then they would not be funny either. They matter; and they do not matter at all; realization of this twofold truth is the vision of comic play. And this applies from the subtlest piece of wit down to the broadest uproar of slapstick and knock-about. It is a breath-taking manifestation of the glory of man that he should be able to perform the amazing feat of walking upright. But the diabolical temptation to pride in such greatness is exorcised when you can greet with rejoicing laughter the fact that this towering monument can be brought down by a humble piece of soap or banana-skin. The very opposite of roaring with laughter when you (in the person of the clown) slip on a banana-skin is smiling grimly when you (in the person of some existentialist hero) commit some appalling *crime gratuit* only to find that no one takes you any more seriously than before—rather like the hero of M. Sartre's *Les Mains Sales*.

Laughter, then, is joy at war; its explosion is our weapon for continually blasting a way through the unsmiling forces of pride to the joyful realism of accepting our creaturely condition, in all its greatness and all its helplessness and dependence. It makes the utterly serious battlefield of this world also a playground, where the limitations of the absurdity barrier are the outlines that give our freedom its shape, and not the imprisoning walls that trap us alive. And it is within this context, not that of any repressed sadism, that we must place Chesterton's lifelong fascination with fighting and violence and the warlike virtues. It was not a dark pathological underside to the extreme kindliness, friend-

liness and gentleness which were his obvious characteristics in daily life, and which made him, for a public
and controversial figure, so remarkably free from real
enemies. Rather, it was the indispensable complement
of these qualities. There are, granted, some serious
criticisms to be made. Part of his thrill to the panoply
and mythology of war was impregnably entrenched in
the fact that he didn't know what he was talking about.
It is all very well to talk about the barricades "flaring
smoke above and slaughter below" when you haven't
had the opportunity of seeing and smelling what the
slaughter of human beings is like in fact. Never having
seen a shot fired in anger, it was easy for him to get all
excited about "Don John pounding from the slaughter-
painted poop"—if he had ever seen a slaughter-painted
poop, or a slaughter-painted anything for that matter,
he would, like most men, have felt less like going and
writing a poem about it than like being sick at the very
memory. But in all this he was in part the child of his
time. Before the war of 1914–18 European civilization's
increasing sense of security produced—as well it might—
a certain nostalgia for more daring and adventurous
kinds of living. Perhaps one of the deepest sources of
the First World War was the simple fact that there were
so many young men about who wanted a chance to pit
their utmost manhood and courage against some kind of
supreme test which raising the standard of living, or
going in for drainage reform, doesn't usually offer us.
Men like Wilfrid Owen learnt most horribly that there
is a side to war which the schoolboy's imagination knows
nothing of; Chesterton never had the opportunity of
that experience. As a matter of fact, I think it extremely
likely that had he ever been put to the test he would
have shown no lack of physical courage. But in the event
he knew nothing of war at first hand, any more than did

Belloc; and in consequence his banging and brandishing tends, at times, to become embarrassing to anybody who does have that knowledge, on however modest a scale.

But this is only a part of the truth, and not the most important part. For all its occasional irritating aberrations his simple and honest thrill at the theme of military heroism was in essence an intuitive appreciation of that healthy violence which, the Gospels tell us, takes by storm the heaven of the peace that passeth all understanding. And his passion for swords and flags and drums and all the rest of it does in fact answer Mr. Eliot's

> Where are the eagles and the trumpets?
> Buried beneath some snow-deep Alps.
> Over buttered scones and crumpets
> Weeping, weeping multitudes
> Droop in a hundred A.B.C.'s.

For all its surface incongruity with the world of poison gas or intercontinental missiles, it is the intuition of a vital truth at a deeper level: that the hard, arduous and testing things which make a man put forth his strength to the utmost must be done with some kind of flourish and style if they are to be done with a good heart. The soldier is traditionally decked out in gay colours as a symbol of our admiration; and we admire him, not so much because he kills the enemy as because he exposes himself to being killed by them, and because that act of courage we instinctively sense as being something to do with the essential colour of life. We associate looking death in the eye with some kind of splendour, some kind of particularly flamboyant proclamation of human dignity; and I think that in fact any man who has faced violent death without losing that dignity will always feel afterwards a certain rightful pride in having

218

measured up to an unusual chance of affirming his human value. The risked life is a life made doubly precious by the risking. As Chesterton puts it with superb bread-and-butter simplicity in *Orthodoxy*:

"He that will lose his life, the same shall save it," is not a piece of mysticism for saints and heroes. It is a piece of everyday advice for sailors or mountain-eers. It might be printed in an Alpine guide or a drill book. This paradox is the whole principle of courage; even of quite earthly or quite brutal courage. A man cut off by the sea may save his life if he will risk it on the precipice. He can only get away from death by continually stepping within an inch of it. A soldier surrounded by enemies, if he is to cut his way out, needs to combine a strong desire for living with a strange carelessness about dying. He must not merely cling to life, for then he will be a coward, and will not escape. He must not merely wait for death, for then he will be a suicide, and will not escape. He must seek his life in a spirit of furious indifference to it; he must desire life like water and yet drink death like wine . . . Christianity . . . [has shown] the distance between him who dies for the sake of living and him who dies for the sake of dying. And it has held up ever since above the European lances the banner of the mystery of chivalry: the Christian courage, which is a disdain of death; not the Chinese courage which is a disdain of life.

The fascination which the soldier's dreadful calling has exercised throughout history on innumerable men who were neither inhuman, nor fools, nor knaves, nor sadists, can be traced to the fact that like everything else in human life its deepest significance lies in its relation to

H*   219

the Redemption. The glamour of the fighting man's profession lies in the fact that he takes death and forces it into the service of a more colourful life—which is, though in a very different way, exactly what the First Knight of Christendom did with it at the Crucifixion. Chesterton's capacity for more abundant life—his peaceful wonder at every blade of grass and every morning of a new day—was maintained by the exhilaration of unceasing conflict with all the nightmares and lunacies which this world's evil can produce. Such a war for the possession of peace is something Mr. Eliot saw deep into when he wrote

> We, who are only undefeated
> Because we have gone on trying . . .

But Chesterton, in virtue of his very "childishness" and "crudity", saw even deeper when he wrote: "There is a vital objection to the advice merely to grin and bear it. The objection is that if you merely bear it, you do not grin. Greek heroes do not grin; but gargoyles do—because they are Christian." He restores to our grim and guilty struggles something of the innocent gaiety of the child playing Roland and the Saracens with a wooden sword and the heads of dandelions in a meadow. The happy peace of childlike wonder at the goodness of being and the fiercely tragic war of adolescent revolt against the overwhelming mystery of evil—these are integrated in the second childhood that is Christian maturity.

This resolution of the sweet and bitter wonders in terms of the sweet is in fact nothing more complex than the right relating of two obvious and inescapable truths: that it is good to be, and terrible to suffer. The right relation is not in itself any more difficult to see than the two truths it relates. That it is good to be is the primary truth; the other must be reconciled with it as best we may. You can exist without suffering, but you cannot suffer without existing; being is primary, suffering is secondary, and it is good to be. In the peaceful periods of our lives, when suffering is absent, this can be plainly and reposefully seen. In the burning hurricane of deep suffering, the vision remains, but only on the condition of the continued conflict of the will with the temptation to despair. Yet even appalling experiences of the kind recorded in Gerard Manley Hopkins's "Carrion Comfort" can make ultimately a positive contribution to joy. For it is agony to suffer precisely because it *is* so good to be, and sometimes it is only when a man has suffered to what seems the limit of his capacity that he comes to full realization of how good it is to be, and how absolutely anterior that truth is to that of the reality and horror of evil. The struggle is not to establish the fact of ultimate goodness, but to retain the free gift of it.

In this world, the victory over despair is never definitely completed. No matter how many actions the Christian wins, the very persistence of his obstinate joy goads on the laughterless and destructive forces of evil to ever-repeated counterattack. Yet just because in this world the war can never be finally won, so also it needn't ever be finally lost. Victory is certain as long as, by God's grace, you keep up the fight: "He that shall persevere unto the end, he shall be saved." Since every defeat can be for the Christian a potential lesson in humility and the realism that implies, he who has fought and run away can live to fight another day, like Mr. Bob Hope among the Redskins. To be knocked down is to learn the lesson of "He that thinketh himself to stand, let him take heed lest he fall". Defeat is defeat, but

221

refusal to admit defeat is victory. Rejection of the temptation to despair is the triumph of hope; and in hope, the keyhole peep through the axis of the cross, joy is genuinely possessed in the very teeth of sorrow.

Curiously enough, the supernatural Christian undefeatableness is the fulfilment of that strange natural undefeatableness which we have noted especially in the old pagan tragedians. The Christian fight to a finish against despair is one of those points of simplification where the supernatural finds it easy, for once, to perfect the natural, and nature and grace go hand in hand. The struggle is desperately hard—because of the brute horror of evil, and the smashing impact of its power on our weakness; it is also curiously easy, because our natural thirst for happiness makes it against our nature not to hope. When Chesterton developed what one who knew him well called "a sort of mystique of defeat" he was doing something very different from Wagner when he wrote *The Twilight of the Gods*. When Gerard Manley Hopkins wrote (clearly, out of terrible first-hand experience)

. . . I can;

Can something, hope, wish day come, not choose not
   to be

he was formulating a spiritual attitude which, in the very depth of its tremendous seriousness, is twin brother to that refusal to choose the unreality of tragic self-assertion which is expressed in man's affectionate laughter at himself. There is a healing violence in the grimmest of refusals to "untwist these last strands of man"—the back-to-the-wall stand where the supernatural virtue of hope fights side by side with the natural thirst for happiness. And there is the same healing violence in laughter—a violence done to man's conceit, his tendency to take himself too titanically seriously. Certainly, it would be nauseatingly superficial to equate with any sort of backslapping breeziness the Christian's back-to-the-wall stand against the brutal, overwhelming and nightmarish onslaught of despair. But heartiness is a thousand miles from the gaiety which is an essential ingredient in all gallantry; and the laughter and joy that go with true gaiety are the inseparable reverse side of the deadly seriousness which puts up an undefeatable resistance against the most diabolical horrors that this world can produce. This is not mere theory, nor is its practice confined to the saints: I think most people could think, as I do now as I write, of cases known to them of men who have endured the kind of misfortunes from which one hastily averts the mind, and yet emerged cheerful, humorous and compassionate, their fighting spirit annealed to a bright edge of gentleness. The most endearing absurdities that a loving appreciation of the ridiculous ever took delight in are an integral part of the most attractive kind of Christian courage there is—the gay, humane and chivalrous courage of a St. Thomas More or a St. Francis de Sales. It is the courage which, whether in the mental home, or on the battlefield, or in the dark night of the soul, or in the wearing anxieties of everyday living, comes fighting out of the corner trap against the most impossible odds that temptation to despair can put in the field, with some bright rag of finery fluttering for a flag and some silly crack to sound the charge.

"In my beginning is my end"; Chesterton sees a cosmic joke at the start of the human story and the same heavenly laughter at the end of it; the two are linked by the gladly accepted crucifixion of comic irony, and the kind of laughter which is the gunfire of joy at war. And this in-my-end-is-my-beginning formula—from comedy through tragedy to comedy—has in fact a certain natural affinity with the process of growth in the individual personality.

In the world of our childhood, even if it is protected only by a purely natural goodness in those who look after us, we are able to taste with extraordinary vividness the sheer goodness of our existence, and of the world in which it unfolds. To prove the fact, you needn't do more than watch any normally happy child running and shouting over the grass on a spring day for the sheer joy of running and shouting, or a baby gurgling with delight when its mother plays with it. Here is possible a primarily acceptant and appreciative vision of existence in which all things are seen as if bright with the dew of the morning of the world. The vividness of the goodness of their being makes them so many sources of fascination which draw the personality out of itself in simple ecstasy—such as you can see, again, easily for yourself if you watch any two-or-three-year-old absorbed in making sand pies or ladling treacle into its best shoes. The consciousness of the self, possession and enjoyment of the self, is experienced most intensely in the act of self-giving: the contemplative surrender which is our natural homage to, and love of, things. A baby gazing open-mouthed at its first Christmas-tree lights is at exactly the opposite pole to some *Angst*-ridden John Donne of the twentieth century, muttering to himself in the embraces of his mistress, "We are committed to consciousness." In such a springtime vision the bitter wonder that life is so painful—even if only in terms of a grazed knee or a broken toy—is still in principle resolved within the wider context of the greater sweet wonder that life should be at all—in Chesterton's example, "at the magnificent soapiness of soap".

It is at the end of childhood, at adolescence, that the bitter wonder gains in strength, so that the activity of the critical masculine "right-hand side of the mind", dominative and analytical, steadily overpowers that of the acceptant feminine "left-hand side", with its power of acceptance and intuitive appreciation. The dominative tragic critique of existence succeeds to the comic contemplation of it. Consciousness of the self begins to become selfconsciousness; something primarily experienced not in the outgoing of contemplation but in the inward-turning of reflexion, thought turning back upon itself and the thinker; not in intuition, but in analysis. The life that was so fully held through being delightedly and playfully lost is now sensed as something in danger of loss and in consequent need of saving; it is the phase of self-defence against the pressure of the power and personality of others. The isolation of acute selfconsciousness succeeds the communion of un-self-consciousness; the loneliness of individuality succeeds the fellowship and security of the parent-centred world. What had seemed most familiar now becomes most bewildering; what had been most unquestioningly accepted—the teachings of authority, the dictates of common sense and social custom, even, indeed, the very existence of the self and the exterior world—is now fundamentally challenged and tested just *because* these things have previously been accepted with so little question. It is a mirroring on a small, individual scale, of that criticism of experience which dominates the story of European philosophy from Descartes to Kant; also, perhaps, of the transition from epic to dramatic poetry.

This adolescent crisis of self-assertion and unsparing critique is, of course, something which has to happen if the individual is to pass from healthy childhood to healthy adulthood. And such an adulthood is, ultimately, a rediscovery of the childhood which had seemed lost for ever. But that rediscovery only becomes possible when the apparently destructive tragic analysis, with its accompanying sense, greater or lesser, of isolation, desolation and insecurity, has in some way been pushed home honestly to its logical conclusion of absurdity. At that flash-point of crisis, where the horrific and the funny meet, it becomes possible for a man to see once more the point of the cosmic joke which he once saw so clearly before, when as a child he laughed at ducks and squidgy mud and whirling autumn leaves, at the spring sunshine on the grass, or the winter sunshine on the snow, or the wind through his hair when he ran. Then, and then only, he can repossess with full adult comprehension the lost world of simple acceptance, vivid appreciation and undestructive vision, gladly saying things like: "But I *do* exist", or "But there *is* an external world", or "But I *am* a creature, and not a potential or a frustrated god". It is after a sort of death of reason—Nietzsche's "good Friday of speculation"—that there occurs the resurrection of reason. In it it becomes clear that the most reasonable of all the things you can do with reason is to acknowledge reason's limits; to open yourself to the possibility of revelation, on the one hand, and, on the other, accept as a gratuitous gift the foundations of sanity, which sanity itself cannot lay. It is after man's mastering powers of critical

226

analysis have probed his own creaturely limitations to the very inside skin of their shell that he becomes aware of this fact: that the uttermost exercise of that power of self-assertion lies not in a triumphant despair but in a hope that survives continual defeat.

This reversed version of what we are accustomed to accept, implicitly at least, as the picture of human greatness, emphasizes once more the indispensably childlike quality of true maturity.[1] The world of Iago and "Machiavel" and the motiveless malignity of the *crime gratuit*, is, in contrast to, say, that of the *Divine Comedy*, a desperately grown-up world—as George Santayana once emphasized[2] (though he drew, I think, precisely the wrong conclusion from his perception of this). It is as deadly serious as the stand-out-of-my-way aggressivity of Verocchio's famous statue of Bartolommeo Colleone. Yet Shakespeare, who works out past its logical conclusion the whole potential development of the Renaissance mind, doesn't come to a stop in this world of the titan, as we have seen. And if you contrast for a moment the jutting-chinned monument of Colleone with the great soldiers of the Middle Ages, sleeping upon their tombs after their last battles, with hands folded in prayer, it strikes you, I think, that it is the earlier attitude which has the greater human dignity—precisely because it lacks the note of "Look at *me*!" At surface level it is the medieval effigy, with its comparatively naïve formalization, which is the more childish, and the Renaissance statue that is adult. But under the surface childishness lies the adulthood of a greater spiritual realism. And under the surface adulthood, with its determination to impress the onlooker, lies a

---

[1] "Childlike", not "childish". We're commanded, not to stick fast in childhood, but to "become as little children"; both the "become" and the "as" are very important.

[2] "Tragic Philosophy", *Scrutiny*, vol. iv, no. 4, Cambridge, 1935.

regression into that attitude which the nannies of all ages have tersely summed up as "showing off".

If you reject the concept of maturity as an ever-lonelier trajectory away from the condition of childhood, and accept a concept of it as the rediscovery of that point of departure,[1] then you are obliged to revalue the tragic vision, particularly as worked out in reaction against the divine comedy of the first Christendom. It ceases to be a magnificently lonely and starlike flight of the adult into an ever deeper cosmic darkness and an ever greater estrangement from all other similarly courageous voyagers. Instead of being the desolate emancipation of the adult from the last clinging shreds of parental security, it becomes essentially a transitional stage through which the child journeys towards that rediscovery of his own childhood—his own creaturehood—which is the full inheritance of it. In a word, it is essentially adolescent, and in consequence any attempt to make of the tragic vision a hallmark of maturity is in fact an attempt to canonize a failure in development; an arrestation, however magnificent, however understandable, however brilliant, in adolescence; the ultimately sterile prolongation of a state whose whole value consists in being transitional.

To say this is not, I must emphasize, to imply some attitude of facile superiority towards the tragic concept of maturity or the secular humanism in which it is rooted. Any such attitude would be, quite simply, silly. Arrestation in the tragic agony is, certainly, at bottom, an

---

[1] A concept superbly expressed, of course, by Mr. Eliot at the level of his explicit poetic thought, in

> We shall not cease from exploration
> And the end of all our exploring
> Will be to arrive where we started
> And know the place for the first time.

arrestation in adolescence, with all the implications of wisdom's disintegration into cleverness which this can carry. Yet it would be a presumptuous man indeed who attempted to disentangle the part played in this fixation by sheer desperate honesty from that played by less reputable factors. And to choose arrestation in a condition of anguish rather than attempt a futile crawl back into the womb is hardly the action of a knave, a fool or a coward. True, it is the height of absurdity to reject something because it's too good to be true. And to that extent there's an uneasy kinship with the diabolical in any pride which *refuses* to follow the nostalgic pull of the instinct for joy through to the other side of the tragic vision, and back again into the comic one from which it was born. Yet any heroic adolescent attempt to cut free altogether from childhood's roots is usually, I think, not so much a prideful determination to reign in hell rather than serve in heaven, as the result of a failure to grasp the nature of the Christian resolution of forces. There can be something utterly and blissfully simple about the childhood state of happiness and security. And there can be something utterly and appallingly simple about the crisis of disillusionment and lonely individuation in which that first childhood can come to an end. The tragic experience, for all its apparent complexity of conflicting opposites, does in fact try to substitute—in the name of realism and integrity—the adolescent simplicity for the childhood simplicity. It tries to accept the suffering condition of humanity as absolute, through the resolute and uncomplaining exposure of the individual to the destructive stress of its tensions at their highest pitch. But this attempt at absolute acceptance of suffering is as much playing false to our humanity as would be the attempted absolute refusal of it implied in any "return to the womb". Consistency with, and loyalty to, our own humanity (which, it must be remembered, is, according to Christians, an image of God) demands that we both accept suffering and reject it; that we accept both sorrow and joy. And the cruciform Christian "complex of opposites" does in fact have about it, as I have tried to show, an essential element of symbolism, of pointing-beyond. In this world, if our hope is to keep airborne it has to keep moving; always in creative conflict with the dark side of existence and passing through it to a target beyond.

If we accept this revised view of tragic vision then it is not unreasonable to revise in the light of it the picture still commonly held of the post-Renaissance age as European man's entry into adulthood. To the medieval mind the idea of existence as part of a divine comedy was so much in the blood that the playful aspect of the Catholic faith was hardly reflected on; and the bases of commonsense philosophy were similarly, in principle, accepted as worthy of clarification but beyond the necessity of being established. Fundamentally, this attitude was healthy; but it was a source of potential weakness as well as of actual strength. For as we have seen, it seems to be, generally speaking, a normal law of human development that nothing is truly possessed until it has been apparently lost—a psychological law spiritually underwritten by the Gospels. The Middle Ages had behind them—historically speaking, that is, in the "folk memory"—an experience of what it is like to be a non-Christian; but they did not have any similar experience of what it is like to be an ex-Christian. They inherited memories of what it was like to be searching for that answer to the problem of evil which would make the world make mysterious common sense. But they had none of what it was like to challenge the claims of mysterious common sense itself.

If we view things in this way, the secularized modern Europe we are accustomed to regard as an awakening to adulthood undergoes a revaluation similar to that which placed the tragic vision as a transition stage between two comic ones, an interlude in the cycle of "in my end is my beginning"; not the ex-Christian new development destined to succeed the Christian world-picture which gave birth to it, but a protracted adolescent crisis which marks the death of the first Christendom and the birth of the second.

All this might seem to indicate that it is the age which lies ahead that is destined to be one of man's true adulthood. I don't think we should necessarily dismiss this idea out of hand, just because during the last two or three decades the European intelligentsia has developed a certain masochistic gusto in telling itself and everyone else that we are living in the twilight of Western civilization. But if we do accept for the moment the possibility that the idea may be true, it is important to realize what it doesn't mean as well as what it does.

This can be seen more clearly if you go back for a moment to the level of the individual. We have talked about the alternation of a first "feminine" phase of childhood, and then a "masculine" phase of adolescence, and then a second-childhood adulthood in which these two phases are integrated. An important thing about that third state of balance is that the successive phases reconciled in it are manifestations of opposed elements present in the personality throughout the whole development. The second childhood of full maturity is the stage in which the individual's psychological progress resolves its dynamism in the repose of his definitive psychological structure.

It is commonplace knowledge today, of course, that there are both masculine and feminine elements in the

231

psychological makeup of both men and women, and that the fulfilment of a member of either sex involves the successful assimilation of strong elements of the other. Whether in the intellect or the passions or in the employment of both in action, the "masculine" capacity for dominative assertion of the self can be healthily realized only when complemented by a balancing "feminine" capacity for submission to life and acceptance of it. Similarly, the "feminine" capacity for intuitive contemplation is always in danger of opening the floodgates to chaos unless it is balanced by a "masculine" power of critical analysis and discrimination. Without the perpetual refreshment of intuition, reflexive analysis becomes a gritty machine for "murdering to dissect"; without the discipline of the dominative power of the mind, acceptant intuition becomes a malignly proliferating monstrous growth. Split the two things apart into a caricature state of "pure" isolation and you pays your money and takes your choice between rusty machinery and amorphous fungus.

Speaking of the sphere of natural psychological maturity, then, the whole point of the development is an end of progress in dynamic repose; the oscillation between the two poles ends in balance between them—a balance which, of course, necessarily implies a persisting distinction between the elements balanced. And the natural psychological maturity of the individual is something which can be more or less complete; once you reach it the condition is a relatively stable one, and you are unlikely to regress.

There is thus an immensely important difference between psychological and spiritual maturity. For the latter isn't a resolution of successive movements in final repose; it is the re-liberation of repose in endless dynamic movement. The whole point about spiritual

232

maturity is its incompleteness and dynamic striving. As St. Bernard pointed out, the perfection of man consists not in being perfect but in trying to be; and that trying implies, of course, continual failures. The saints describe them in terms so blunt that we, who tend to equate sanctity with faultlessness, think it must be pious rhetoric, mock-modesty. The repose of spiritual maturity is one whose very nature consists in being lost and found and lost and found again: "The just man shall fall seven times and shall rise again." "In my end is my beginning"—here, the whole point of the end is that it is a perpetual beginning-again, as St. Thérèse of Lisieux saw so clearly. The pattern is not quite the cyclical one of a Christian psychology nor the linear one of a titanist psychology; it's the tilted-spiral of a Christian spirituality, in which we are always going lower in order to rise higher towards the centre.

If we translate this from the terms of the individual into those of European history and culture, it is not hard to see the limitations of what is implied in saying that the present crisis may be the entry of Western man on his adulthood. We shall be well advised not to let any cyclical Christian interpretations of history make us over-apocalyptic in our approach to the immediate future; for if the next generation or so does indeed see the entry of Western man on his maturity, this may well be no more than the starting-point of the most important period of his story.

This mysterious inconclusiveness of the state of spiritual maturity is the reason, of course, why the principle of the resolution of forces which underlies it is also the dynamic principle of hope; the virtue of hope is the secret weapon of human weakness, and this can be seen equally in strictly spiritual aspiration and in that will to civilization which is one of its expressions. And

233

this fight to the finish against despair is, as I have tried to show, one in which laughter provides some of the heaviest artillery.

Yet it would be a thundering lie to pretend that for most of us, most of the time, "the joy of the cross" isn't one of the most suspect of all the traditional pious phrases. Between talking about suffering and undergoing it there's the same sort of difference as lies between reading about an earthquake and having the city come down about your ears in one. The primary quality of all experience of serious suffering is the naked and brutal power with which it usually snaps like a match the spine of such discipline as we have managed to prepare against its coming, and leaves us simply hanging on by blind agonized instinct, we don't know how or even why, against a nightmare tidal wave of despair. And the savage revolt against talk of religious consolation which is easily evoked by realization of this fact can be made all the easier because there are two easy false simplifications of the true Christian "complex of opposites".

The first oversimplification of the complexity of Christian joy is the tragic one, corresponding to the tragic simplicity of the adolescent crisis. It consists in simplifying the joy of the cross by eliminating, for practical purposes, the joy, and is another aspect of what I have described earlier on as the Eliotian translation of the old titanism into new Christian terms.

> Who then devised the torment? Love.
> Love is the unfamiliar Name
> Behind the hands that wove
> The intolerable shirt of flame
> Which human power cannot remove . . .

This at first sight seems the expression of an attitude

234

which has in it far more spiritual greatness than Chesterton's

> They *may* end with a whimper
> But *we* will end with a bang.

But the greatness is of a dangerously ambiguous kind. Even when you have taken into account the poetic condensation and rhetoric involved, you still, I think, feel compelled to point out that love in fact devises no torment, and that you need to watch your step very carefully indeed if you are going to start talking, however paradoxically, as if it did. To try to remodel your natural power to love, and thirst for happiness, upon this contradiction in terms is to run a very grave risk of saddling yourself with a titanically distorted picture of Christian heroism; and this is, I think, a temptation to which Mr. Eliot has in fact most honourably succumbed.

If you want to see how the problems of Anglo-Saxon culture, and the Anglo-Saxon Catholic's possible contribution to it, are related to this distortion of the true nature of Christian joy, it's essential to look for a moment at the way in which this Eliotian "swing past the centre" at the spiritual level manifests itself at the cultural level. It is from the very heart of the world of the titanic great man, with its magnificence of tragic pride, that Mr. Eliot originally comes. His subtle transmutation of Catholicism's spontaneity into the language of the strained dominativeness of secular humanism has been mirrored in the whole approach which he has instinctively made in his contribution towards the redemption of English culture; a clerkly and esoteric redemption from above. And that situation is faithfully reflected by the ambiguity and limitation in the Englishness of his poetry.

First, there has been the world of

> We have been, let us say, to hear the latest Pole
> Transmit the Preludes, through his hair and finger·
> tips

—a world not only superciliously sophisticated but
sufficiently supersophisticated to be supercilious about
its own superciliousness. Then there has been a very
real change, to produce the world of

> The only sort of wisdom we can hope to acquire
> Is the wisdom of humility; humility is endless.

Yet this latter world is, still, a world of royalism,
exclusive High Anglicanism, the select club, the college
common-room and the country-house weekend—the
world of *The Cocktail Party* and *The Confidential Clerk*
and *The Elder Statesman.* It is a world very remote,
for good or ill, from the main living reality of the England
of its day; and I am not sure that Mr. Eliot's diametrical
opposition to the Marxism and left-wingery of the
thirties didn't have in it not a little similar simple
determination not to ride ten to a carriage, on principle.
Just as his Catholicism is (to put it crudely) more-
Catholic-than-the-Pope's, so his Englishness is more
English than that of the English themselves. In this,
just as he has a certain affinity with Milton, whom he
has so strongly criticized, so he has a certain affinity
with those men who brought about in England the
Reformation crisis many of whose effects he so sincerely
deplores. For these men were also more English than
the English, in that they sought to realize English
particularity, both politically and spiritually, in opposition to Catholic universality rather than in terms

of it—an Either-Or at the cost of Both-And. There is a "swing past the centre" in Mr. Eliot's brilliant, super-deliberate attempt to relate the individual talent of England to the general tradition of Europe. His royalism, for example, is the symbol of an authoritarian and anti-democratic tendency[1] which is one more aspect of a general distaste for the common; it is far removed from that peculiar Both-And blend of hierarchy and democracy which England has worked out in her practice of constitutional monarchy. His High Anglicanism is rooted in a tradition which was originally—among other things —one of attack upon the popular "idolatrous" lower element in English Christianity, and has been distinguished throughout its development by a progressive recession from the broad sweep of the popular life of the nation. Where the English have maintained a steady, if somewhat muffled, resistance to the stern restraints of Puritanism, Mr. Eliot has cultivated to a point of extreme refinement something of that aristocratic distaste for the lower manifestations of human vitality which has for long been an essential ingredient in the popular Continental picture of the English tourist. In fact, the simplest way to sum up the ambiguity and ambivalence in Mr. Eliot's lovingly cultivated English-ness is to say that it has resulted not in his becoming a typical Englishman so much as what an intelligent and sympathetic Latin might conceive as the picture of a typical Englishman; something very like the reality but very different from it because it is more like the reality than the reality is. For all his Bloomsbury cosmopolitanism, Lawrence could put his fingertip on the pulse of living England as Mr. Eliot has never been

---

[1] It is fair, I think, to comment here on his use of Maurras, though as Mr. F. O. Matthiessen points out in his *The Achievement of T. S. Eliot*, this antedated the full manifestation of Maurras' Fascist tendencies.

able to; his vision makes that of Mr. Eliot take on an uncomfortable air of the tourist's brochure.

If, in fact, as Chesterton believed, the true English centre is Catholic, it is not surprising that Mr. Eliot's Englishness should show the same characteristic as his Christianity—the old dominative machinery put into reverse gear. The strain and tension of the eroding cosmopolitanism of the early poems is still being used, in reverse, to hold together by deliberately directed force the carefully assembled elements of a constructed Englishness. The attempt to break out of an isolation of cultural disinheritedness through to the English subsoil of American culture is as magnificently self-defeated as the attempt to break out of the limits of the dissociated clerkly sensibility. In a word, it is a false, though magnificent, concept of the Catholic supernatural mould which has led to an equally false and equally impressive concept of the natural national character. And all this is one workout of the adolescent over-simplification of the joy of the cross.

We must now go on to see what lessons are to be drawn from the second type of oversimplification—the kind which simplifies the complex joy of the cross by getting rid of the cross.

Just as the tragic simplification corresponded to the simplicity of the adolescent crisis, so this "super-comic" simplification corresponds to the simplicity of the first childhood, with its vision as yet unclouded by real aware-ness of evil. It produces the sort of cheeriness which is all the more infuriating because it seems to imply that what we feel might be a life-saving truth—"All shall be well and all manner of thing shall be well"—is an affirmation possible only to those who can manage, somehow, to keep suffering at a level of comparative unreality. The man who puts suffering breezily in place with "Ah, well, it's all God's will" or "These things are sent to try us" or "It's probably all for the best in the long run" seems *ipso facto* to rob such statements of the truth they can possess, even for those who find them the hardest of hard sayings. The delicate but steely and dynamic balance of the complex Christian truth is turned into the flat-bottomed inertness of sit-down-plump platitude, and the man who really knows what the face of horror can look like turns away in an agony of contempt.

Just as Chesterton criticized Mr. Eliot for going out with a whimper, so Mr. Eliot once criticized Chesterton for going out with a bang. The criticism isn't a simple one to refute. You can't help respecting the viewpoint of any man who says that real experience of the full blast of evil will *always* hurl a man into the open deep of despair, and that anyone who says different can do so only in ignorance: who says, in fact, that the only valid spiritual technique is to accept the hell of our existence as redemptive.

Indeed, in a way this is quite true. Suffering is, in its own way, an absolute; insofar as it is going on, there is no comfort; if there were, it wouldn't be suffering. It was not without reason that Chesterton grated on the nerves of the new generation. He was the child of his time, and that time had been, for England, one of quite unusual and unreal security, comfort and self-confidence —at least, for those who were socially fortunate; the disillusion and dread of the postwar generation was history's harsh corrective to this unreal frame of mind. And also there was in Chesterton both something of the perpetual child and a strong element of conflict.

Some critics have accused Chesterton of a truly infantile unawareness of the dark side of life. Others, noting in his work its elements of violence and the macabre, have interpreted its positive aspect as a tormented overcompensation for a basic morbidity which is none the less sinister for being only too sadly in accord with the real facts of life. But both these views can be accepted in principle without damage to Chesterton's status if we recall the peculiar nature of that complex of opposites which is the cruciform pattern of Christian joy and Christian sanity. Chesterton's Catholic centrality and balance are, as he put it, the point of "the still crash of two extremes ".[1] There was in him a truly childlike serenity and a truly ferocious struggle. But these were not mutually contradictory; they were complementary. How this was so I have tried to explain a little earlier on when I discussed his linking of the cosmic joke and the cosmic war.

His innocence was achieved not basically at the cost of experience but through it—as seems the case with not a few English artists. There was a real underside of darkness and violence to his work; and the horror of everything which he would have associated with the devil is, in his artistic vision, none the less sinister for being formulated in the bright colours and simple shapes of his "peasant art". For although he did not—as far as an outsider can judge—undergo really savage encounter with evil in the concrete instance—for example, anything like Dostoevsky's near-execution—he did certainly undergo a very profound intuitive apprehension of the essence of evil. And that is no light matter.

It is certainly difficult to graduate acute mental suffering on one scale of intensities with, say, acute physical pain or the endurance of extreme human malice. But it is also certain that a real look over the edge of the

---

[1] I am reminded of Mr. Eliot's

. . . Except for the point, the still point
There would be no dance, and there is only the dance.

"mind's mountains" is a state which can only be described, in all sober literalness, as indescribably appalling. It is capable of wholly absorbing a man's capacity for suffering at the time; a pinhole can be quite enough to afford a glance into the depths of hell. And it was an initial experience of that kind—of a condition of utter and apparently self-induced lucid insanity—which provided the persistent dark counterfoil to Chesterton's glowing vision of the wonder of sanity and the glory of common sense and common reality: the holy communion of the ordinary. He symbolizes it with his customary simplicity in the darkness behind the raised monstrance at Benediction which closes the last of the Father Brown stories. The conflict with it was continual precisely because it had been, in principle, resolved within a wider context; Chesterton emerged triumphantly from his early crisis vision of horror because he did not, at the time or afterwards, try to run away from it. It was a continual conflict, joyful but very real, with the powers of darkness which was his dynamic peace. If you glance through some of his best-known works— *Orthodoxy* in particular, but also *The Napoleon of Notting Hill*, *The Man who was Thursday*, or *Manalive*, for example—you will see how often he uses a description of the unreal world of insanity as a means of revealing the nature of that of sanity. Indeed, his whole continual proliferation of joke and paradox is one long development of this principle. And his depiction of the insane world is always authentic. Anyone who, to however modest a degree, shares his first-hand acquaintance with the "private world" of thoroughgoing unreality will know that the process of acquiring such understanding can, as I have said, be incommunicably horrible. Yet the determination "not to choose not to be" which can be born of it—the determination never to surrender to the powers of horror and despair—is not merely dogged, but a thing of unequivocal joy, exhilaration and zest; of "eagles and trumpets" just as we imagined them when we marched round the nursery beating a drum. To Mr. Eliot's

> We only breathe, only suspire
> To be redeemed from fire by fire

Chesterton would, I think, have made the comment that the basis of Christian life is not loving to suffer but loving to be, despite suffering; and that it is a noble error to try to remedy the presumption of secular-humanist titanism by baptizing the despair in which it collapses and embracing that purgatorial condition as the essence of Christianity.

There still remains, however, a qualification to be made concerning Chesterton's achievement if we are not to run the risk of still appearing to exalt a lesser artistic achievement over a greater on illegitimate theological grounds. His "Christian barbarism" is every bit as much a limitation and a witness to a condition of cultural disease as is the aristocratic overcivilizedness of Mr. Eliot. To realize just how great a dis-integration of society is implied by the gulf between these two artists it is only necessary to look back to Chaucer, where the two worlds are integrated, and clerk and clown in more or less full communion (despite the intensely hier-archical structure of medieval society). Chesterton's own work provides a full synthesis of the disintegrated elements in potentiality only, not in actuality. The choice of the peasant world of bread-getting was the right one, but it is deeply regrettable that a choice had to be made. The absence of high sophistication *is* an absence. The escape from the "clerkly" restrictions and the provision of a new voice for those who had not spoken yet—high culture's maternal underworld of common life and common sense—was achieved at a cost: loss of the complex enrichment of self-consciousness (for increased self-consciousness *is* an enrichment of the personality) which had been the work of the clerkly world in its increasing isolation. To have effected a redemptive Christian protest against the destructive humanist split between the "high" and "low" in man which could have drawn clerks and people together into one integrated audience—that would have demanded a second Shakespeare, with a power of creating a previously non-existent unity equal to Shakespeare's power of exploiting a previously existent one. Such a man would be a sort of "culture hero" indeed, creating an art which would in itself be a primary tool for re-creating a civilization. Considering the rate at which Shakespeares have been rationed up to date it is not exactly surprising that we didn't get one; yet if Chesterton and Mr. Eliot could have been boiled together we shouldn't, perhaps, have been all that far off it.

Things being as they are, however, we must learn from both men. We may agree that in the last analysis Chesterton's comparatively crude achievement is potentially more fruitful than Mr. Eliot's. But if we thus accept the idea that the real basis of human maturity is the childlike simplicity which was one characteristic of the Middle Ages, we are not in any way committed to denying that this simplicity is most fully realized when it contains within itself—as, for example, in *The Tempest*—all the adolescent complexity associated with the Renaissance. It is very important to remember, when trying to get in perspective the more extremely Romantic aspects of Chesterton's love for the Christian past, that his whole devotion to it was rooted in his devotion to

243

the present, to his own age just as it was. And this
capacity for appreciating the positive enrichments of
man's mind by the modern age has, I think, a very
important lesson for his co-religionists today. It is
understandable enough that Catholics, struck by the
obvious fact of the modern world's enormous tensions,
and the equally obvious fact that these derive from the
atomic fission of medieval Christendom, should be
tempted to cry that the whole development of the modern
age has been a progress in catastrophe, and that our
only hope of salvation lies in retracing our steps, as far
as possible, towards that more elemental state of greater
simplicity which preceded it. But although it is quite
true that there is nothing deceptive about the impression
of fundamental order and repose which the Middle Ages
give us, it is also true that this order and repose were in
no way placid, but, rather, a dizzy structure raised out of
the balance of vast and powerful opposing forces. And
the next Christendom, repeating this resolution of forces
in a new creation of matter from energy, will have to
integrate within itself all the new elements discovered by
the ex-Christian Europe which intervened between the
two. Had there been nothing to criticize in the old
Christendom, there could never have been so widespread
and successful a revolt against it. For men as a whole
do not lightly forsake the ways that are familiar to them.

The sixteenth-century crisis did, in the event, work
itself out in terms of a revolt against the Church. But
as we draw further out of the dimension of the post-
Renaissance world and deeper into that of the new one,
there begin to appear increasingly solid grounds for
questioning whether the fact of revolt against the Church
is really the most fruitful aspect of the sixteenth-century
crisis for us to concentrate upon today. An intense
probing and testing of all that has previously been taken

as axiomatic is an unavoidable stage in any progress deeper into truth, as we have seen. If (where Catholic dogma is concerned) it gets out of hand into total rejection, then the Catholic can never say anything else but that this is in essence unjustifiable; but he should never feel himself obliged to argue that the Church doesn't suffer something as a result, and not merely the loss of those who secede.

Here the polarized nature of Chesterton's thought becomes particularly important. He found that from one standpoint the loving dialectic he was bound to conduct with his non-Catholic fellow-countrymen naturally worked out principally in terms of the Church's either-or. That was something he had to affirm, all the more uncompromisingly for the charity with which he did it, against the increasingly chaotic version of both-and which had been the logical workout of the sixteenth-century rejection of the Church's key claim—the right to wield, and the indispensableness of, religious authority. And undeniably it is just such an emphasizing of the hard-edged aspect of the Church's teaching which has, since the Counter-Reformation, loomed large in the development of the Church's own thought until comparatively recent times. The social, political and cultural consequences of this general tightening and stiffening worked themselves out in the nature of the traditionally Catholic societies of the *ancien régime*. And the explosive reaction between that Latin tradition of authoritarianism and the Anglo-Saxon exaltation of individual freedom blasted open what remains one of the biggest historical rifts between the English Catholic and his fellow-countryman.

Yet in due course these officially Catholic societies too passed through a delayed-action version of the crisis which had convulsed England earlier on—as in the

France of the Revolution and the Italy of the *Risorgimento*. And once history had thus drastically forced the Church free from the fossilized encrustations of the old order of things, the way was made far easier for a fresh development of the complementary aspect of the Church's teaching—her both-and.

For though either-or is of course an essential element in Catholicity, Catholicism is not an affair of either-or alone, in that isolated state of spurious "purity" which, I have argued in this book, is a hallmark of disintegration. A humanely tolerant society can only be built upon intolerance towards certain things—the idea that might is right, for instance; yet the tolerance that can be built on that foundation is real, and just as important as the intolerance that is its basis. So, in the Catholic view, it is only on an uncompromising basis of spiritual either-or that we can unfold the full breadth of spiritual both-and; but here too the superstructure is just as real as, and no less important than, its complementary basis. It is this primal wedding of both-and with either-or, each revealing its true shape in the embrace of the other, which makes Catholic doctrine no mere bleak rationalism eerily exoticized with a dash of holy water behind the ears, but the rational formulation of elemental and unplumbable mystery.

In the world of growing spiritual disorder and confusion which arose, brilliant and tragic, out of the crisis of Renaissance and Reformation, Catholic thought and practice responded to the growing chaos of both-and run riot by an insistence on either-or so strong as to be at times frankly brutal. At the purely human level (through which, after all, the world largely experiences the Church) this reaction was a thing of mixed motives. A tough and ruthless line offered to the administrator and legislator a grimly effective way of offloading onto outsiders the heavy load of Catholic guilt incurred by all the scandals and inadequacies which had helped to fan the revolt; the guilt which the front-line martyrs took upon themselves with such heroic love and forgiveness. Yet the repressive reaction was also the expression of a desperate concern with vital issues in a situation of tragic emergency; and however little we may like some of the ways in which that emergency was met, the historic fact remains that it *was* met, in essence. But again, although this narrowing and tightening of the structure of Catholic thought was in fact effective as an emergency measure, it cannot, for all that, be regarded as anything else but a tragic price paid for the no less tragic failures and misdoings, in thought and action, which played so important a part in bringing about the state of emergency in the first place. An operation, however successful, cannot in itself be regarded as anything but a misfortune for the patient.

It is, consequently, a clear sign of another great forward swing in the rhythm of the Church's vitality and love when her truly creative thinkers show a strengthening instinct to balance more equally against her fundamental either-or its complementary both-and. And it was precisely because Chesterton learnt so thoroughly and instinctively the lesson which five centuries of Catholic either-or had been struggling (not always in the wisest way) to teach, that he could so strengthen with it the grasp he had always had of the both-and which is its corollary. It was this which made his reaction to the modern age not simply a violent attempt to reverse its "pure" naturalism into "pure" supernaturalism, but an attempt to fulfil, not destroy, its most magnificent and desperate ambitions by reintegrating it, in all its enriched selfconsciousness and developed individuality, with the timeless foundations first historically embodied in the world of the Middle Ages. And this is not a question of salting childhood's vision with the bitter irony of adult tragic experience, but of grasping at greater depth than before just how true to reality the childhood vision is. The capacity to see that can become possible through some kind of temporary exile from the paradise of innocence such as occurs when in adolescence there clash behind us the gates of the sweet and the bitter wonders.

All this is perhaps made clearer if you consider for a moment how inconceivable to Dante would have been the kind of tragic experience worked out by Shakespeare. Yet it is precisely in Shakespeare that there is probably the greatest of all progressions through a kind of Christian tragedy to a yet deeper Christian comedy. And it is in Shakespeare the conservative revolutionary that we can find focused, I think, the quality that is the key to Chesterton's position with regard to the English and the Catholic traditions: the quality—to borrow Blake's terms—of innocence in experience. This is the hallmark of the English comic genius, which makes England's greatest dramatist end up writing fairy-tale plays; and it is also the hallmark of that repossession of the medieval thought-world which is the true end of the development and enrichment of the European mind in the post-Renaissance era.

In this perspective you can see a new significance in a characteristic closely connected with English child-likeness and comicality: amateurishness. The over-sprawling of the moulds of classical symmetry which marks the English refusal to stay put on the "tragic heights" becomes, on this view, something more positive than a mere failure in artistic discipline and the failure in spiritual discipline which that implies. The "semitic" bursting of the inexorable restraint of the classical Latin tragic logic, and the outrageous overrunning of the classical forms in literature, become an entry into a new dimension, just as the passionate uprush of Gothic architecture, with its vivid rocket-trail of the grotesque and the primitive, is something quite other than an inability to recapture the poise and serenity of classical Greece. The overboiling richness of English literature's comic genius is the symbol of a life that is larger than artistry, and a vitality which is something greater than good taste. The sentimentality and purple-patchery that flaws the work of Dickens transmits something that freezes up in the inhuman perfection of Flaubert, rather as the incompleteness of the *Summa* of St. Thomas Aquinas is part of the message of the work itself, and a symbol of its superiority over the works of the neat system-builders. "Spiritually, we are all Semites," said Pope Pius XI. It is a thought as potentially dynamic as the atomic bomb, when you pause to think how uncritically, both inside and outside the Church, Roman Catholicism tends to be identified with the Latin cultural tradition alone; and in the working out of its implications England, with her semitically concrete synthesizing and intuitive linguistic tools, will have much to contribute.

The English capacity for not taking things "too seriously", the English caution before ruthlessly logical conclusions and ruthlessly tidy systems—all these can produce results that are ugly, results that are shameful, results that are sheer mess. Yet in essence the fundamental genius for play which expresses itself equally in English humour, and English democratic institutions, and English art and thought, is a very Catholic instinct; and its "game" is in essence the complement of a very real "earnest". The apparently childish comicality which you find in Chesterton thus has in it a very great deal more than immediately meets the eye—all the more because this "great deal more" does not, by its additional depth, alter the delightful quality that first strikes you. To grasp this fully you need to glance at one or two further aspects of English life and society in the light of the English tradition of comic play.

It's possible, I think, that the present somewhat masochistic national mood of England may be drawing towards its close, and thus opening the way for attitudes which may, let it be hoped, be none the less positive for having thoroughly absorbed the very necessary lessons of their preceding bout of self-questioning. And if this should prove to be so, there will be no more vital part of the changeover than a developing appreciation of the surprisingly deep significance—spiritual, cultural and political—of the peculiar Anglo-Saxon genius for play with the absurd. If we are to secure for the Anglo-Saxon clowns their rightful place alongside the great unintelligible German metaphysicians and the great deadly-dignified French men of letters, we must certainly never allow ourselves to be frowned out of the English wisdom of childlikeness—the true "joyful wisdom"—by the grimmest Continental titanism that ever blinded itself with deadly serious science. But we have to be careful. We have to remember that if we have indeed retained in our capacity for laughing at the absurd a vital element of sanity often signally deficient in the thought of the Continent, the fact should be an occasion for much humble thanksgiving as well as some realistic self-approval. The thing is very much our good luck as well as our achievement. For despite the aeroplane, the rocket and the hydrogen bomb, the Channel remains twenty miles of water; and if we have managed to cultivate a richer sense of humour than some of our Continental neighbours, this is in part at least because an accident of geography has preserved us from the full impact of the political tragedies which have, century by century, repeatedly torn Europe from end to end. Our country has not been a battlefield, properly speaking; our citizens have not been deported; we have not seen the proclamations of foreign military governments on our walls or had our police stations turned into torture chambers. Behind the wall of the sea we have enjoyed a remarkable degree of peace and security in which to concentrate our energies on those problems of internal government which the nations of Europe have all too often had to struggle with exposed to the full blast of violent external interference. The comparatively peaceful and playful social and political atmosphere in which our particular search for wisdom has been conducted is a geographical gift as well as a historical achievement. There is, I think, a definite connection between the either-or tendency in modern Continental thought, with its tendency to absurd extremisms, and the political absolutisms of Europe; but we have to remember that such systems of government, with all the worst in the way of tyranny they could run to, often came into being under the pressure of external threats far more immediately deadly than those with which England has been accustomed to cope. Strong naval power provides any island community with maximum security at the cost of a minimum absorption of social resources. The comparatively relaxed atmosphere within which English empiricism and the English comic tradition and English political democracy were all able to pursue their own peculiar developments was created, in part at any rate, because English society was able to defend itself from external interference with the minimum of internal tension. In judging the horrific world in which the secular humanist tradition finally found its ironic "godhead"—the universe of absurdity as depicted

251

by M. Sartre—we have to give due weight to the back-cloth of Nazi Germany and occupied Europe.

Yet when we have said all this and firmly turned our backs on the picture of a flattering contrast between our humbly wise selves and the cleverly perverse Continent, the fact still remains that the difference between the English and the Continental attitudes to the absurd cannot be explained away simply by the existence of the Channel. Particularly as far as the artist is concerned, the tragic and horrific aspect of life is not confined to war, conquest, revolution and tyranny, fearful as these things are. "I will show you fear in a handful of dust", wrote Mr. Eliot; whatever the varying intensity of suffering may be as between this person and that, the basic wonder and tragedy of the human condition remains the same all the world over; and it is towards this basic human situation, rather than any particular intensification of its problems, that we take up an attitude either of comic acceptance or tragic challenge. Here, perhaps, is the appropriate place for a comment on an objection which can very easily and most pertinently be brought against the kind of thesis I have been developing throughout this book. To write about the duty and justification of joy is all very nice and very easy, it may be said—provided you have been lucky enough to escape all really nightmarish intensity of the horrors which life can inflict. It is easy enough, for example, for a lucky Englishman. But supposing political oppression were not something that one read about in the newspapers as happening somewhere else? Suppose, instead of reading about the pile of tens of thousands of children's shoes still rotting outside Auschwitz, one remembered what it had been like to witness the fate of their owners?

There are several partial answers here, chief among which is, perhaps, that it is not always safe to assume that individuals who have not endured obviously appalling ordeals have therefore escaped wholly without experience of life's horror. Mr. Custance, in the book to which I have already referred, describes how at some stages in his mental sickness the folds of a pillow could assume the lineaments of a manifestation of indescribable horror; and this is symbolic; it is, in fact, possible for a man to be shown sufficient horror in a handful of dust to make him literally retch with terror. Even without concentration camps, children still get burnt; without brainwashing, mental sickness can still produce a solitary confinement in hell; without secret police, cancer can torture. Such things are just as fiendishly efficient as the cruelty of men in making the statement "It is good to be" seem a nightmare mockery. Any one of us can think in seconds of innumerable things that could happen to him—still worse, to those he loves—which would, he feels, break his spirit utterly.

But a thing does not become false because it is easy to say, any more than it becomes false because it seems impossible to say. The comic affirmation, if true, remains true whether or not we have the power to make it. You do in fact find individuals who have retained the capacity for taking joy in life, in the face of experiences which you would have thought would have driven any man mad. Yet even apart from this, *if* it is good to be it continues to be so whether or not we have the heart to say it. It is possible to laugh again in heaven, where God shall wipe away all tears from our eyes, even if it is not possible to laugh any more on earth. And in actual fact that knowledge can, I think, even in this life, bring back the echo, and more than the echo, of joy to people who have felt that they could never smile, or sleep an untormented sleep, again. The knowledge that the smile can be so appallingly easily wiped off our faces should

253

not stop us from smiling; it should simply make us smile
with humility and not complacency.

There is in actual fact no necessary direct correlation
between historically tragic situations and the formulation of tragic attitudes, or historically "comic" situations
and the formation of comic attitudes. It was out of the
death of the medieval order that Cervantes created *Don
Quixote*. Lewis Carroll threw up the first surrealistic
comic defences of sanity against the coming philosophic
nihilisms in the heyday of Victorian self-confidence. It
was in the prosperous first flush of the German Empire
that Nietzsche hatched out his titanic and tragic scheme
for the transvaluation of all values. Baudelaire wrote
Les Fleurs du Mal within the framework of a decidedly
secure and prosperous French society. And the first
full revelation of the ironic "divinity" of the Sartrian
humanist—*La Nausée*—was written, not under the
Nazi occupation, but in 1938. The English capacity for
laughing at the absurd is more than the mere by-product
of historical and geographical good luck; it is a genuine
self-shaping of the national genius. And we are no more
entitled to undervalue the contribution which it has to
make to the common human achievement than we have
to be complacent about the strong English tendency to
woolly-mindedness. There is something of intrinsic
positive value in the English disinclination to accept a
tragic concept of human maturity and "tragic", all-
or-nothing, either-or, absolutist systems of social and
political organization. In their comic literature, in their
empiricist and pragmatist tradition of philosophy, in
their capacity for bloodless social revolution and their
paradoxical games between Right and Left within the
Constitution, and between people and Crown within
the framework of constitutional monarchy, the English
display a particular aptitude for that play within the

limits of sanity which is safely controlled by the capacity for laughter. And it is perhaps particularly significant that our deepest admiration is reserved for our humorists, rather than our satirists. For the humorist offers us a vision in which we laugh at ourselves in others, while the satirist offers a vision in which we laugh at others inasmuch as we are enabled to feel ourselves apart from them.

It was because he was able to recognize the Catholic implications of this civilization of comic play that Chesterton was able to see deeper into the peculiarities of English culture than either men like Lawrence and Mr. Eliot, on the one hand, or many of his co-religionists on the other. Holding as he did that it is Catholic Christendom which is the abiding matrix of Christian England, and that England is England because she is at root Christian, he was well placed to see not only how much his country had been alienated from her true self since the sixteenth-century rupture, but also how far she had remained true to it. He would undoubtedly have maintained that nothing essential can be brought to the Catholic synthesis from outside, and thus that any return of nations to the Faith, on however large a scale, could never restore to the Church something essential she had been deprived of, or add something essential she had previously lacked. Yet the intensity of the patriotism which was complementary to his loyalty to the Church and Christendom points to a lesson which it is particularly vital for English Catholics of the future to learn: that in the process of aberration from the Catholic norm a culture may work out implications of Catholic principle which the "officially" Catholic cultures may have missed. Which is, of course, no more than we should expect if God does indeed permit evil only to draw from it a greater good.

255

Here again Chesterton holds opposites in the balance of play. He affirms the aristocratic hierarchy of an authoritatively teaching Church and the Christian democracy of all redeemed sinners, who, from Pope to prostitute, stand on equal terms before the love, mercy and justice of God. He affirms the principle of personal loyalty (symbolized in monarchy) as the key element in the structure of the humane society, and its bulwark against the impersonal tyranny which is the worst tyranny of all; but he also affirms the common man's indestructible right to freedom, and his terrible right to hurl down political authority, in the last resort, should this try to violate it. And just because his thought was formed in a milieu which stands right outside the social and political quarrels of the officially Catholic nations, his criticism of that milieu is also an appreciation of Catholic principles which it has preserved and which the actual history of the Catholic countries has sometimes half-obscured. He is able, for example, to see in the French Revolution not simply an abominable onslaught of wicked freethinkers on altar and throne; he sees—at greater depth—a blind, despairingly hopeful outbreak of instincts fundamentally Christian against abominable suppression at the hands of nominal Christians. He stands outside the conflict between the elements of truly Christian humanitarianism implicit in the revolt of Voltaire and the Encyclopaedists, and the elements of truly diabolical cruelty sanctioned by the Most Christian Kings of the sacral *ancien régime*. He stands outside the political ramifications of the Continental quarrel between anti-clerical liberalism and reactionary sacristy Catholicism; and thus he can look back to St. Benedict and St. Robert Bellarmine to see in constitutional monarchy a type of political system nearer in fact to Catholic patterns than any of the consecrated despotisms of the seventeenth and eighteenth centuries. Despite his Catholic criticism of British culture and society, he is hot to preserve all the vital lessons that a Protestant and then ex-Protestant England has learnt. His vision of England's true self—both historically and ontologically—as Catholic was also a vision of Catholicism and Catholic Christendom as including and reaffirming all that he found best in the ways of England. And in that vision, which should, I think, be that of all his Catholic fellow-countrymen who truly love their Church, their Christendom and their own country, there is summed up the answering pattern to our original jigsaw puzzle.

In a world where the worship of man and nature in opposition to God has resulted in the unmanning of the one and the rape of the other, the occupational disease is despair. It seems fitting if in such a situation the Church's healing mission should formulate itself increasingly in the cultivation of hope, the defence of laughter, and the confirmation of the common man's childish insistence on the necessity of joy. And this fittingness is also a fittingness as between the English thing and the Catholic thing.

This means that for the Catholic artist of the future there waits a vast creative task, immensely demanding, immensely difficult and therefore immensely stimulating. In the past, great artistic achievement has been largely associated with the prior existence of a rich cultural deposit which the artist has been able to exploit; a common vision, providing those common assumptions and common symbols in virtue of which artistic communion of a really full-bodied kind, with a thick texture of universal associations to each particular thing, has been possible between men. The exploitation may have been constructive, like the work of a good farmer on

257

his land; as when Chaucer fused rich Anglo-Saxon and Latin elements in the mould of the Catholic world-picture to create a new linguistic and poetic synthesis. It may have been destructive, consuming irreplaceable matter in a dazzling but transitory firework display of mental atomic fission; as in Donne's baroque cerebral exploitation of the full-blooded vitality inherited from the world of the Middle Ages. But it has been, in the main, an exploitation, whether basically healthy or unhealthy, of primal cultural potentialities already there.

That situation has now, I think, changed. I am very far indeed from joining the chorus of those who have chanted for some years past now, with a certain gloomy relish, the dirge of the decay of European civilization. On the contrary, I think that if the West does collapse on itself, this will be largely because we've spent a sight too much time sitting on our bottoms and telling ourselves, in ever more elegiac accents, that we have had it. But it is, I think, true that the process of disintegration has gone sufficiently far for yet further brilliant pyrotechnics of tragic critique to become almost impossibly difficult. The tragic critique can only bite, so to say, as long as it has not yet gnawed everything in pieces with its analysis, and there is still something left sufficiently plump in substance to get your teeth into. Once that point is passed, then the universal wolf has indeed nothing left to do but eat up itself. Things fall apart and the centre cannot hold; when that has really happened, you have to call a halt to playing atom bombs with the spiritual world you have inherited, and begin to try to reharness the vast energies you have released into reconstituting a new one.

The great English literature of the future will have to be, not a display of a culture's exploitation, but a living instrument of recivilization. Its great artists will have to combine a Homeric simplicity of vision with a Proustian wealth of self-awareness. In place of the brilliantly and subtly mechanical screwing-together of dissected parts practised by Joyce and Mr. Eliot, they will need to develop to the *n*th degree the grafting and cross-pollinating skill of the great gardener. The great poet will always be a clerk, *ipso facto*; but instead of tormenting himself with the problem of how to become ever more titanically clerkly, the poet of the future must learn that the whole burden of revitalizing his culture doesn't rest on the shoulders of the artist alone. It rests also, and even more widely, on those of the "people of England, that never have spoken yet"—or, as Mr. David Jones puts it in the dedication to his *In Parenthesis*, "all common and hidden men and . . . secret princes".

The poet of the future must, in a word, learn to play again. Indeed, both people and clerks can only learn to play properly when they determine once more to establish communion with one another, at whatever transitional cost. For where contact with the people is lost, clerkly cultural vision fades; and where the people are deprived of the clerkly vision, their vitality is made blind. Truly joyful creative play demands the wedding of elemental vitality and refined insight.

This final return to the affirmation of joy brings me to the tailpiece of this odd book. It is a tailpiece because it implies a level of discussion rather different from that which I have maintained throughout the rest of my pages; and yet it is far from irrelevant, for many people would consider that in this particular case the real sting of the problem is, in fact, in its tail.

I have been arguing throughout that the natural desire of the child and the common man for joy and for the happy ending are fundamentally endorsed by the Catholic faith. But many people who would perhaps find themselves in agreement with me to a considerable extent will still, I think, emerge regretfully from this state of pleasant accord to say that although all this is very nice as far as it goes, in the last resort it hasn't got us anywhere. Despite all efforts in this particular direction, the ultimate bad joke, the ultimate nightmare, still remains; remains all the more grimly because we have perhaps been able to forget it for a moment. For the Catholic Church uncompromisingly teaches the doctrine of hell. And if in fact it is true that the basic constitution of things includes the existence of some created beings—even were it only of one—in a condition of perpetual torment, then, they will say, no matter what ingenious and subtle mental contortions we may go through, the plain blunt fact is that horror is something ultimate and unresolvable, and we're back in Rats' Alley, with a vengeance.

Now, it is true that a good deal to meet this contention can be done by stripping away from the theological essentials of the doctrine of hell the appalling and dubiously-motived imaginative wallowing in crude anthropomorphic horrors, which has in the past often been regarded as an indispensable weapon of the popular preacher and the instructor of little children. You can sweep away the identification of God's justice with that of the medieval torture chamber; you can get rid of pictures like the pair of scales in which good deeds and bad deeds are weighed up (regardless of the present disposition of the soul, of course) by a merciless divine Accountant; you can clear away the idea of God's dealings with the hardened sinner as those of a patient policeman who finally gets his man, or an arbitrary nursery governess—doing eeny-meeny-miney-mo to decide whether or not to grant or withhold the grace necessary for repentance. In a word, you can strip away all the crude oversimplifications which can in practice distort the doctrine in terms sadistic, vindictive or callous; and concentrate on its theological essentials. That is to concentrate on the concept of the wholly free, wholly deliberate, wholly cold-blooded and open-eyed definitive rejection of God's love by a being who would rather endure eternal suffering than admit his creaturehood so far as to make the admission of the prodigal son—"I have made an absurdity of my being by trying to assert my will against yours; have mercy on me." It is to concentrate on the concept of one who would rather reign as a "god", even if only over the appalling private universe of his own utterly isolated self, than participate in the life of God himself on the terms of a wholly dependent creature's glad acceptance of a wholly undeserved free gift. It is to see hell as an expression of God's absolute respect for the freedom of his creatures, which refuses to violate them, even in welfare-state fashion, "for their own good", and pays the last compliment it can even to those who freely use that freedom to reject him totally. All this is something very different from Dante's appalling gusto in formulating God's justice in the most brutal terms of man's vindictiveness.

Yet even when you have done all this there will still be many who say: "Granted, you've eliminated the cruder elements in the problem. Yet for all that nothing is really changed; the same nightmare is merely restated in a subtler form. If, as you say, man needs God more than anything else in the world, and thus self-alienation from him for good must mean a greater suffering than any we know of, the same blasphemous horror is still left right at the very centre and heart of all things. If 'omnipotent love' is to possess any meaning for us at

261

all, and not simply to be made a mysterious X which bears as much relation to what we can understand of love as do the gods of the Aztecs, how *can* it be reconciled with eternal suffering on the part of what it has created? How *can* eternal happiness persist in the face of eternal nightmare, if it is not either callous or sadistic, or again some kind of incomprehensible X which has no connection whatsoever with anything we can understand?"

Now, this is no foolish objection, and it is very foolish indeed to dismiss it airily as mere sentimentality, such as we didn't suffer from in the good old ages of faith (which also didn't suffer from any difficulties about boiling coiners in oil and roasting heretics alive). It is not an unreasonable answer to say that if the rest of the Christian revelation seems to us to fit the facts of our world's case uniquely, then we are entitled to accept this part of it too, whatever our difficulties about it, on the grounds of our general trust in the indisputable goodness of God, as something which must fit in somehow, even though we may have only the most inadequate idea as to how. For it is perfectly reasonable to accept the fact that our own minds are not the measure of the universe, and that acceptance of mystery is, here as elsewhere, the very condition of sanity and reason.

Yet still there would, I think, be many who would reply that while they are perfectly prepared to admit that they cannot, in the nature of things, master wholly with their minds the mystery of existence, they can at least keep honest faith with their reason as far as it will go; and that to believe this doctrine *is*, for them, a violation of reason. If, they will say, omnipotent love and eternal happiness can be reconciled with the eternal suffering of some creatures, then they are for us simply "X", and "anything goes"; you can reconcile anything with anything, and chaos is come again. Far from

finding in this an occasion for cheap anti-Christianity, a
great many such people would, I think, find it one of
acute distress of mind—all the more so because they
may be by no means unsympathetically disposed towards
the Catholic faith, and by no means so shallow-witted
as to suppose it can lightly be weighed in one hand while
you do the crossword with the other. Those sincerely
so minded can have to endure what is perhaps the
heaviest mental cross a man can bear; that sense of lucid
lunacy in which the reality of hell seems to spread like a
monstrous blot right over the reality of heaven, and to a
mind appalledly paralysed there seems to have happened
the unbelievable catastrophe which Flaubert evoked
when he once wrote: "Suppose the absurd were true?"
That indescribably dreadful condition of mind is thumbnailed with his usual uncanny intuition by Chesterton in
his Father Brown story "The Honour of Israel Gow",
when he makes the little priest say (though admittedly
in a less absolute context), "Something has fallen on us
that falls very seldom on men; perhaps the worst thing
that can fall on them. We have found the truth; and the
truth makes no sense."

However reasonable it may be to say that this gravely
difficult doctrine may be honestly accepted in virtue
of our knowledge of, and trust in, God's goodness, and
our admitted inability to see to the bottom of the problem of evil (as of anything else), it is not of much
help to say this under such circumstances. For the whole
natural basis of our knowledge that God exists, and is
God, lies in the rationality of ourselves and of God's
pattern in the universe, and the capacity of the first to
apprehend the second. And here the whole trouble is
that the appalling truth of hell seems to be smashing
up alive the essence of rationality itself—the very image
of God and the very mind of the man. In such a state

indeed, a man can feel a certain detached astonishment that his mind should not yet have collapsed into sub-human chaos, and even a certain impatient longing for it to do so, so that he may be spared the agony of consciousness. This situation has to be faced. For if our Christian joy can only survive at the cost of averting the eyes from this problem, then it is a cowardly phoney and the human situation does after all seem to be Rats' Alley. Where do we go from here, if anywhere? Or are we waiting for Godot? What more can be said, if anything?

My personal opinion is that while in a sense nothing more *can* be said, the same things as before can be said in slightly different terms, and in such a way as to be, I hope, of some genuine help to those for whom Catholic teaching here seems to imprison them, in the last analysis, in a truly Sartrian nightmare. As I have said, the problem presented to the human mind by the doctrine of hell can, in its acutest form, present itself as a ghastly and incredulous conviction that God is the devil, and a consequent experience of horror quite incommunicable in its absoluteness. But as I have tried to show, when the onslaught of despair becomes so overwhelming as to drive us right into the last corner, the supernatural duty of hope forms one force with the natural instinct to preserve ourselves, our sanity and our thirst for joy. The whole point about hope is that its fire-power is laughter; that it is joy at war. And the whole point of joy at war is that it will not admit defeat under any possible circumstances. The more utterly deafening the propaganda roar of "You're beaten" the more dogged the reply, "But I'm still fighting". As Chesterton says, the more hopeless the situation, the more hopeful the man must be; St. George can still shake his sword at the dragon, he says, even if the very earth and sky are no more than the opening of its gigantic jaws. The more overwhelming the temptation to despair, the more point there is in the fantastic common sense of hope, even if the charge is made with two men and a boy against a million million monsters. Here we can put a judo throw on our very perversity, against the root cause of it: we can say truly and cheerfully "I'll be damned if I'll be beat".

Here, then, where the whole racking problem of evil comes to its ultimate cruciform and crucifying focus, we find as before that the very centre of the cross is the point of the resolution of forces which is the pinhole way out of the rat-trap, the point of breakthrough in hope. And it is above all in the perspective of hope, I think, that we must view this matter. In the ultimate context of God's dealings with the sum total of creation, as in the context of our own personal salvation, we must never despair of the mercy of God.

We know what God has told us as necessary to know for the purpose of our salvation. And we know that what he has told us will never be falsified by anything else there may be to know. But what there may be more to be told, and the further depths of its relation to what we can now grasp—of this we know nothing. And it is into this darkness, warm and friendly with the simple goodness of God, that our hope dynamically rises through the very heart of the cross. The moment we try to treat that release as something in the dimension of knowledge, we move towards the kind of position which the Church cannot but repudiate as heretical: either explaining away God's justice as something merely formal, or explaining away his mercy as something merely ironic. But as long as we realize that hope's final victorious charge into the black heart of the armies of despair will mean a fight in the dark—that dark in which, says Chesterton, the men of Christ go gaily—then we shall see how it is precisely *because* we've no idea what we are hoping for that our hope can be limitless. It is in such a hope that is finally secured the indestructibility of joy.

As it passes through the analysis of our minds, God's image is broken down into different attributes—love, mercy, justice and the rest. But what is distinct in our minds remains one in God himself. And it is love which is his primal definition, and mercy which is above all his works. And if it is mercy especially that is associated with us his works fallen and redeemed, then it is very fitting that laughter should be the sign of our struggle to be true to the divine image in us. For mercy is joy's incentive never to surrender to despair; and there is in mercy a kind of laughter.

There is no greater possible assertion of human freedom than man's refusal to despair of his God.